MOZART

and His Operas

MOZART
and His Operas

EDITED BY STANLEY SADIE

MACMILLAN REFERENCE LIMITED, LONDON
ST. MARTIN'S PRESS, INC, NEW YORK, NY

Published in Great Britain by
MACMILLAN REFERENCE LTD
25 Eccleston Place, London, SW1W 9NF

Basingstoke and Oxford
Companies and representatives throughout the world

British Library Cataloguing in Publication Data
Mozart and his operas - (Composers and their operas)
1. Mozart, Wolfgang Amadeus, 1756—1791.   2. Operas.   3. Composers - Biography
I. Sadie, Stanley, 1930—
782.1′092
ISBN 0-333-790197

Published in the United States and Canada by
ST. MARTIN'S PRESS, INC
175 Fifth Avenue, New York, NY 10010

ISBN 0-312-24410X

A catalog record for this book is available from the Library of Congress

Typesetting by The Florence Group, Stoodleigh, Devon, UK

Printed and bound in Britain by Cambridge University Press, Cambridge.

CONTENTS

Cities

PREFACE

This volume is one of a series drawn from *The New Grove Dictionary of Opera* (1992). That dictionary, in four volumes, includes articles on all significant composers of opera and on their individual operas (as well as many other topics). We felt that it would serve the use of a wider readership to make this material available in a format more convenient for the lover of opera and also at a price that would make it accessible to a much larger number of readers.

The most loved, and most performed, of opera composers are (in chronological order) Mozart, Verdi, Wagner and Puccini, who form the central topics of these volumes. The volumes each include chapters on the composer's life (with particular emphasis on his operatic activities) and a chapter on each of his operas. In some cases, the availability of additional space has made it possible for us to include, additionally, information that provides a fuller context for the composer and his work. Not for Verdi, who (perhaps unfortunately) composed so many operas that space did not permit any additions. And in the case of Wagner, whose operas demand quite extensive discussion, it was possible to add material only on his original singers and of course on Bayreuth.

For the Mozart volume, however, in which only a relatively modest number of operas call for extensive treatment, we were able to include material on virtually all his singers (excluding only those on whom we are almost totally ignorant) and on his interesting array of librettists, as well as some background on cities in which his music was heard. And for Puccini, there is material not only on librettists and singers but also on the most important composers among his Italian contemporaries, men whose music is still in the repertory (for instance the composers of *Cavalleria rusticana* and *Pagliacci*).

The authors of the chapters in these books are leading authorities on their subjects. The Mozart volume is chiefly the work of Julian Rushton, the Verdi of Roger Parker and the Wagner of Barry Millington, while the Puccini principal author is Julian Budden. Writers of the shorter sections are individually acknowledged within the book. We are grateful to all of them for permitting the re-use of their work.

STANLEY SADIE
London, 1999

ILLUSTRATIONS

Plate 1 – A scene from *Die Zauberflöte* at the Bregenz Festival, 1985 [Bregenzer Festspiel]

Plate 2 – Autograph score of '*Le nozze di Figaro*' (1786): part of the Act 2 trio, showing the upper line (extended to c') assigned initially to the Countess; as elsewhere in the opera, the upper line may eventually have been taken by the Susanna (Nancy Storace). A German text is written into the score. [Deutsche Staatsbibliothek]

Plate 3 – *Il re pastore*, Act 1 scene i (the countryside beyond the walls of Sidon, as described in the libretto); engraving from the *Opere* of Pietro Metastasio (Venice, 1758) [Fototeca dell'Istituto per le Lettere, il Teatro e il Melodramma, Fondazione Giorgio Cini]

Plate 4 – Playbill for *Die Entführung aus dem Serail* [Stanley Sadie]

Plate 5 – '*Le mariage di Figaro*': engraving by J.-P.-J. de Saint-Quentin showing the final denouement, from the first authentic edition of Beaumarchais' 'La folle journée, ou Le mariage de Figaro' (Paris, 1785) [Bibliothèque Nationale de France]

Plate 6 – Angelica Catalani as Susanna and Giuseppe Naldi as Figaro in *Le nozze di Figaro* at the King's Theatre, London 1812: anonymous drawing [Theatre Museum/Board of Trustees of the Victoria & Albert Museum]

Plate 7 – Wolfgang Amadeus Mozart: unfinished portrait (probably 1789) by Joseph Lange [Internationale Stiftung Mozarteum; in the Mozart Museum, Salzburg]

Plate 8 – Luigi Bassi in the title role of *Don Giovanni*: engraving by Médard Thoenert (1787) [Mary Evans Picture Library, London]

CONTRIBUTORS

A.H.K.	Alec Hyatt King
B.A.B.	Bruce Alan Brown
B.D.M.	Barbara Dobbs Mackenzie
B.M.	Betty Matthews
C.H.	Clemens Höslinger
C.R.	Christopher Raeburn
D.E.M.	Dale E. Monson
D.H.	Daniel Heartz
D.L.	Dorothea Link
D.N.	Don Neville
G.C.	Gerhard Croll
H.G.	Harald Goertz
H.J.-W.	Harrison James-Wignall
H.S	Herbert Seifert
J.A.R.	John A. Rice
J.L.	Jitka Ludov
J.R.	Julian Rushton
K.J.S.	Klaus J. Seidel
K.K.H.	Kathleen Kuzmick Hansell
L.T.	Linda Tyler
M.C	Mosco Carner
M.D.	Mariangela Donà
P.B.	Peter Branscombe
P.C.	Paul Corneilson
P.L.G.	Patricia Lewy Gidwitz
P.W.	Piero Weiss
R.K.	Rudolf Klein
R.W.	Roland Würz
T.B.	Thomas Bauman
T.C.	Tim Carter
W.E.R.	Walter E. Rex

CHRONOLOGY OF MOZART'S LIFE AND OPERAS

1756

27 January — Born in Salzburg, the son of Leopold Mozart and Anna Maria Mozart (née Peterl)

1763 – 66 — Travels with his family to Vienna, France, England and the Netherlands

1767 — Dramatic début in Salzburg with the oratorio *Die Schuldigkeit des ersten Gebotes*

13 May — Première of *Apollo et Hyacinthus* in Salzburg, Benedictine University

1768 — *Bastien und Bastienne* performed in Vienna, at the home of F.A. Messer

1769

1 May — *La finta semplice*, Salzburg, Archbishop's palace

1770 — Mozart's first visit to Milan

26 December — *Mitridate, re di Pontò*, Milan, Regio Ducal Teatro

1771

17 October — *Ascanio in Alba*, Milan, Regio Ducal Teatro

1772

May — *Il sogno di Scipione*, ?Salzburg, Archbishop's palace

26 December — *Lucio Silla*, Milan, Regio Ducal Teatro

1775

13 January — *La finta giardiniera*, Munich, Salvatortheater

23 April — *Il re pastore*, Salzburg, Archbishop's palace

1777 – 78 — Mozart's stay in Paris

1779/80 — *Zaide* composed, although not performed in Mozart's lifetime; the première was in Frankfurt on 27 January 1866

1781

29 January — *Idomeneo, re di Creta*, Munich, Residenztheater

1782

16 July — *Die Entführung aus dem Serail*, Vienna, Burgtheater

4 August — Marries Constanze Weber

1783 — Starts composition of *L'oca del Cairo*; abandoned in early 1784

1783 – 84 — *Lo sposo deluso* composed but remained unfinished

1786

7 February	*Der Schauspieldirektor*, Schönnbrunn, Orangery
1 May	*Le nozze di Figaro*, Vienna, Burgtheater

1787

28 May	Leopold Mozart dies in Salzburg
29 October	*Don Giovanni*, Prague, National Theatre

1790

26 January	*Così fan tutte*, Vienna, Burgtheater

1791

6 September	*La clemenza di Tito*, Prague, National Theater
30 September	*Die Zauberflöte*, Vienna, Theater auf der Wieden
6 December	Mozart dies in Vienna

Biography

Wolfgang Amadeus Mozart

Johann Chrysostom Wolfgang Amadeus Mozart was born in Salzburg on 27 January 1756; he died in Vienna on 5 December 1791. He was the son of Leopold Mozart, Chamber Composer and Deputy Kapellmeister to the Prince-Archbishop of Salzburg. Mozart is the first composer whose operas have never been out of the repertory. His comprehensive mastery of three genres, *opera seria*, *opera buffa* and Singspiel, is unmatched in operatic history; and although he wrote no operas in French, *opéra comique* is represented in translation by *Bastien und Bastienne* and *tragédie lyrique* by his first masterpiece, *Idomeneo*. This achievement is founded on his genius for assimilation and in the circumstances of his life and early experience of operatic genres.

OPERATIC CAREER   Although Mozart's formative experiences in opera lay away from home, the musical life of Salzburg included serenata performances (operatic though not fully staged), plays with music at the University and Gymnasium and *opera buffa* and spoken drama from visiting troupes. Mozart composed three operatic works for Salzburg, as well as his only incidental music to a play.

First, however, Mozart's travels with his family to Vienna, France, England and the Netherlands (1763–6) displayed him as a keyboard prodigy and composer of instrumental music. He quickly became acquainted with opera, which in Austria and Germany was mostly Italian. In Paris the unreformed Opéra, bastion of a tradition particularly disliked by Leopold Mozart, contrasted with the more modern *opéra comique* dominated by Duni, Philidor and Monsigny. In England Mozart met J.C. Bach and imitated his instrumental works; Bach was also at the centre of London's almost entirely Italian operatic culture.

Mozart's early experience of Italian opera is documented in Daines Barrington's report (published 1769) to the Royal Society in London: at nine, the prodigy could already, in improvised recitatives and arias, ape operatic styles suited to anger and tenderness. In London and

The Hague Mozart composed his first known arias, including his first settings of Metastasio (K21/19c and 23).

Mozart made his dramatic début in Salzburg (1767) with the first act of an oratorio, *Die Schuldigkeit des ersten Gebotes* (K35), and began his lifelong practice of inserting numbers into other composers' operas. His first complete dramatic work was the Latin intermezzo *Apollo et Hyacinthus*. From September 1767 the Mozarts spent 15 months based in Vienna, where they heard Gluck's *Alceste*; its profound impact emerged later, in *Lucio Silla* and especially *Idomeneo* and *Don Giovanni*. Mozart's first real operas, written in Vienna, mark the principal division of his output, between operas in Italian with recitatives and operas in German with spoken dialogue. The *opera buffa La finta semplice*, written with imperial encouragement, was not performed until the return to Salzburg. The Singspiel *Bastien und Bastienne* is said to have been given privately in 1768 at the Vienna home of Dr Franz Anton Mesmer, whose 'magnetism therapy' is pilloried in *Così fan tutte*.

Whereas most of his contemporaries specialized, sometimes writing over a hundred operas, Mozart's mature output is punctuated by gaps which resulted from circumstances rather than inclination. Four serious Italian operas followed between 1770 and 1773, three produced in Milan, then under Austrian rule. The Mozarts were welcomed by the plenipotentiary, Count Firmian, and obtained a commission for Carnival 1771. They travelled widely in Italy; Mozart saw serious operas by Hasse, Guglielmi, Piccinni and, in Naples, Jommelli's late opera *Armida* of which he said: 'beautiful, but much too elaborate and old-fashioned for the theatre' (letter of 5 June 1770). The blow is directed at the structure, and particularly the 'pompous' ballets, rather than the music; Mozart had to conform to similar tastes in Milan.

In October he complained that his fingers were aching from writing recitatives. Composition of arias waited until he was in Milan, where he could discuss them with the singers: referring to the primo uomo Leopold wrote that 'Wolfgang refuses to do the work twice over and prefers to wait for his arrival so as to fit the costume to his figure' (letter of 24 November 1770). Several arias had to be revised, a circumstance that does not seem to have recurred. Yet with *Mitridate re di Ponto* Mozart achieved mastery of *opera seria* in a single stride, a fact recognized by the immediate commission for another *opera seria* two years later.

In the meantime, he gained experience with an oratorio, *La Betulia liberata* (K118/74c), intended for Padua, and a serenata, *Ascanio in Alba*, for a royal marriage in Milan. The return to Salzburg in December 1771 just preceded the death of Archbishop Schrattenbach, whose successor, Archbishop Colloredo, was far less generous in allowing leave of absence. But, probably after helping to inaugurate his reign with another serenata, *Il sogno di Scipione* (originally written for Schrattenbach's anniversary), Mozart obtained leave to present *Lucio Silla* in Milan (Carnival 1773), scoring a triumph on which he was never allowed to capitalize.

Over a year later Count Seeau, theatre Intendant to the Elector of Bavaria, asked Mozart to write another opera, *La finta giardiniera*, performed in Munich early in 1775. It occupies a special place in Mozart's output as his first opera to enter the German repertory, adapted as a Singspiel, and the first whose musical and dramatic qualities have encouraged more than an occasional modern revival. Almost immediately afterwards Mozart set Metastasio's *Il re pastore* as a serenata for a royal visit to Salzburg.

Mozart wrote no more Italian dramatic music (concert arias apart) for five years, the major hiatus of his career. During his traumatic stay in Paris (1777–8) the *opéra comique* repertory provided themes for instrumental variations and Mozart experienced the regenerated repertory of the Opéra; but the 'Querelle des Gluckistes et Piccinnistes' preoccupied the public and the management, and his only theatrical music was a ballet, *Les petits riens*. Yet the period between *Il re pastore* and *Idomeneo* was not entirely wasted for him as a dramatic composer. Affected by his love for Aloysia Weber in Mannheim, he poured out substantial concert arias (their texts usually taken from operas), and he worked out dramatic ideas in his first great concertos. The experience of the Mannheim and Paris orchestras was seminal in the development of the orchestral aspect of his later operas.

Mozart's interest turned to German opera on hearing of Joseph II's establishment of the National Singspiel in Vienna. In 1778 he became interested in melodrama, words spoken to instrumental music: of Benda's *Medea* he wrote 'nothing has ever surprised me so much, for I had always imagined that such a piece would be quite ineffective! ... I think that most operatic recitatives should be treated in this way – and only sung occasionally, when the words *can be perfectly expressed by the music*' (letter of 12 November 1778). He may have composed a *Semiramis* (1778) in this form; if so, it is lost. Melodrama is used in the incidental music to Gebler's *Thamos, König in Ägypten* (K345/366a), written between 1773 and 1779 when Schikaneder's troupe was in Salzburg, and in his next opera, the unfinished *Zaide*. The neglect of melodrama in later German works may reflect the need to conform to Viennese expectations, or may represent disenchantment with the medium.

Carl Theodor, formerly of Mannheim, became Elector of Bavaria in 1778 and brought singers and his unrivalled orchestra to Munich. Count Seeau may have been induced to commission *Idomeneo* (1781) by musicians who knew Mozart, including the elderly tenor Raaff. It is Mozart's first undoubted masterpiece and marks a watershed in his career. After this close approach to Gluck's development of *tragédie lyrique*, he could never again write so dramatically for chorus, so pictorially for instruments, or provide such an extended ballet; the solo arias and ensembles banish display for its own sake, and have enhanced dramatic impact because they arise directly from the dramatic situations.

The composition of *Idomeneo* gave rise to a fascinating correspondence; this and subsequent letters about *Die Entführung* give us the clearest indication of Mozart's aesthetics, as well as demonstrating his acute dramatic intelligence. Although documentary evidence is lacking (for instance with the Da Ponte operas and *Die Zauberflöte*), it seems legitimate to assume that Mozart subsequently took a guiding role in the dramatic construction of his librettos: after *Die Entführung*, only *La clemenza di Tito* was not written specially for him, and even there Metastasio's text was 'turned into a proper opera' by Caterino Mazzolà.

Mozart's absence from Salzburg tested his employer's patience to the limit. Colloredo summoned him to Vienna, where he was happy to go and still happier to stay when dismissed (June 1781). His remaining operas were composed for the capital of the Empire or for the neighbouring capital of Bohemia, Prague. Mozart was quick to make friends, among them Gottlieb Stephanie the younger, director of the National Singspiel. Instead of accepting *Zaide*, however, he offered Mozart a similar libretto, *Die Entführung aus dem Serail*; Mozart's setting was performed two weeks before his marriage, on 4 August 1782, to Constanze Weber. It became popular throughout Germany. Had there been royalties on performances, Mozart's subsequent financial problems would hardly have arisen.

The replacement of the National Singspiel by an Italian troupe was popular with the Viennese, but it led to the last serious break in Mozart's operatic output. He was eager to contribute to the Italian repertory, mostly *opera buffa*, and studied it avidly; he also got to know the performers and was impressed by several of them, notably the *buffo* Francesco Benucci and Nancy Storace, later to be the first Figaro and Susanna.

Paisiello was the most performed opera composer in Vienna during the mid-1780s. The repertory included his *Il barbiere di Siviglia* (1783), and Haydn's *La fedeltà premiata* (1784), an example of the sentimental genre of *La finta giardiniera*. More persistent rivals, whose output was concentrated in Vienna, were Salieri and Martín y Soler, both of whom worked with Lorenzo da Ponte. Martín's operas were particularly successful, but he and Mozart were on amicable terms. Salieri's intrigues against Mozart have probably been exaggerated, but he wielded considerable influence, and Mozart's perception of the situation is clear (letter of 7 May 1783):

[Da Ponte] has promised to write an entirely new libretto for me. But who knows whether he will be able to keep his word – or will want to? For, as you are aware, these Italian gentlemen are very civil to your face. Enough: we know them! If he is in league with Salieri, I shall never get anything out of him.

Mozart honed his skills by working on librettos without commission. He read more than a hundred without finding anything suitable,

7

and in the same letter asks his father to persuade Varesco to write a comedy:

The most essential thing is that on the whole the story should be really *comic*: and, if possible, he ought to introduce *two equally good female parts*, one of these to be *seria*, the other *mezzo carattere* . . . The third female *character* may be entirely *buffa*, and so may all the male ones.

The prescription for three contrasted female roles is fulfilled in varying degrees in the Da Ponte operas, especially *Don Giovanni*.

Varesco began *L'oca del Cairo*, and Mozart drafted several numbers before abandoning it. A little later he worked on *Lo sposo deluso*, which also remains fragmentary. In 1783 he wrote three arias for Anfossi's *Il curioso indiscreto* (K418-20), two in the two-tempo rondò form which he later put to significant use in his own operas; in 1785 he added two lively comic ensembles to Bianchi's *La villanella rapita* (K479-80). In 1786 *Der Schauspieldirektor* was performed at Schönbrunn alongside Salieri's *Prima la musica*: Mozart's work was buffoonery about German theatre folk, Salieri's a sophisticated consideration of the relation of music and poetry. The contrast might have been galling, but Mozart soon demonstrated his mastery of the Italian genre in *Le nozze di Figaro*.

According to Da Ponte, Mozart himself suggested basing a libretto on Beaumarchais' play, and he again composed much of it before obtaining permission to stage it. Despite an initially good reception *Figaro* was not an unqualified success except in Prague; in Vienna it was soon outstripped by Martín's *Una cosa rara*. *Figaro*, however, marks the last watershed; from now on Mozart was a recognized opera composer and in his remaining five years he produced four major works. The longest interval, between *Don Giovanni* (first performed in Prague in October 1787) and *Così fan tutte* (Vienna, January 1790) was bridged by the Vienna production of the former (1788) and the 1789 revival of *Figaro*, both requiring new music. Adapted as a Singspiel, *Don Giovanni* soon joined *Die Entführung* in the German repertory.

Figaro has lost nothing of its freshness in over 200 years. The preparation for this epiphany in operatic history included, of course,

Mozart's previous operas, but also, typically and perhaps more importantly, local conditions including the presence of a large group of expert singers, and Vienna's recent experience of *opera buffa*: Paisiello's *Il barbiere di Siviglia*, a model for 'really *comic*' opera with a fast-moving, realistic plot and precise characterization, and Martín's operas, which display the virtues of a popular, song-like idiom. Memories of *opéra comique*, until recently part of the Viennese operatic scene, may have contributed to the masterly action ensembles, while the long finales are the culmination of an *opera buffa* tradition associated with Goldoni's Venice. Yet Mozart's own genius is needed to account for the radical nature of the transition from the uncompromisingly extended musical developments of *Die Entführung*; from now on, the symbiotic harmony between music and drama is complete.

The last phase of Mozart's career marks a climax in three genres, each transformed by his dramatic insight. *Opera buffa* reached an unsurpassable peak in the three Da Ponte operas, *Figaro*, *Don Giovanni* and *Così fan tutte*. Their length and intensity, although there is no shortage of humour or even farce, make them unique in the literature of 18th-century comedy, and it is no exaggeration to call them the foundation of the modern repertory. Mozart wanted to show his strength in *opera seria* and, contrary to an opinion often expressed, the commission for *La clemenza di Tito* (for the Prague coronation of Leopold II) was far from unwelcome; it enabled him to produce a concise drama which had remarkable success over the next 20 years. His last opera in order of composition, *La clemenza* was performed before *Die Zauberflöte*. Here Mozart transformed the Singspiel into an allegory of his own quasi-religious commitment to Freemasonry, while retaining the popular element appropriate to his only opera since *Bastien und Bastienne* not composed for a court theatre. The loss opera suffered by his early death is incalculable; nevertheless the level and range of his achievement is rivalled only by specialists in the genre such as Verdi and Wagner.

STYLE   Mozart's stylistic development in opera parallels that of his instrumental music, but appears less consistent. Until *Il re pastore* his aims and methods were representative of his time; thereafter he composed individual masterpieces whose qualities have affected operatic composition ever since they became widely known. While the excellence in relation to prevailing standards of all but his earliest operas should be emphasized, the following observations refer mainly to his mature work.

In *opera seria* and Singspiel Mozart's masterpieces stand in direct opposition. The musical riches of *Idomeneo* contrast with the austerity of *La clemenza di Tito*, as does the profuse invention of *Die Entführung*, redolent of court opera, with the demotic *Zauberflöte*. The earlier pair displays the exuberance of invention found in his instrumental works up to about 1785, the Vienna piano concertos and wind serenades, the quartets dedicated to Haydn. The first Da Ponte operas, *Figaro* and *Don Giovanni*, have the riper mastery of the 1786 concertos, the last four symphonies, the string quintets; the style of *Così fan tutte* moves towards the operas of 1791 which share the effortless lucidity, the virtual concealment of what is nevertheless real complexity, of the late instrumental works (the 'Prussian' quartets, the last concertos).

While insisting on the primacy of music in opera, Mozart never lost sight of its dramatic context. He intended his arias to suit both the available voices and the dramatic situation, and fed the appetites and expectations of his audiences rather than defying them; if his greatest works were not an immediate triumph, it was not because their forms or dramatic content were unacceptable, but because of the elaboration of his fundamentally conventional musical language. Mozart explained his priorities in a letter to Leopold (26 September 1781) concerning 'Solche hergelaufne Laffen' (*Die Entführung*):

Osmin's rage is rendered comical by the use of the Turkish music. In working out the aria I have . . . allowed Fischer's beautiful deep notes to glow. The passage 'Drum beim Barte des Propheten' is indeed in the same tempo, but with quick notes; and as Osmin's rage gradually increases, there comes (just when the aria seems to be at an end) the Allegro assai, which is in a totally different metre and in a different key; this is bound to be very effective. For just as a man in such a towering rage oversteps all the bounds of order, moderation and propriety and completely forgets himself, so must the music too forget itself. But since passions, whether violent or not, must never be expressed to the point of exciting disgust, and as music, even in the most terrible situations, must never offend the ear, but must please the listener, or in other words must never cease to be *music*, so I have not chosen a key foreign to F major (in which the aria is written) but one related to it – not the nearest, D minor, but the more remote A minor.

Osmin is comical, but represents a threat to the sympathetic characters. To convey this Mozart takes advantage of instrumental possibilities and the capabilities of his singer, and acknowledges the right of expressive exigencies to overrule musical decorum. The resulting blend of serious purpose and comedy is one of his most characteristic dramatic achievements.

Perhaps unwittingly, Mozart followed Gluck's precepts on overtures, even in comedies; as early as *La finta semplice* he joined the last movement to the first scene, and from *Idomeneo* he abandoned the three-movement sinfonia, although a slow central section interrupts the Allegro in *Die Entführung* and three later overtures have slow introductions. Except in the two operas of 1786, the overtures go beyond mere appropriateness to incorporate important musical ideas from the opera. Instrumental expression reaches its zenith in orchestral recitative (and the melodramas of *Zaide*), enhancing its expressive penetration by harmonic daring and increased use of wind instruments. Conventionally reserved for soliloquy (a notable example is Donna Elvira's 'In quali eccessi' in the Vienna version of *Don Giovanni*), obbligato recitative was used for long dialogues in *Idomeneo* (the sacrifice scene) and *Così*, where it also gives rise to measured music in a recitative context (arioso). Mozart was also imaginative in his use of *recitativo semplice*. Occasionally, but not so often as to become predictable, the bass line has a pertinent shape; a descending scale over a diminished 4th is characteristic of *Idomeneo* (ex.1a: Ilia contrasts the woes of Troy with the gods' defence of Greece; ex.1b: Idamante sings of Arbace's approach bearing evil tidings). Even ostensibly conventional declamation sometimes makes use of shapes related to formal numbers. Before 'Là ci darem' Don Giovanni makes repeated allusions to the pitch-contour A–C$^\sharp$–F$^\sharp$ (preceding recitative, bars 1–4, extending F$^\sharp$–B by bar 7; bar 10; bars 14–16), ending with a direct anticipation of the melody (ex.2); similarly, B$^\flat$–D–B$^\flat$ in recitative immediately precedes 'Fin ch'an dal vino' (the main motif, $b^\flat$–$b^\flat$–$b^\flat$–d'–$b^\flat$ repeated, appears at 'voglio divertir').

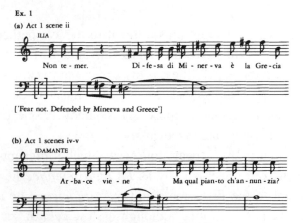

Ex. 1

(a) Act 1 scene ii

ILIA

Non te - mer.   Di - fe - sa di Mi - ner - va è la Gre - cia

['Fear not. Defended by Minerva and Greece']

(b) Act 1 scenes iv-v

IDAMANTE

Ar - ba - ce vie - ne   Ma qual pian-to ch'an - nun - zia?

['Arbace approaches. But what complaint does he announce?']

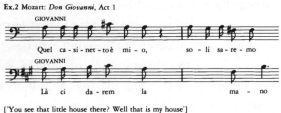

Ex.2 Mozart: *Don Giovanni*, Act 1

GIOVANNI

Quel ca - si - net-to è mi - o,   so - li - sa - re - mo

GIOVANNI

Là ci da - rem la   ma - no

['You see that little house there? Well that is my house']
['You'll lay your hand in mine']

Mozart's choice of musical forms was dictated by dramatic requirements, ensuring that the musical numbers emerge from the inner drama of character or the outer drama of action. His ensembles and finales are usually assumed to be more original or significant than the arias, but even in the late comedies solo expression is of paramount importance. Mozart always found a place for arias which explore a character's mental state and contribute to dramatic understanding by changing our perception of the personality; such arias occur even in his fastest-moving comedies, although beside comparable scenes in *opera seria* they gain intensity through their relative brevity and the absence of display.

Writing for a Viennese *buffo* troupe, or for Schikaneder's company, Mozart not only eschewed cadenzas but developed a precision and conciseness of expression which may be gauged by comparing *La finta giardiniera* with *Figaro*, or Belmonte's love song in E$^\flat$ (*Die Entführung*: 'Ich baue ganz') with Tamino's (*Die Zauberflöte*: 'Dies bildnis'). Yet he can still indulge the voice: Susanna's 'Deh vieni, non tardar' (*Figaro*), Zerlina's arias (*Don Giovanni*) or in a tragic context Pamina's 'Ach ich fühl's' (*Die Zauberflöte*) penetrate to the core of feeling partly because they are so grateful to sing. Virtuosity – the grotesque depths of Osmin, the fireworks of the Queen of Night, the fioriture of Konstanze, Fiordiligi or Sextus – also plays a part in characterization. Shorter arias may be highly dramatic without recourse to structural modulation; often they only briefly visit the dominant before returning to the tonic, a tonal 'flatness' also found in the late chamber music. Mozart prolongs pieces by obsessive repetition (Figaro: 'Aprite un po''), alluring melodic extension (Zerlina: 'Vedrai, carino'), or sensitive play on expectations by cadential postponement, which can be comical and satirical (Don Alfonso's 'Vorrei dir', Dorabella's 'Smanie implaca-bili'), or project the most intense pathos ('Ach, ich fühl's').

Most arias are composed in close correspondence with the lyrical verse forms (usually two strophes of three or four lines each) supplied by the librettists; but they also take forms peculiar to a situation. In 'Aprite un po' quegl'occhi', Da Ponte provided Figaro with 26 lines. Mozart worked through two quatrains in tonic and dominant sections (to bar 48); then, assisted by changes in verse metre, he ran through the remaining 18 lines in a mere 21 bars (from bar 49), largely on tonic harmony. The first quatrain returns on dominant harmony (bar 71); the incomplete repetition of the remaining text is punctuated by the nagging 'il resto nol dico'. The whole cadential period (57–70) is repeated exactly, with a mocking coda (85–102). Such a form resists classification, but is unlikely to be experienced as unorthodox, since it combines musical solidity with dramatic directness.

Mozart used all available forms, selecting the simplest (such as the sectional rondo) for single states of mind (Zaide's 'Trostlos schlutzet Philomele'; *Die Entführung*: Blonde's 'Welche Wonne, welche Lust'). Ternary form, descended from the da capo, is appropriate to the controlled fury of Donna Anna's 'Or sai chi l'onore' (*Don Giovanni*). 'Cavatina' implies an aria that is short (*Figaro*: Countess Almaviva's 'Porgi amor') but not always simple in feeling (*Così*: Ferrando's 'Tradito, schernito'). Binary arias, in design resembling sonata form and equivalent to the first section of a full da capo aria, represent a complex of feelings unresolved at the end; this type, prevalent in *Idomeneo* (including Ilia's 'Padre, germani, addio!'), appears also in comedies (*Così*: 'Smanie implacabile'). Additional text may be accommodated in a middle section, sometimes a complete contrast (Titus's 'Se 'all'impero'), sometimes a modulatory section corresponding to a sonata development (Idomeneus's 'Fuor del mar').

Complex feelings which modify in the course of the aria give rise to additive structures. The essential design of the majestic 'rondò' (*Figaro*: Countess Almaviva's 'Dove sono'; *Così*: Fiordiligi's 'Per pietà'; *La clemenza*: Vitellia's 'Non più di fiori') lies in the alternation of tonic areas and episodes, a system which spans both tempos although the mood of the Allegro supersedes that of the preceding slow movement. Less conventionally, Fiordiligi ('Come scoglio') accelerates to a third tempo, her single-mindedness paradoxically demanding such extreme expression; musical coherence resides largely in continuity of key. A similar plan is used in Sextus's 'Parto, parto' (*La clemenza*). Leporello, however, proceeds from fast (numerical) to slow (taxonomic) cataloguing of Giovanni's conquests.

Such additive forms commonly occur in ensembles where the final tempo, normally faster, corresponds to the concluding phase in the action which brings the voices together. A simple device of musical form in 'Ah guarda, sorella' (*Così*), this procedure marks Zerlina's complete acquiescence to Don Giovanni in 'Là ci darem la mano'. The slower sections usually contrast tonic and dominant areas, but (unlike the rondò) the faster music is a single section entirely in the tonic, requiring no thematic reprise. The unusual fast-slow pattern is used for the first finale in *La clemenza* (action: despair), and turns from humour to numinous beauty in the quintet (no.5) of *Die Zauberflöte*. Such progressive schemes reach a pitch of complexity in the chain finales, which both in action and musical duration (often over 600 bars) bulk hugely in the comedies.

Mozart's welding of action to musical continuity is usually most appreciated in ensembles and finales, but the action aria can also develop a situation (*Figaro*: 'Non più andrai', 'Venite, inginocchiatevi'; *Don Giovanni*: 'Ho capito', 'Metà di voi quà vadano'). Mozart certainly exploited the necessities of musical language for dramatic ends, but where character and feelings rather than action are concerned careful analysis is required to define what is really happening – or to resist definition, since Mozart's own position frequently appears ambiguous, and allows interpretative scope to the singers and director.

In the often-cited first duet of *Le nozze di Figaro* (ex.3), a marked opposition appears between Figaro's theme and Susanna's gracious melody; he is counting, she admiring her hat. Figaro moves towards the dominant, sufficiently established by the perfect cadence (bar 30) for the music to continue there; instead Susanna enters in the tonic. Figaro resumes counting, and articulates the dominant more decisively (underlining its dominant, bars 45–6). Susanna develops this tonal situation but forgets her melody, resorting to pettish repetition over the pedal A. Figaro sings her tune in the dominant (bar 50), but her insistent 'guarda un pò' (bars 55, 57) suggests that his attention is elsewhere. Susanna leads the music back to the tonic for restatements of her melody, which Figaro now dutifully doubles. These musical processes are usually held to demonstrate Susanna's greater force of personality and intelligence. Yet, conventionally, strength is considered to reside in the establishment of the dominant, here accomplished only by Figaro: Susanna's music twice relaxes to the tonic. Is Figaro, after all, the stronger? Hardly, since Susanna finally seduces him from his work. The rest of the opera tends to support Susanna's claim to superior wit, but the duet itself may be read as striking a balance emblematic of the compromises which make a successful marriage.

Ex.3 Mozart: *Le nozze di Figaro*, Act 1

[Figaro: 'Five ... ten ... twenty ... thirty ... thirty-six ... forty-three ...' Susanna: 'Now like this I'm happy']

Action may be less ambiguously wedded to musical events than character, but even in Mozart's busiest ensembles it does not develop at a rate comparable to recitative. In the *Figaro* sextet, a 24-bar ensemble expands the situation reached at the end of the previous recitative. 16 bars of dialogue follow Susanna's entry, half mingled with further ensemble. Susanna sees Figaro embracing Marcellina and slaps him; this takes 14 bars, reaction to it 20. From bar 74 (reprise of the opening) the misunderstanding is explained (with humorous repetitions);

from bar 102 the rest is commentary, embodying contrasted views (Count Almaviva and Don Curzio are angered by what rejoices the others). Commentary exceeds action in a proportion of about 3:2. Often such frozen tableaux, during which the music is extended before the next event or to make a decisive conclusion, are still more prevalent, notably in the closing (and fastest) sections of finales.

The relationship of certain ensembles to sonata form has frequently been described (notably in the trios and sextets of *Figaro* and *Don Giovanni*), and is undoubtedly a remarkable synthesis of styles. But additive designs are also common (*Die Entführung*: quartet-finale; *Così*: sextet). The *Don Giovanni* sextet has been compared in structure to a finale; Rosen (1971) justifies the huge closing·section (147 bars entirely in $E^\flat$) by the need for tonal resolution of the extreme modulations of the first part. Here sonata form is merely an analogy; unlike the *Figaro* sextet, this has no thematic reprise, and the dramatic effect would be the same if it ended in C rather than $E^\flat$ major, a licence the harmonic situation before the Allegro (a dominant of C minor) would certainly permit, exceptional though such a procedure would have been.

Starting from primitive chain finales (*La finta semplice*), Mozart enriched the musical and dramatic content (*La finta giardiniera*); but the action remains slow and the tonal architecture primitive. The realistic *opera buffa* produced swifter action, and Mozart devised appropriate tonal schemes, beginning and ending in the same key and moving between sections by a 5th or 3rd. Landon (1989) postulates influence from the tertial key-changes in Haydn's *La fedeltà premiata*. In *Figaro* and *Don Giovanni* Mozart used this device better, because more sparingly: 5th-progressions are normal and shifts down a 3rd mark a peripeteia (entries of Figaro, Act 2: $B^\flat$ to G, and the masked trio, *Don Giovanni* Act 1: $E^\flat$ to C). A more complicated scheme lies behind the first finale of *Così* (see Table 1). It begins with the ladies alone in the garden (*A*). The men rush in, taking poison (*B*); Alfonso and Despina go for the doctor (*C*), leaving the frightened ladies to tend the 'dying' men (*D*). Despina as the doctor cures them (*E*). Feigning to believe they are in paradise, the men plead love to the ladies (*F*), who reject them with renewed energy (*G*).

17

Table 1: *Così fan tutte* Act 1 finale

section	A	B	C	D	E	F	G
key	D	g	E♭	c	G	B♭	D
tempo	Andante	Allegro	(continued)		Allegro	Andante	Allegro
metre	2/4	¢	(continued)		3/4	C	¢

In sections *A* to *E*, all key-changes also involve change of mode; in *E* to *G* the shifts are chromatic. The still more active second-act finale is tonally almost eccentric: at one point the key-sequence is A♭, E, D, E♭. Weaker tonal architecture in comparison with *Figaro* and *Don Giovanni* perhaps reflects the deceptiveness of the dramatic situation.

Mozart's key-schemes can never be completely systematized as signs of character, social class, affect or even musical form. Social structures, however, are more reliably encoded through associations of metre with dance. The contredanse in the Act 1 finale of *Don Giovanni* is the meeting-point between aristocratic minuet and plebeian waltz. Figaro's 'Se vuol ballare' accelerates from minuet to contredanse; Susanna mocks Count Almaviva by emerging from the closet (Act 2 finale) to a minuet. This system has less applicability in *Così* or *opera seria*, but a parallel hierarchy of musical types (including counterpoint) governs the complex society of *Die Zauberflöte*.

But for each instance of affective key-symbolism a counter-instance can be produced. 'Regal', 'heroic' D major (besides being available for trumpets, it is particularly brilliant on strings) can embody the tenderest feelings (*Così*, opening of the first finale). 'Rustic' G (peasant choruses in *Figaro* and *Don Giovanni*; Papageno) appears in *Idomeneo* for Electra's 'Idol mio' and (in comedy) for arias of Marcellina and Despina, who are far from bucolic. E major is used for gentle breezes in *Zaide*, *Idomeneo* (twice) and the trio in *Così*, but also for deep introspection (*Così*: 'Per pietà') and for a *buffo* duet in a graveyard (*Don Giovanni*). Instrumentation and tempo, harmony, melody and rhythm, contribute more to mood and characterization than tonality or absolute pitch.

It is certainly interesting that 14 Mozart operas begin and end in the same key (the latest exception is *Il re pastore*). Eight are 'in' D and five in another 'trumpet key'. But to relate other keys to this 'tonic' proposes a scheme too vast to be grasped unless fully supported by secondary evidence such as thematic reprise or instrumentation; both can deceive (in the first finale of *Don Giovanni*, music first heard in F recurs in G; in the sextet, the trumpets enter in D, a semitone below the tonic). The claims of affective key symbolism and tonal architecture are virtually irreconcilable, and it is not self-evident that such systematic structures are appropriate to dramatic forms; they are best understood as an aspect of Mozart's musical language. Dramatic criticism is more appropriately founded on the interaction of elements than single cohesive theories.

The statue music in *Don Giovanni*, the folkishness and solemnity of *Die Zauberflöte*, resonated throughout the 19th century; even the gaiety of *Figaro* was occasionally evoked, as in Berlioz's *Béatrice et Bénédict*. But while Mozart's influence was widespread, composers took what they needed – the inspiration of colourful orchestration, an idea like the dance scene in *Don Giovanni* which resurfaces at the opening of *Rigoletto* – rather than imitating his dramatic methods. Mozart's transmutation of the sonata into a vehicle for drama may appear his most radical achievement; yet it was not developed even by Beethoven in *Fidelio* (as distinct from its overtures). The chain finale anticipates 19th-century continuous opera, nowhere more than in *Die Zauberflöte*; the first finale is tonally simple, using only the closest relations to C major, but it includes obbligato recitative building to expressive arioso (Tamino and the Orator), lyrical song (Tamino with the flute), action ensembles and choruses. The second finale incorporates popular and learned styles as well as spectacular scenic effects. Nevertheless the operatic styles engendered by the French Revolution, and the continuity of Italian traditions, played at least as great a role in forming Romantic opera. The musical languages of Rossini and Weber were not sonata-based; Wagner had more immediate models; *Falstaff*, *Der Rosenkavalier* and *The Rake's Progress* are spiritual descendants too remote in time to constitute a tradition.

In every genre Mozart built on existing conventions to point a new way: his Singspiel accommodates heroism and religious quest, as well as a huge musical expansion; *opera seria* is purged of artificiality and humanized; *opera buffa* provides the framework for serious explorations of society and sexuality. His influence on the next century's opera is perhaps the victim of the very perfection of his works. Yet from Goethe and E.T.A. Hoffmann he affected the minds of poets and philosophers as well as musicians; he is the first operatic composer whose work as a whole has never needed to be revived. It is likely to remain the touchstone of operatic achievement.

J.R.

Operas

Apollo et Hyacinthus
('Apollo and Hyacinthus')

Intermezzo in three acts, K38 set to a Latin libretto by Rufinus Widl; first performed in Salzburg, at the Benedictine University, on 13 May 1767.

Mozart's first stage work, *Apollo et Hyacinthus* is an intermezzo, written for performance by students with the five-act Latin tragedy *Clementia Croesi* by the Benedictine Gymnasium teacher, Widl.

Hyacinthus (boy soprano), son of Oebalus (tenor), King of Lacedonia, is murdered by Zephyrus (boy alto) to incriminate Apollo (boy alto), his rival for the hand of Oebalus's daughter Melia (boy soprano). She denounces Apollo; but the dying Hyacinthus, in a moving recitative, reveals the truth. Zephyrus is banished, Apollo and Melia marry, and the god turns Hyacinthus into the flower that bears his name.

The musical idiom is not yet characteristic, but is never less than expressive. Although the singers were aged between 12 and 23, the solo numbers (an aria for each character, two duets and a trio) are neither short nor particularly easy. There is a single-movement overture and an opening chorus.

J.R.

Bastien und Bastienne
('Bastien and Bastienne')

Singspiel in one act, K50/46*b* set to a libretto by Friedrich Wilhelm Weiskern and Johann Müller and revised by Johann Andreas Schachtner after Marie-Justine-Benoîte Favart and Harny de Guerville's *opéra comique Les amours de Bastien et Bastienne*. It was first performed in F. A. Mesmer's house in Vienna, sometime around September and October of 1768.

Favart and Guerville's realistic parody of Rousseau's *Le devin du village* appeared in Vienna in 1755 and was translated in 1764. It was used in children's theatre and was possibly performed in Salzburg in 1766. For Mozart, Schachtner made alterations and improvements, including versification of the dialogue. The performance in Vienna at Mesmer's house in 1768 used spoken dialogue; Mozart later set some of it as recitative. The opera may have been revived in Salzburg in 1774.

Bastien (tenor) has shown signs of fickleness but Bastienne (soprano), advised by the 'magician' Colas (bass), wins him back by feigning indifference, even encouraging him to drown himself. Pastoral innocence is reflected in the short melodious arias (*La finta semplice* shows that their unsophisticated style derives from the subject, not Mozart's youthfulness). Variety is given by Colas's pseudo-magical invocation; by dividing a two-section aria between the angry lovers; and by a short recitative-arioso at the crux (the threat of suicide). A longer duet includes quarrel and reconciliation, and leads without a break into the final trio.

J.R.

La finta semplice
('The Pretended Simpleton')

Opera buffa in three acts, K51/46*a*, set to a libretto by Carlo Goldoni with alterations by Marco Coltellini; first performed in Salzburg, at the Archbishop's Palace, probably on 1 May 1769.

La finta semplice was rehearsed in Vienna in 1768 but not performed, because of doubts about its genuineness and other intrigues (indignantly, but not circumstantially, outlined by Leopold). Its only performance in Mozart's lifetime was in Salzburg the next year, with local singers including Maria Magdalena Lipp, Michael Haydn's wife (Rosina). Coltellini's revisions tighten the intrigue and ensure a good third finale.

The three-movement *sinfonia* K45 became the overture, its final cadence elided with the opening *coro*. *La finta semplice* is a comedy of love overcoming obstacles through deceit, its roots in *commedia dell'arte*. Cassandro (bass) and Polidoro (tenor) forbid their sister Giacinta (soprano) to marry Fracasso (tenor) and their maid Ninetta (soprano) to marry his servant Simone (bass). Fracasso's sister Rosina (soprano), the major role whose range of sentiment includes the longest and most serious arias, wins Cassandro's heart by her feigned simplicity (hence the title) and Polidoro's by instructing him in wooing. The brothers' resistance is finally broken by the threat of a duel and the theft of their gold. The lovers succeed in forcing assent to their marriages, and Rosina marries Cassandro.

By Mozart's own standards, rhythmic squareness, lack of ensembles and monotony of key in the long finales may be seen as signs of immaturity. Distinctions of class are not fully reflected in the music. Nevertheless *La finta semplice* shows a complete grasp of the idiom and can stand comparison with contemporary *opera buffa* by such composers as Piccinni.

J.R.

Mitridate, re di Ponto
('Mithridates, King of Pontus')

Dramma per musica in three acts, K87/74*a*, set to a libretto by Vittorio Amedeo Cigna-Santi after Giuseppe Parini's translation of Jean Racine's *Mithridate*. Its first performance was at the Regio Ducal Teatro in Milan, on 26 December 1770.

Mitridate was commissioned for Carnival 1771; Mozart wrote the recitatives and overture while touring Italy in 1770. Reaching Milan on 18 October, he was forced to write and rewrite the arias quickly; the castrato Pietro Benedetti caused anxiety by his late arrival (1 December) and someone tried to persuade the prima donna to introduce arias from Gasparini's *Mitridate* (1767, Turin: with the same libretto). As in Vienna in 1768 there were those who condemned the work in advance because of Mozart's extreme youth. They were silenced by the first performance. Despite its length – six hours, with the ballet – *Mitridate* was repeated 21 times. Some music not by Mozart may have been included in the performances, and some lines of recitative are missing in every source. No further performances are known until the present century.

The setting is at Nymphaeum, in 63 BC; the scenes, for which designs by the brothers Galliani were applauded, include the palace, a temple, the port, hanging gardens and a military encampment. Mithridates, who long defended his empire against the Romans, and his son Pharnaces (who in Racine's play remains treacherous to the end) are historical personages; but the plot is fiction.

*

ACT 1 Mithridates (tenor, originally Guglielmo d'Ettore), twice married and with two sons, is betrothed to Aspasia (Racine's Monime; soprano, Antonia Bernasconi). He is reported dead resisting the Romans. Both his sons, Sifare [Xiphares] (soprano castrato, Benedetti) and the elder Farnace [Pharnaces] (alto castrato, Giuseppe Cicognani) are in love with Aspasia; she reciprocates only the love of Xiphares. Thwarted ambition leads Pharnaces to conspire against his father with the Roman Marzio [Marcius] (tenor, Gaspare

Bassano). Defeated by Pompey, Mithridates unexpectedly returns, bringing Ismene, a Parthian Princess betrothed to Pharnaces (soprano, Anna Francesca Varese; she does not appear in Racine). Mithridates fears he has returned to two ungrateful sons, but is reassured by Arbate [Arbates] (Governor of Nymphaeum; soprano castrato, Pietro Muschietti) concerning Xiphares. Mithridates' second aria, in a regal D major, ends the first act.

ACT 2   Pharnaces spurns Ismene; she complains to the King who says Pharnaces is worthy to die. Mithridates doubts Aspasia's fidelity; he has to leave to do battle with Pompey, but proposes to marry her first. His aria alternately thanks loyal Xiphares (andante) and hurls accusations at Aspasia (allegro). Xiphares decides he must leave Pontus and bids Aspasia a moving farewell ('Lungi da te, mio bene': one of the three extant versions has an obbligato horn part). Aspasia laments her fate in a soliloquy (aria in two tempos, 'Nel grave tormento'). When Mithridates accuses Pharnaces of treachery he admits his guilt ('Son reo: l'error confesso'), but betrays Xiphares's love for Aspasia. Mithridates imprisons both his sons; the lovers bid a last farewell (the only duet).

ACT 3   Mithridates prepares for his final battle ('Vado incontro al fato'; Gasparini's setting is the one in the standard Mozart scores). Spurned by Aspasia, he sends her poison, which she accepts (monologue: recitative framing a cavatina); but Xiphares prevents her from drinking it. He prepares for worthy death in battle ('Se il rigor d'in-grata sorte', a noble *Sturm und Drang* aria in C minor). As the Romans attack, Marcius frees Pharnaces; in a magnificent *scena* (aria, 'Già dagli occhi') he resolves to support his father and goes to burn the Roman fleet. Mithridates is victorious but mortally wounds himself; he unites Xiphares with Aspasia, and forgives Pharnaces, who marries Ismene.

*

Fitting the arias for demanding singers did not prevent Mozart introducing ample variety of expression. Aspasia's second aria is a powerful lament in G minor; Xiphares' second combines short *andante* sections with vehement *allegro* passages. All his, Aspasia's and Ismene's music is characterized by extreme virtuosity. Mozart skilfully abbreviated the required ternary forms and used a large number of arias in which contrasting affections are expressed by alternating tempos. The overture is a three-movement sinfonia in D major and the finale a very short 'coro' of soloists. *Mitridate* is an astonishing achievement for a boy of 14; it makes the best use of conventional forms of expression and presents a drama which, if artificial, contains scenes of real intensity.

J.R.

Ascanio in Alba

Festa teatrale in two acts, к111, set to a libretto by Giuseppe Parini; first performed in Milan, at the Regio Ducal Teatro, on 17 October 1771.

Mozart's second Milan opera, following *Mitridate* (1770), is in the courtly genre beloved of the Habsburgs. It was included in the celebrations for the wedding of Archduke Ferdinand to Maria Ricciarda Berenice d'Este, with Hasse's *Il Ruggiero* which (according to Leopold Mozart) it put in the shade, and it was repeated three or four times.

Ascanio (soprano castrato; originally sung by Mozart's former singing instructor, Giovanni Manzuoli) is the son of Aeneas and grandson of Venere [Venus] (soprano, representing Maria Theresa). He is destined to marry Silvia (soprano), a descendant of Hercules (alluding to Duke Ercole d'Este). In an allegory of arranged marriage, Venus contrives to have Silvia fall in love with a dream-image of Ascanio, while he is allowed to see her but may not identify himself. This slender plot develops amid pastoral scenes with shepherds, votaries of Venus led by Fauno (soprano castrato) and the priest Aceste (tenor). During an entr'acte (a ballet, for which only the bass parts have survived), the city of Alba Longa miraculously springs up; in Act 2 a little dramatic tension is generated by Silvia's uncertainty about whether her beloved really is Ascanio. Several scenes are structured by repeated choruses, there is one trio. The arias, particularly Fauno's second and those for Ascanio and Silvia, are exceptionally brilliant. Mozart's growing maturity is revealed in the solo scene for Silvia (aria, 'Infelici affetti miei') and in the skilful blend of counterpoint and homophony in what is perhaps the work's most distinctive feature, its choral writing.

J.R.

Il sogno di Scipione
('The Dream of Scipio')

Azione teatrale in one act, K126, set to a libretto by Pietro Metastasio; its first performance was possibly in Salzburg, at the Archbishop's Palace, in May 1772.

It seems likely that *Il sogno di Scipione*, Mozart's first full-length Metastasio setting, was planned for the 50th anniversary of Archbishop Schrattenbach's ordination, and accordingly was composed before *Ascanio in Alba*. Schrattenbach however died in December 1771, and it may have been performed as a serenata in the Salzburg palace the next year during the installation ceremonies for Archbishop Colloredo.

Il sogno di Scipione belongs to the Viennese court tradition of moral theatre pieces. In his dream Scipio (tenor) is claimed by Fortuna [Fortune] (soprano), promising earthly rewards, and Costanza [Constancy] (soprano), representing unselfish virtue. In Elysium he meets his adopted father Publio [Publius] (tenor) and his real father Emilio [Emilius] (tenor), but they will not dictate his choice. Fortune impatiently demands an answer; Constancy is more persuasive and despite the threats of Fortune (the only obbligato recitative) Scipio elects to follow her. There follows a *licenza* in praise of the Archbishop.

The solos are arranged symmetrically round the aria for Emilius, the other singers each having two. The series of abbreviated da capo forms is mitigated by variation of tempo and metre, the short second aria for Publius and two choruses. The overture, lacking a third movement, is linked to the first scene; Mozart later added a finale to make a separate symphony, K141a. The final recitative is harmonically and instrumentally adventurous; otherwise, as befits its function, *Scipione* is elegant rather than dramatic.

J.R.

Lucio Silla
('Lucius Sulla')

Dramma per musica in three acts, K135, set to a libretto by Giovanni
De Gamerra; first performed in Milan at the Regio Ducal Teatro on
26 December 1772.

The original cast was: Bassano Morgnoni (Sulla), Venanzio
Rauzzini (Cecilius), Anna de Amicis-Buonsolazzi (Junia), Felicità
Suardi (Cinna), Daniella Mienci (Celia) and Giuseppe Onofrio
(Aufidius).

Lucius Sulla *dictator of Rome*	tenor
Giunia [Junia] *daughter of Gaius Marius,* *betrothed to Cecilius*	soprano
Cecilio [Cecilius] *exiled Roman senator*	soprano castrato
Lucio [Lucius] Cinna *his friend, a conspirator*	soprano
Celia *sister of Sulla*	soprano
Aufidio [Aufidius] *tribune, friend of Sulla*	tenor

Guards; nobles; senators; people of Rome

Setting Rome, 79 BC

The contract for *Lucio Silla*, dated 4 March 1771, required Mozart
to deliver the recitatives in October 1772 and to be in Milan by
November to compose the arias and rehearse 'with the usual reser-
vations in case of theatrical misfortunes and Princely interventions
(which God forbid)'.

The primo uomo Venanzio Rauzzini (Cecilius) arrived only on
21 November, the prima donna (Junia) still later. Morgnoni was a
last-minute replacement (so his role is relatively simple). Mozart had
to make alterations in the light of Metastasio's comments on the
libretto. Archduke Ferdinand's letter-writing delayed the première
two hours; it was immensely long (there were three ballets), but
nevertheless was followed by 25 more performances, a major
triumph. The libretto was set by other composers including J. C. Bach

31

(1775, Mannheim), but Mozart's opera was not revived until 1929 (Prague, in German).

*

The successful general Lucius Sulla seized total power in Rome but unexpectedly laid it down the year before his death. Some of the characters are historical, but the plot is fiction.

ACT 1 *A neglected grove* The banished Cecilius reappears secretly in Rome and learns from Cinna that Sulla, declaring him dead, proposes to marry Junia. Cecilius may see her when she goes to mourn her father; love promises a better future ('Vieni ov'amor t'invita'). Cecilius is prey to fear and joyful anticipation (the first of many fine obbligato recitatives) as well as feelings of tenderness ('Il tenero momento').

In Sulla's palace Celia agrees to persuade Junia to accept Sulla (in minuet style, 'Se lusinghiera speme'); no girl will resist for the sake of the dead. Junia rejects the tyrant who has deposed her father and banished her lover. Sulla, at first not unkind, says the price of obstinacy may be death. Junia responds ('Dalla sponda tenebrosa'): in an *adagio* section she invokes her father and lover, then (*allegro*) pours scorn on his love. Sulla decides he must overcome the weakness of affection and, like a true tyrant, condemn her (obbligato recitative and aria, 'Il desio di vendetta').

The mausoleum The rest of Act 1 uses no simple recitative. After the fiery D major of Sulla's aria, Mozart sets the new scene by sombre music which modulates obliquely to C minor. Cecilius's mixed feelings bring varied figurations and rapid tempo changes. Junia enters with mourners; within their funeral chorus she sings a G minor lament ('O del padre ombra diletta'). Cecilius is taken for a ghost. Their duet ('D'Eliso in sen m'attendi'), a moving Andante and brilliant Allegro, ends the act on a note of hope.

ACT 2 *A military arch* Aufidius tells Sulla that as Junia has many supporters in Rome he should publicly declare her his wife ('Guerrier, che d'un acciaro'). Sulla permits Celia's betrothal to Cinna. Cecilius pursues Sulla with a sword but Cinna restrains him; rashness will gain nothing. Cecilius mingles hope and despair in snatches of obbli-gato recitative, but his aria ('Quest'improviso tremito'), a concise Allegro in D, shows his fierce desire for revenge. Celia tries to declare her love for Cinna but is tongue-tied (an appealing Grazioso, 'Se il labbro timido'). Cinna is more concerned with plotting; but Junia refuses to marry Sulla and murder him in bed. He must care for Cecilius (obbligato recitative), whose danger freezes her heart. Her aria ('Ah se il crudel periglio') is a grandiose Allegro of stunning virtuosity. Cinna decides that he must take communal vengeance upon himself (obbligato recitative and a vigorous aria, 'Nel fortunato istante').

Hanging gardens Struggling with contradictory feelings, Sulla again assures Junia that refusal means death. His aria ('D'ogni pietà mi spoglio') explodes without ritornello. Drained of pity, he will assuage his hurt by killing. In a short middle section he is overcome by tenderness towards her, quickly suppressed. Cecilius tells Junia that he must kill the tyrant; if he dies his shade will watch over her ('Ah, se a morir mi chiama'). Exceptionally, the main section is Adagio, nobly arching in wide leaps (up to a 15th), and the middle section a tender Andante. Celia urges Junia to marry Sulla ('Quando sugl'arsi campi'). Her cheerful A major is followed by the tragic D minor of Junia's soliloquy on the conflict of duty and love. She will kill herself rather than submit, and gasps out her despair in an agitated aria ('Parto, m'affretto') with a daring harmonic shift ($E^\flat$ from G, the tonic being C) at the reprise.

The Capitol The chorus hopes that Sulla's glory will be crowned by love ('Se gloria il crin ti cinse'). Sulla publicly claims Junia as the token of civil peace; she is prevented from killing herself when Cecilius vainly attacks Sulla. In a trio ('Quell'orgoglioso sdegno') Sulla declares that he will humble his enemies, Cecilius is defiant, and Junia, joined by Cecilius, anticipates the consolation of death.

Act 3 *Before the prison* Cinna excuses his failure to support a futile assassination attempt. He agrees to marry Celia if she can persuade her brother to have mercy; she promises to achieve this whatever storms arise ('Strider sento la procella'). Cinna expresses

33

optimism (Cecilius has supporters) in a heroic aria in D ('De' più superbi il core'). Junia appears for a last farewell; she will not save Cecilius by yielding to Sulla. Aufidius comes to take Cecilius to public judgment; in a melting, rondo-like aria ('Pupille amate') in minuet tempo he says her tears will make him die too soon; his soul will return, dissolved in a sigh. Junia is left to her premonitions, her obbligato recitative richly scored and anticipating the motif of the aria ('Frà i pensier più funesti'), in which she imagines Cecilius dead, lamenting over a throbbing muted accompaniment; then with a determined Allegro she runs after her lover.

A hall in the palace   The denouement takes place in simple recitative. Even as Sulla condemns Cecilius, Junia publicly proclaims her betrothal. Baffled, even moved, the tyrant decides to forgive her and permit the two couples to marry. He retires from public life (finale); the chorus praises his devotion to Rome, and the soloists sing of love and freedom.

*

Mozart constructed the first two acts cleverly, gradually abandoning the conventionally formed and very long arias liked in Milan for more flexible designs perhaps suggested by Gluck's *Alceste*. Despite the magnificent mausoleum scene, *Lucio Silla* remains an unreformed type of *opera seria*. Several D major arias with trumpets and drums are contrasted with remarkable richness of expression in the splendid roles of Cecilius and Junia while Celia's lightly scored music provides relief. Although its plot is turgid and its denouement unconvincing, *Lucio Silla* is musically the finest work Mozart wrote in Italy, and ranks with *opera seria* by the greatest masters of the time.

J.R.

La finta giardiniera
('The Pretended Garden-Girl')

Opera buffa in three acts, K196. First performed at the Munich, Salvatortheater on 13 January 1775.

The casting of the first production remains unknown. Rosa Manservisi sang Sandrina and the soprano castrato Tommaso Consoli, Ramiro, although the range suits the modern (female) mezzo. Other likely singers include Teresa Manservisi (Arminda or Serpetta), Johann Walleshauser (Belfiore), Augustin Sutor (the Mayor) and Giovanni Rossi (Nardo).

Ramiro *a knight*	soprano castrato
Don Anchise *Mayor (Podestà) of Lagonero*	tenor
Marchioness Violante Onesti *disguised as Sandrina,* *working in the Mayor's garden*	soprano
Roberto *her servant, disguised as Nardo, a gardener*	baritone
Serpetta *the mayor's housekeeper*	soprano
Arminda *a Milanese lady, the Mayor's niece*	soprano
Count (Contino) Belfiore	tenor

Setting The Mayor's estate at Lagonero near Milan

No published libretto of *La finta giardiniera* acknowledges its authorship. The first setting, by Anfossi, was given at Rome during Carnival 1774; Mozart's followed within a year.

The Mozarts left Salzburg three weeks before the planned first performance (29 December), which was postponed, Leopold wrote (28 December), to allow more time to learn the music and actions. Three performances took place, the first and third with great success in the old court theatre; the second, in the Redoutensaal, was truncated because one singer was ill.

The first revival was as a Singspiel, *Die verstellte Gärtnerin*. Mozart probably helped with the adaptation, which was performed by Johann Böhm's company in Augsburg (1 May 1780). Böhm took it to other German centres including Frankfurt (1782; the first Mozart opera given in North Germany). After 1797 it was not heard until 1891, in Vienna. Until recently, 20th-century revivals necessarily used the German form since no source survived of the Italian first act. Its rediscovery (in time for the Neue Mozart-Ausgabe, 1978) permits revival of the original version (Munich and Salzburg, 1979; several subsequent productions). English performances have been given under the title *Sandrina's Secret*.

*

ACT 1 *The Mayor's garden* In an *Introduzione* the characters introduce themselves and their situations, and develop their initial feelings. Ramiro, spurned by Arminda, finds love a snare; the Mayor compares his love for the garden-maid to a series of musical instruments ('Dentro il mio petto', an aria which had some currency outside the opera). Sandrina (Violante) reminds Nardo (Roberto, pretending to be her cousin) of the background to the story; she is seeking her lover Belfiore who a year ago stabbed her and fled, leaving her for dead. Her pastoral aria maintains her disguise in front of Ramiro. Nardo is in love with Serpetta, but she intends to marry her master. Arminda clamours for attention until the arrival of her betrothed, who proves to be Belfiore, singing the praises of female beauty. Arminda threatens punishment for any unfaithfulness. Belfiore traces his pedigree to the heroes of Greece and Rome. Serpetta engages in banter with Nardo (each sing a verse of an aria); she adds a sprightly aria of her own.

Hanging Gardens Sandrina bewails her fate in an eloquent cavatina. She still hopes to find and forgive her lover. On learning the name of Arminda's betrothed she faints. In the finale Belfiore recognizes her, but she denies her identity. Nevertheless their behaviour seems compromising. In a brilliantly varied multi-movement 'ensemble of perplexity', Ramiro is pleased, Nardo concerned, Serpetta and Arminda jealous, Sandrina upset, Belfiore bemused and the Mayor vexed by the upset to his household.

ACT 2 *Hall of the Mayor's house* Having dismissed Ramiro, Arminda turns on Belfiore for his faithlessness (an aria in a vibrantly emotional G minor). Nardo woos Serpetta in Italian, French and

English, but she is too jealous of his 'cousin' to admit to liking him. Sandrina muddles Belfiore still more by giving an eyewitness account of her own death; in his amorous aria in response he accidentally pays court to the Mayor, from whom Sandrina has to repel a further advance. Ramiro appears with a warrant for Belfiore's arrest for killing Violante; the Mayor cannot allow a murderer to marry his niece. Ramiro pleads his cause in the warmest melody of the opera ('Dolce d'amor compagna').

Another room Belfiore is confronted with the accusation. Sandrina defends him: there was no murder, for she is Violante. The others only half-believe her and to Belfiore she denies it again, saying she spoke only to save him. This finally unhinges him (obbligato recitative and aria). Meanwhile we learn that Arminda has had Sandrina abandoned in the wild woods; everyone hastens to the rescue. Serpetta's roguish aria leads without a break into the new scene; the music is now continuous to the end of the act.

A dark wood, with rocks and caves Sandrina cries out in fear (Agitato in C minor; 'Crudeli, fermate'; cavatina and recitative). She hides in a cave and in the finale the others appear one by one and pair off in a comedy of mistaken identity revealed when the practical Ramiro brings a light. But the noble lovers find harmony in madness, acting the part of mythological characters amid general consternation.

ACT 3 *A room* The lunatics mistake Nardo for each other. He makes his escape, leaving them prey to imaginary disasters (aria and duet). The Mayor complains that he cannot understand what is going on. Arminda is still determined to marry Belfiore; Ramiro gives vent to his feelings in a powerful C minor aria ('Va pure ad altri').

The garden Sandrina and Belfiore are sleeping. They awake restored and take leave of one another in a long recitative and duet, then decide, with ecstatic finality, that they must never part. This news reconciles Arminda with Ramiro; Serpetta, seeing that the Mayor will always sigh for Sandrina, marries Nardo. In a short finale all sing Sandrina's praises.

*

La finta giardiniera is Mozart's first mature *opera buffa*, but it is a far cry from the swiftly unfolding, ensemble-driven plots of the Da Ponte operas. Its ancestry lies in Goldoni's librettos, mingling serious emotions with comedy; apart from the finales it consists almost entirely of arias. The *Serva padrona* tradition remains in the Serpetta–Nardo–Mayor intrigue, and the disguised noblewoman, victim of jealousy, descends from Piccinni's *La buona figliuola*. Whereas the Count, who seems decidedly weak in the head, is both comic and pathetic, Ramiro is entirely serious, while Arminda appears to caricature *opera seria*.

The music is almost too elaborate, but it is an astounding achievement for an 18-year-old: richly coloured, distinctive in characterization, alternately good-humoured and searchingly expressive in the arias, and brilliantly inventive in the finales. Characterization includes class distinction. The nobles employ a more developed musical idiom, including obbligato recitative and a greater degree of coloratura, than Ramiro and Arminda (despite the vehemence of their minor-mode arias) and the Mayor. The servants bring a simpler melodic style, largely syllabic word-setting, and lighter orchestration.

The opera contains an almost wilful variety of emotional entanglements but its resolution remains obstinately symmetrical, like that of *Così fan tutte*. Love-ties across class barriers (Arminda–Belfiore; Serpetta or Violante/Sandrina–Mayor) do not work out. The restoration of the aristocrats' wits, and the union of social equals in three couples, symbolize restoration of the order threatened by the aftermath of Belfiore's rash attack on Violante.

J.R.

Il re pastore
('The Shepherd King')

Serenata in two acts, K208, set to a libretto by Pietro Metastasio; first performed in Salzburg at the Archbishop's Palace, on 23 April 1775.

Il re pastore was written immediately after Mozart's return from Munich to oversee the performance of *La finta giardiniera*. It was one of two short works performed in honour of Archduke Maximilian, who broke a journey from Vienna to Italy at Salzburg (the other was *Gli orti esperidi* by Fischietti). The reduced form of Metastasio's libretto compresses Acts 2 and 3 into one, cutting five arias and reducing the recitatives so that what was originally a pastoral *opera seria* is scaled down to the proportions of a serenata. This version of the libretto had been devised for a performance in Munich in 1774, with music from Guglielmi's 1767 setting for Venice, and was Mozart's principal source; further alterations may have been made by Giambattista Varesco.

The performance took the semi-staged form, without scenery, appropriate to a serenata. The castrato Tommaso Consoli came from Munich to sing Aminta [Amyntas]; with him came the flautist Johann Baptist Becke. The exact disposition of the other roles, taken by members of the Salzburg Hofkapelle, is unknown.

*

Il re pastore, based on an episode in the career of Alexander the Great, is designed to show the magnanimity and understanding of this imperial archetype. The title role is the shepherd Amyntas (soprano castrato) who, unknown to himself, is Abdalonimo [Abdalonimus], legitimate heir to the kingdom of Sidon. He is betrothed to Elisa (soprano), despite her noble birth.

The first act is almost unchanged from Metastasio's. As in Gluck's setting (1756), the single-movement overture runs into Amyntas's first aria ('Intendo amico rio'), really a short song in a pastoral 6/8; it is interrupted in turn by the arrival of Elisa. Amyntas is worried by the proximity of Alexander's army; Elisa is sanguine ('Alla selva, al prato'); the country and her beloved will provide a sanctuary.

39

Alessandro [Alexander] (tenor) comes disguised with the Sidonian nobleman Agenore [Agenor] (tenor) to question Amyntas, who praises the simplicity and honesty of his pastoral existence (obbligato recitative and aria, 'Aer tranquillo', a replacement text present in the 1774 Munich libretto).

Alexander looks forward to restoring the instinctively noble young man to his rightful station (the martial aria 'Si spande al sole in faccia'). Tamiri [Tamyris] (soprano), friend of Elisa and daughter of the tyrant Straton whom Alexander has deposed, is in hiding, but she comes to Agenor, her betrothed. He assures her of his love ('Per me rispondete'); she, however, fears the wrath of Alexander ('Di tante sue procelle'). Agenor tells Amyntas of his change in fortune; he fears parting from Elisa but she remains confident (obbligato recitative). The lovers' duet ends the first act.

In this compressed form of the libretto the lovers' problems are quickly resolved. First Agenor is obliged to prevent Elisa from seeing Amyntas; her anguish is expressed in her second aria ('Barbaro, oh Dio!'), a lamenting Andante in which the coloratura is deeply expressive, and a protesting Allegro. Amyntas is likewise prevented from following Elisa. Alexander sends him to deck himself like a king.

On learning from Agenor that Tamyris is near, Alexander announces his intention to marry her to Amyntas; through his conquests he wishes people to be made happy (a virtuoso aria in F major, 'Se vincendo vi rendo felici'). In Amyntas's next aria ('L'amerò, sarò costante'), a ravishing rondò with violin obbligato, muted strings, two flutes and two english horns, the noble arches of his melody support a declaration of the constancy of his love. Elisa and Agenor believe that he is talking of Tamyris, who, however, accuses Agenor of faithlessness ('Se tu di me fai dono': surprisingly, a Grazioso in A). His misery induces the only minor-mode aria, a vehement Allegro protesting his constancy ('Sol può dir'). Alexander enters, his final aria ('Voi che fausti ognor donate') a kingly showpiece. Tamyris and Elisa throw themselves on his mercy, and as soon as he understands he unites the four lovers and declares that the Shepherd King and Elisa will rule in Sidon, while Agenor and

Tamyris will be granted another kingdom. All join in a 'coro' in praise of the unconquered Alexander ('Viva l'invitto Duce').

*

The second and third arias of Act 2 add two flutes to the standard Salzburg group of two oboes and two horns; the virtuoso flourishes in the first of these were doubtless intended for Becke. Trumpets appear in Alexander's other arias, so that all three are distinguished instrumentally. So, however, are the crucial arias in the roles of the characters who are facing real dilemmas: Amyntas (see above) and Agenor ('Sol può dir', where the minor mode is supported by two horns in different keys). The arias with strings only (Agenor's first and Tamyris's second) act as a foil to these more elaborate movements. Mozart shows equal resource in the handling of the now standard aria design, the 'modified da capo' or small-scale sonata-form aria. If *Il re pastore* is not as original as *La finta giardiniera*, it nevertheless makes the most of its slender dramatic basis, and helped Mozart to develop characterization in the serious style, a useful preparation for *Idomeneo*.

J.R.

Zaide
[*Das Serail*]

Singspiel in two acts, K344/336*b*, set to a libretto by Johann Andreas Schachtner after Franz Josef Sebastiani's *Das Serail*; first performed in Frankfurt on 27 January 1866.

Mozart wrote *Zaide* in Salzburg between autumn 1779 and mid-1780, perhaps for J. H. Böhm's touring company or Schikaneder's, but surely with the National Singspiel in mind. In April 1781 Stephanie rejected it as too serious for Vienna. The autograph is untitled. The source, a Singspiel by Sebastiani, is called *Das Serail*; '*Zaide*' was chosen by Johann Anton André for his 1838 publication, and avoids confusion with *Die Entführung aus dem Serail*. Schachtner's libretto was evidently more than a revision, but it is lost apart from incipits in the autograph score. *Zaide* was first performed at Frankfurt (Mozart's birthday, 1866), as completed by André, who had added an overture and finale, and with new text by Friedrich Carl Gollmick. Other versions followed, in German, French and English, often with additional music from *Thamos, König in Ägypten*, K345/336*a*. There is no evidence for the missing overture being the G major Symphony K318; D is a more likely tonic for the opera, the instrumentation does not correspond, and Mozart is unlikely to have written the overture first.

*

ACT 1   begins with the slaves (tenor solo and unison chorus) cheerfully finishing work for the day ('Brüder, lasst uns lustig sein'). Gomatz (tenor), exiled and enslaved, laments his bitter fate in what is Mozart's greatest melodrama ('Unerforschliche Fügung!'): the opening Adagio anticipates Mendelssohn, and other passages are of unusual enharmonic daring. Gomatz sleeps, watched by Zaide (soprano), the beautiful favourite of the Sultan. Her aria ('Ruhe sanft') is an image of peacefulness, a floating J. C. Bachian melody recurring after each episode. She leaves her portrait, which inspires Gomatz to defy the ragings of fate ('Rase, Schicksal'). Zaide reveals herself and they declare mutual love (duet, 'Meine Seele hüpft von Freuden') in a short and gentle Allegretto.

Allazim (bass), betraying the Sultan, helps prepare their escape. Gomatz ('Herr und Freund') is almost embarrassingly grateful; he returns during the exitritornello offering further thanks. Allazim bids his heart take courage ('Nur mutig, mein Herze'). They set out (trio, 'O selige Wonne', in E major): the sea is calm at sunrise, though Zaide imagines thunder; in a final Allegro they pray for future happiness.

ACT 2   begins as the Sultan Soliman (tenor), assisted by the only appearance of trumpets and drums, fumes, in a melodrama: Zaide has spurned his love to fly with a Christian slave. An officer tells him that their recapture is imminent. Soliman rails against all women. In his huge aria ('Der stolze Löw'', 246 bars) his anger twice boils over into a headlong Presto. A proud lion may be tamed, but treat him shamefully and he becomes a tyrant. There follows a comic scene for the overseer Osmin (bass) with a laughing aria ('Wer hungrig bei der Tafel sitzt').

Soliman tells the captives that he rewards service but punishes defiance ('Ich bin so bös' als gut'). Zaide acknowledges his bounty, but he did not offer freedom ('Trostlos schluchzet Philomele'); the caged nightingale sings only of her sorrow. This melting rondo fails to move him, and she turns to attack ('Tiger! wetze nur die Klauen') in a G minor aria of splendid fury. The contrasting middle section ('Ach, mein Gomatz') looks forward to release through death; but her anger extends to the last bar, with its final cry of 'Tiger!'.

Allazim (whose life is spared) lectures Soliman ('Ihr Mächtigen seht ungerührt'): the mighty should recognize slaves as brothers. In the quartet ('Freundin, stille deine Tränen') Gomatz asks Zaide to calm her tears; death will crown their love. Allazim's heart is breaking. Taking the blame (like Konstanze in *Die Entführung*), Zaide pleads for Gomatz's life; Soliman remains vindictive. This resourceful ensemble worthily anticipates the *Idomeneo* and *Entführung* quartets.

*

Zaide herself is Mozart's first three-dimensional character. In *Das Serail* Zaide and Gomatz are revealed as siblings, children of Renegat (Allazim); Soliman forgives them (Renegat once saved his life).

Despite its origins in Voltaire, Mozart may have planned a less perfunctory denouement. With the quartet as finale the two acts are of equivalent length, and conceivably a third was intended. In *Das Serail* Soliman is a spoken role, like Selim in *Die Entführung*; here parts of his arias imply a more compassionate personality, suppressed in the quartet. Although not viable as it stands, *Zaide* marks a striking advance and at its best reaches the level of Mozart's maturity.

J.R.

Idomeneo, re di Creta
('Idomeneus, King of Crete')

Dramma per musica in three acts, K366, set to a libretto by Giovanni Battista Varesco after Antoine Danchet's *Idomenée*; first performed in Munich's Residenztheater on 29 January 1781.

The original cast included Anton Raaff (Idonmeneus), Dorothea Wendling (Ilia), Elisabeth Wendling (Electra), Vincenzo dal Prato (Idamantes) and Domenico de Panzacchi (Arbaces).

Idomeneus *King of Crete*	tenor
Idamante [Idamantes] *his son*	soprano castrato
Ilia *Trojan princess, daughter of Priam*	soprano
Elettra [Electra] *princess, daughter of Agamemnon*	soprano
Arbace [Arbaces] *confidant of the king*	tenor
High Priest of Neptune	tenor
Oracle	bass

Trojan prisoners; sailors; people of Crete

Setting Mycenean Crete: the Royal palace at Kydonia (Sidon), by the sea, and the temple of Neptune

Mozart received the commission from the Munich Intendant, Count Seeau, during the summer of 1780. Danchet's five-act libretto of 1712 was adapted by the Salzburg cleric Varesco in three acts, on the pattern of the 'reformed' operas of Jommelli and Gluck, balancing the introduction of Italian arias by retaining a strong choral element, ballet, a high proportion of orchestrated recitative, scenic effects, and some ensemble writing. The influence of Gluck's *Alceste* is felt in hieratic scenes, particularly the speech for the High Priest and the utterance of the oracle, but also in the prevailing seriousness. Mozart had witnessed the synthesis of French forms and Italian music in Piccinni's *Roland*, the effect of which, and perhaps of Jommelli, was to encourage what Gluck tended to repress: highly developed aria forms with the bloom of italianate lyricism.

45

Raaff may have been instrumental in obtaining the commission for Mozart, and other singers, as well as the orchestra, were known to Mozart from Mannheim. He was therefore able to start work before leaving Salzburg on 5 November. His completion of the work in Munich is documented in letters home; his father, besides supplying trumpet mutes, had to act as intermediary between composer and librettist. Mozart is constantly concerned with theatrical effect and timing. The libretto required severe pruning: the oracle must have fewer words; the recitatives were too long; there were too many arias (at the last minute, two were dropped from the third act).

Mozart also reported the singers' reactions, and the elector's approval of the music in rehearsal. The first performance, attended by Leopold Mozart, was well received. The designs were by Lorenzo Quaglio and the ballet-master was Le Grand, who in the absence of the librettist may have acted as director. Raaff, by then 66, was tactfully nursed by the composer; Idomeneus's music contrives to be brilliant and expressive without placing exceptional demands on breath-control. The Wendling sisters-in-law were capable and experienced; Elisabeth, the younger, must have been a formidable singer to have inspired Electra's music. Unfortunately the Idamantes was relatively inexperienced; Mozart had to teach him his part 'as if he were a child'; and the Arbaces insisted on the unnecessary development (with two arias) of his role.

There were three performances in 1781. In September of that year Mozart wrote to his father from Vienna that he would like to revise *Idomeneo* 'more in the French style', but with a German text (by J.B. van Alxinger, who had translated Gluck's *Iphigénie en Tauride*). Idomeneus was to be a bass (Ludwig Fischer). Various numbers were included in concerts in his first year in Vienna, as if sowing seeds for a new production; but the only other performance in Mozart's lifetime, at Prince Auersperg's palace in Vienna, was probably a concert performance, given by amateurs. The chief alteration actually made was to recast Idamantes as a tenor. Mozart added two new numbers, rewrote the ensembles involving Idamantes, produced a simplified version of Idomeneus's showpiece ('Fuor del mar'), and made further cuts including Arbaces's arias and a good deal of recitative: so much, that at times intelligibility was endangered.

Idomeneo was not performed again until the 19th century, when various translations appeared in the repertory of German companies. The first of these was in Kassel (1802), followed by Vienna and Berlin (1806). The music was occasionally employed in 19th-century *pasticcios*, but there were few recognizable performances outside Austria and Germany until the 20th century, the first in Paris (in concert form) being in 1902, in Britain (Glasgow) 1934, in Italy and the USA 1947. The 150th anniversary (1931) was mostly recognized by productions in German, still more or less 'arranged', notably Richard Strauss's version for Vienna (published in vocal score). In the last 30 years most major companies have produced *Idomeneo*, but as an opera in need of perpetual revival rather than a repertory item.

*

The Trojan war is over; the legendary misfortunes of the returning Greek chieftain Idomeneus closely parallel the biblical story of Jephtha. Ilia and other Trojan captives have been sent to Crete ahead of him. Electra is there, following the murder of Agamemnon by her mother. Both have fallen in love with Idamantes.

The overture, in D major, is a boldly truncated sonata movement expressing majesty and suffering. It ends with a diminuendo making repeated use of a significant motif first heard in the ninth bar, which occurs throughout the opera and has been identified as a 'Sacrifice' or 'Idamantes' motif. The cadence prefigures the tonality of the first aria and allows Ilia to sing without further introduction.

ACT 1 *Ilia's apartment in the palace* Ilia bewails her fate: orphaned, a prisoner, in love with her captor's son and certain that he must prefer his compatriot Electra to a foreign slave. She explores her dilemma in a subdued lament in G minor, its moderate tempo as characteristic of her as an *allegro* is of Electra (recitative and aria, 'Padre, germani, addio!'). When Ilia considers her own disloyalty to her father, Priam, in loving a Greek, Mozart introduces the 'Idamantes motif' in the cellos.

47

Idamantes enters with words of comfort and even affection, but she proudly rejects him. In a short, majestic Adagio Idamantes protests that he has committed no fault, and in a driving Allegro he blames the gods for his suffering ('Non ho colpa'). As evidence of his kindly intentions, he frees the Trojan prisoners (chorus, 'Godiam la pace'). Electra protests at this action and is suspicious of his motives. Arbaces brings news of Idomeneus's shipwreck and Idamantes rushes off. In obbligato recitative, Electra gives vent to her jealousy: with Idomeneus dead, who will prevent his son marrying Ilia? Her D minor aria ('Tutte nel cor vi sento') writhes between fury and self-pity. The daring reprise in C minor not only symbolizes her mental disturbance but anticipates the storm of the next scene: although decorum is restored in that the aria ends in D, the music continues without interruption or change of speed,.

The sea-shore, strewn with wreckage   A distant chorus of sailors echoes the chorus on shore ('Pietà! Numi, pietà'). In pantomime Neptune is seen calming the waters; the king lands and dismisses his followers. He can think only of the impending sacrifice, for the price of his survival is that Neptune must be offered the first person he meets; he imagines himself haunted by the innocent victim ('Vedrommi intorno'). The 'Idamantes motif' reappears in the Andantino, as do images of the storm in the Allegro. The victim appears: it is Idamantes searching for his father. At his ecstatic recognition simple recitative explodes into orchestral figures. But Idomeneus breaks away and leaves Idamantes a prey to fear and longing; the atmosphere of the storm again affects Idamantes' aria ('Il padre adorato'). The Cretan soldiers make land and the populace comes to greet them (ballet sequence with choral chaconne, 'Nettunos' onori').

ACT 2   *A royal apartment*   [1786 only: orchestrated dialogue and aria K490. Ilia yields Idamantes to Electra but asks to be remembered. His reply, 'Ch'io mi scordi di te?', and subsequent rondò, 'Non temer, amato bene', with obbligato violin.]

Idomeneus tells Arbaces everything; he resolves that Idamantes must escape sacrifice by taking Electra back to Argos. Arbaces responds sententiously, in an energetic Allegro ('Se il tuo duol', omitted in 1786). Ilia approaches the king. In Mozart's most tenderly poised melodic vein, she accepts Idomeneus as a second father ('Se il padre perdei'). He now sees that the sacrifice will ruin two lives beyond that of the victim; his recitative underlines his concern by its orchestral use of motifs from her aria. His own aria ('Fuor del mar'), majestic in D major (the opera's tonic), exists in a simplified (1786) version as well as the more flamboyant original destined for Raaff. Freed from the sea, he finds a worse storm in his own heart. In the middle section he asks why a heart so near to shipwreck cannot find it; Mozart risked a heartstopping enharmonic modulation before the full reprise. Electra is transformed by the thought of Idamantes escorting her home; her aria is a serene invocation of love ('Idol mio, se ritroso'), accompanied by strings only, and utterly unlike the remainder of her role. A distant march, beginning with muted brass, grows to *fortissimo* to mark the change of scene.

The port of Kydonia Electra and the chorus welcome the propitious calm ('Placido è il mar, andiamo'). Idomeneus bids farewell to his sorely perplexed son (trio, 'Pria di partir, o Dio!'). As they are about to embark, a tempest breaks out (represented in music of barely repressed violence) and a terrible sea-monster appears (storm, with chorus, 'Qual nuovo terrore'): the people demand who has brought this upon them by angering the gods. Without naming Idamantes, Idomeneus publicly confesses (obbligato recitative) that he is the sinner; he has the temerity to accuse the gods of injustice. Terrified at the revelation, the crowd flies in confusion ('Corriamo, fuggiamo').

ACT 3 *The palace garden* In a tender E major aria, Ilia bids the winds bear her message of love to Idamantes ('Zeffiretti lusinghieri'). When he appears she is unable to suppress her feelings, and they declare themselves (duet, 'S'io non moro' – omitted at the première; replaced in 1786 by a shorter duet with some of the same material, 'Spiegarti non poss'io' K489). Idomeneus and Electra find the lovers. The varied emotions of all four are embodied in the harrowingly beautiful harmonic and contrapuntal web of one of Mozart's supreme achievements, the quartet ('Andrò, ramingo e solo'). Ilia's heart is still divided; Electra is full of suppressed jealousy; Idamantes, again banished without learning the reason, is deeply saddened, and Idomeneus wishes the gods would kill him instead. Each has reached the limit of suffering; their voices unite at 'soffrir più non si può'. Idamantes repeats his opening phrase, an emblem of loneliness and misery, and leaves the stage. Arbaces begs the king to help his suffering people and laments the condition of his country in a magnificent obbligato recitative ('Sventurata Sidon!'), usually retained when the role is reduced. His aria ('Se colà ne' fati è scritto', omitted in 1786) is more conventional, a broadly conceived piece accompanied by strings.

A large public place before the palace   The high priest confronts the king (recitative, 'Volgi intorno la sguardo, o Sire'): the monster has devoured thousands and laid the country to waste. Only Idomeneus can save them by naming the sacrificial victim. To the longest development of the 'Idamantes motif' he confesses the truth; the Cretans are awed and deeply moved ('O voto tremendo'). The collision of triplet violin quavers with the duple rhythms of the voices, the ominous fanfares of muted brass, and a melancholy chromatic fragment, form a picture of desolation without equal in 18th-century music.

The temple of Neptune, both exterior and interior being visible The king and priests process to the temple (march) and prepare the sacrifice (chorus of priests with Idomeneus, 'Accogli, o rè del mar'). A jubilant cry is heard (fanfare); Idamantes has slain the monster. Idomeneus fears worse will befall them, but Idamantes enters robed for sacrifice. Interrupted only by the first of the arias Mozart planned to omit before the 1781 performances, but may ultimately have included (Idamantes's, 'Nò, la morte io non pavento': he has no fear of death but dies willingly), these scenes unfold in orchestrated recitative of unprecedented length and expressiveness. At the moment of sacrifice Ilia enters and offers herself instead; the confusion is ended only when the oracle commands the abdication of Idomeneus in favour of his son, who is to marry Ilia. Electra invokes the Furies (her stupendous rage aria, 'D'Oreste, d'Ajace', was replaced in 1781 by a recitative powerful even by the standards of *Idomeneo*).

Idomeneus welcomes his retirement (recitative, 'Popoli! a voi l'ultima legge'). His exquisitely beautiful aria ('Torna la pace al core') was also cut in 1781, but its serene glow perfectly concludes the action. The brisk final chorus ('Scenda Amor, scenda Imeneo') is followed by an extended ballet.

*

Idomeneo is divided from its French model by the spread of Enlightenment. Danchet's libretto includes another love tangle (Idomeneus loves Ilia), and involves Electra closely in the plot (jealous of Ilia, she reveals to the priests Idomeneus's scheme to save Idamantes). It also ends tragically, with Idamantes dead and Idomeneus driven mad by Nemesis. Varesco, undoubtedly influenced by Metastasio, made myth into *opera seria*, an allegory of enlightened monarchy; flawed by his vow, rather than his failure to fulfil it, Idomeneus is unfitted to reign, but the god permits the organic transfer of power to the new generation and the reconciliation of former enmities by dynastic marriage. This restoration of harmony is movingly captured in Idomeneus's final aria so that Mozart's omission of 'Torna la pace' is particularly regrettable. This theme also reflects the father-son relationship which is considered to have been the source of much creative tension in Mozart.

The letters to his father, and the cuts on which he insisted, demonstrate Mozart's growing theatrical judgment as well as the powers of persuasion he exercised upon the singers. Most remarkable is his willingness at the last moment, following the dress rehearsal, to sacrifice superlative music for a theatrical end. In view of his intended and actual reworkings, it seems safe to say that *Idomeneo* never reached a form with which he would have been completely satisfied. Unfortunately some performances with tenor Idamantes ignore not only the 1786 aria and duet in Act 2 but also Mozart's careful revision of the great Act 3 quartet, whose texture is ruined by simply placing the original line an octave too low.

Even within the repertory of 'reform' opera (Italian, French and German), *Idomeneo* is remarkable for its orchestration. Mozart used clarinets here for the first time in an opera, and four horns, but the music for flutes, oboes, bassoons and trumpets is equally striking, as are the brass mutes in the Act 2 march and the scene where the Cretans learn that the sacrificial victim must be Idamantes. The varied but almost continual use of all the wind instruments creates an unprecedentedly rich palette, although trombones are confined to the oracle's speech (and these may have been omitted: Mozart made four different settings of it. Most remarkable is the deployment of wind instruments during critical passages of recitative, notably those preceding the two final arias. The strings are treated with equal resourcefulness; for instance the tremolando in the High Priest's recitative, the hammering c''' in 'O voto tremendo', responding to the muted trumpet calls, and the harp-like pizzicato in the invocation of Neptune at the beginning of the last scene.

Instrumental inventiveness is matched by harmonic daring; even the simple recitatives make expressive use of enharmonic progressions and remote tonalities. *Idomeneo* is also notable for its continuity, again beyond what was normal in 'reform' operas. Several numbers have no final cadence but move into the next recitative as if to avoid leaving time for applause; Mozart added such an ending to the simpler version of 'Fuor del mar'.

Idomeneo is also the first Mozart opera in which the arrangement of tonalities seems deliberately calculated. Recognition of certain recurring keys is not only assisted by instrumentation but by the use of distinct motifs; the use of these is more highly developed than in any previous opera. Although it is unlikely that every instance was intentional, Mozart cannot have overlooked the 'Idamantes motif': from the overture to the sacrifice scene its most clearly identifiable recurrences all relate to the young hero. Nevertheless, most of the opera consists of discrete numbers which reflect Mozart's determination that music should govern the poetry. With this end in view, he did not reject virtuosity, but turned its musical qualities to dramatic ends. Despite detectable influences within it, and from it (for instance in *Don Giovanni* and *La clemenza di Tito*), *Idomeneo* stands on its own, occupying a special place in the affections of its composer who went on to other achievements as vital and significant, but never returned to its dignified, heroic, yet thoroughly human world.

J.R.

Die Entführung aus dem Serail
('The Abduction from the Seraglio')

Singspiel in three acts, K384, set to a libretto by Christoph Friedrich Bretzner (*Belmont und Constanze, oder Die Entführung aus dem Serail*), adapted and enlarged by Gottlieb Stephanie the Younger; first performed at the Burgtheater in Vienna, on 16 July 1782.

Caterina Cavalieri was Konstanze at the first performance, Valentin Adamberger was Belmonte; Osmin was sung by Ludwig Fischer, Blonde by Therese Teyber, Pedrillo by Johann Ernst Dauer.

Selim *Pasha*	spoken
Konstanze *a Spanish lady, Belmonte's betrothed*	soprano
Blonde *Konstanze's English maid*	soprano
Belmonte *a Spanish nobleman*	tenor
Pedrillo *servant of Belmonte, now supervisor of the Pasha's gardens*	tenor
Osmin *overseer of the Pasha's country house*	bass
Klaas *a sailor*	spoken
Mute *in Osmin's service*	silent

Chorus of Janissaries; guards

Setting The country palace of Pasha Selim, on the Mediterranean coast in an unidentified part of the Turkish Empire

Dismissed from service with the Archbishop of Salzburg, Mozart must have felt satisfaction in writing to his father on 1 August 1781: 'the day before yesterday Stephanie junior gave me a libretto to compose'. Gottlieb Stephanie, director of the National Singspiel, wanted Bretzner's *Belmont und Constanze* set quickly for the visit in September of the Russian Grand Duke Paul Petrovich. Bretzner was a popular librettist, whose name assured interest (*Belmont und Constanze* had been set in Berlin by Johann André). Yet with the postponement of the royal visit (it eventually took place in November, when Gluck's operas were played), *Die Entführung* might have suffered the fate of the Singspiel *Zaide* (1779), which remained unperformed in Mozart's lifetime, had not Stephanie and, no doubt, the singers maintained support for him. Mozart had already composed much of Act 1, and he wrote in detail to his father on 26 September about the arias for Belmonte, Osmin and Konstanze.

Since time was available, he urged Stephanie to enlarge Act 1. By adding an aria at the beginning for Belmonte and making Osmin's opening number a duet, Mozart virtually turned Bretzner's opening dialogue, with Osmin's song originally its only music, into a continuous introduction. He established Osmin as a major force with 'Solche hergelauf'ne Laffen' (Mozart sent Stephanie the music for words to be added), and wrote the overture, musically linked with the opening aria. His comments to his father concerning Osmin's and Belmonte's arias, 'Solche hergelauf'ne Laffen' and 'O wie ängstlich', contain some of his most important recorded views on operatic aesthetics. The Janissary chorus is 'short, lively and written to please the Viennese'; he also admitted that he had 'sacrificed Konstanze's aria ('Ach ich liebte') a little to the flexible throat of Mlle Cavalieri'.

Mozart and Stephanie recast the remaining two acts more extensively. The women and Osmin received one additional aria each ('Martern aller Arten', 'Welche Wonne' and 'O, wie will ich triumphieren'), while Belmonte received two (the second, opening Act 3, often cut in modern performances or nonsensically replaced by the first). They devised a new situation for a long ensemble (finale to Act 2) and a new dénouement: the libretto thus remains essentially Bretzner's (he alone was credited on the original playbill and libretto), but with significant differences. Mozart began setting a quintet which, in Bretzner, covers the whole elopement scene. The loss of such an extended action ensemble is tantalizing; doubtless it was rejected because it could not form a finale. Instead the elopement is in dialogue and reaches a musical climax only after its failure, with Osmin's aria. The enhanced importance of Osmin sharpens the oriental setting and makes him a tangible menace; whether this change resulted from, or merely took advantage of, Fischer's immense range and full deep notes, is impossible to determine.

Mozart finished the score in April 1782. Rehearsals began in June and, despite some delays, an alleged cabal and the difficulty of the music, the first performance was a success. Performances continued until the closure of the National Singspiel early in 1783; the German company at the Kärntnertor revived it (1784–5) with Mozart's sister-in-law Aloysia Lange as Konstanze.

The fame of the new opera spread rapidly. The second production, also in 1782, was in Prague, which at once took Mozart to its heart (the first performance in Czech was not until 1829). *Die Entführung* was the foundation of Mozart's reputation outside Austria. In 1783 there were productions in Warsaw, Bonn (under Neefe, Beethoven possibly assisting), Frankfurt and Leipzig. The first translation (Polish) followed in November, again at Warsaw. In 1784 there were productions in Mannheim, Carlsruhe, Cologne and Salzburg; Dresden, Munich and other German cities followed in 1785. It was given in some 40 centres in Germany and the Austrian Empire, and reached Amsterdam in Mozart's lifetime. The second foreign language used was Dutch (1797, Amsterdam), the third French (1798, Paris, in a version by Gluck's librettist Moline); it was also the first opera ever heard in German in Paris (1801). In Moscow it was given in 1810 in Russian (St Petersburg following in 1816) and in 1820 in German.

The first London performance, in English, was at Covent Garden in 1827, the score arranged by C. Kramer with an altered plot; the setting was moved by the translator, W. Dimond, to a Greek island. Such alterations were standard in 19th-century revivals. In Paris the 1859 revival to a translation by Prosper Pascal reordered several numbers and gave 'Martern aller Arten' to Blonde (no less a Mozartian than Beecham placed this aria in Act 3). Later in the century London also saw it in German and Italian (the title *Il Seraglio* is still often used in English). The American première was in New York in 1860, probably in German. An attempt to produce it in 1840 in Milan came to nothing. The Italian première was not until 1935, in Florence, by which time the 20th-century revival of Mozart was under way; it had already appeared at Glyndebourne.

The background is the territorial and cultural intersection of the Islamic lands and the older Christian civilization of Europe, especially

Spain; Belmonte's father is Governor of Oran on the coast of North Africa. A major stimulus for artistic interest in things Turkish was the menacing but in the end unsuccessful siege of Vienna in 1683, but the action evokes an earlier period when piracy was rife and crossing between religions not uncommon; Pasha Selim is a renegade Christian. The overture is a bubbling Allegro in C major, its 'Turkish' style martial and colourful yet, in Mozart's hands, subject to abrupt changes of mood; a promising crescendo lurches into the dominant minor, anticipating the confusion of the action to come. A slow middle section in C minor brings a foretaste of sentiment, its melody by turns hesitant and passionate, richly clothed in woodwind sound. The Allegro resumes, ending on the dominant.

*

ACT 1   *A plaza before Selim's palace, near the sea*   A major-key version of the middle section of the overture ('Hier soll ich dich denn sehen') forms a short aria by the standards of this opera, but after a hesitating start its lyrical cadences convey Belmonte's ardent desire for reunion with Konstanze. Osmin brings a ladder, and begins picking figs; he sings a moral Volkslied (*lied* and duet, 'Wer ein Liebchen hat gefunden': 'Whoever finds a lover, let him beware'). When Belmonte speaks Osmin refuses to answer, directing the later verses at him instead: plausible strangers bring danger to lovers. Belmonte now enquires for Pedrillo, wrenching the tempo to Allegro, but the wrath of the Turk, enraged by mention of Pedrillo, dominates the ensemble. In a furious Presto, the original G minor yielding to D major, he drives Belmonte away.

Pedrillo asks Osmin whether Selim has returned. Still not answering, Osmin fumes about vagabond fops fit only to be hanged ('Solche hergelauf'ne Laffen'). A full binary exit aria, portentous and often contrapuntal, it flies off the handle in the coda to which Mozart added 'Turkish' music for comic effect. Belmonte reveals himself. Pedrillo assures him that Selim will not force love on Konstanze, but they are in great danger and Osmin watches everything. Belmonte's heart is beating with anxiety and ardour ('O wie ängstlich, o wie feurig'); both melody and orchestra are suffused with feeling as well as detailed imitation of the lover's symptoms.

A march (possibly cut by Mozart, but restored by the Neue Mozart-Ausgabe) announces the arrival of the Pasha in a boat with Konstanze; the Janissaries greet them with a vigorous chorus in 'Turkish' style. Selim asks why Konstanze remains sad and promises that her answer will not anger him. In the Adagio of her aria Konstanze relives her past love ('Ach ich liebte, war so glücklich!'); the Allegro compresses the Adagio's melodic outline into a vehement protest; all happiness has fled (the Adagio text and mood return in the middle of the Allegro). Mozart's sacrifice for Cavalieri brings coloratura to an inappropriate text ('Kummer ruht in meinem Schoss': 'sorrow dwells in my heart'), but this emphatic utterance tells us that Konstanze is a considerable character. Selim is angry, but when she leaves he admits that he loves her all the more for her resistance. Pedrillo introduces Belmonte as an Italian-trained architect; Selim approves his entry into the household. But Osmin has other ideas. A vivacious trio in C minor ('Marsch, marsch, marsch! trollt euch fort!'), ending with a faster major section, forms a comic finale; eventually the Europeans force an entry.

ACT 2   *The palace garden, with Osmin's house to one side*   Osmin is pursuing Blonde, whom the Pasha has given him as a slave; but she will have none of his Turkish ways; tenderness, not force, wins hearts ('Durch Zärtlichkeit und Schmeicheln'). Her Andante aria is the epitome of Mozartean elegance. Osmin indignantly orders her to love him, but she merely laughs, and wards off an assault by threatening his eyes with her nails and reminding him that her mistress is the Pasha's favourite (duet, 'Ich gehe, doch rate ich dir'). Osmin warns her not to flirt with Pedrillo; she mocks his low notes with her own (to $a^\flat$). In a lugubrious Andante Osmin declares that the English are mad to allow their women such liberties; Blonde rejoices in her freedom.

At the nadir of her fortunes, Konstanze turns to the most intense style of *opera seria*, obbligato recitative ('Welcher Wechsel herrscht in meiner Seele', and aria, 'Traurigkeit ward mir zum Lose'). In an exquisite Adagio Mozart paints her sighing breaths, her halting steps. The aria, its orchestra enriched by basset-horns, is a sustained lament in G minor, like Ilia's (*Idomeneo*, Act 1) but attaining a new poignancy through its higher tessitura.

Blonde tries to comfort her mistress. Selim threatens not death, which Konstanze welcomes, but every kind of torture. Her aria ('Marten aller Arten': 'Every kind of torture awaits me; I laugh at pain; death will come in the end') picks up Selim's threat, but not before a 60-bar ritornello with obbligato flute, oboe, violin and cello has unfolded a rich motivic tapestry founded on a march rhythm (with trumpets and timpani). The closing words are given more emphasis by a faster tempo. This magnificent piece, coming imme-diately after another long aria for Konstanze, presents a challenge to the actors and the producer; but as the expression of stubborn resistance to coercion from a woman with no hope of deliverance, it is of immense dramatic power. Selim is baffled; affection and force having failed, he wonders if he can use cunning. (This exit line perhaps prefigured a new intrigue intended for Act 3 but not included.)

Pedrillo tells Blonde of Belmonte's arrival. Blonde's reaction, a rondo with a melody from the flute concerto к314 ('Welche Wonne, welche Lust'), sparkles with unalloyed delight. Pedrillo musters his courage in a martial D major ('Frisch zum Kampfe!'), but a nagging phrase ('Nur ein feiger Tropf verzagt': 'Only a cowardly fool despairs') shows his underlying lack of confidence. He succeeds in getting Osmin drunk (duet, 'Vivat Bacchus'), and sends him to sleep it off so that the lovers can meet. Tears of joy are love's sweetest reward; Belmonte's aria of *galanterie* ('Wenn der Freude Tränen fliessen') is a slow gavotte and then a serenade-like minuet announced by the wind and embellished with wide-ranging passage-work.

The escape is planned before the finale (quartet, 'Ach Belmonte!'). The first mature Mozart ensemble to incorporate dramatic develop-ment begins with a lively D major Allegro. Joy gives way to anxiety (Andante, G minor); have the women yielded to blandishment? In a faster tempo, Konstanze expresses hurt, Blonde slaps Pedrillo's face, and the voices come together in mingled relief and regret. The men ask forgiveness (Allegretto); Blonde withholds it, singing in com-pound time against the simple time of the others (a device Mozart might have picked up from *opéra comique*). But eventually misunderstanding is cleared away and the four join in praise of love.

ACT 3   *The scene of Act 1; Osmin's house to one side. Midnight*
Pedrillo and Klaas bring two ladders. Belmonte is assured that all is ready, but they must wait for the guards to finish their rounds. Pedrillo advises him to sing; he himself often sings at night and no one will notice the difference. In a long Andante, featuring clarinets and extended coloratura, Belmonte builds his hopes on the power of love ('Ich baue ganz auf deine Stärke').

Pedrillo gives the agreed signal, a romance ('In Mohrenland gefangen war ein Mädchen'). The opera's second *lied*, this too refers to the dramatic situation. Its haunting melody, to a plucked accompaniment, rests upon harmonic ambiguity and ends unresolved after four verses when Pedrillo sees a light. Belmonte fetches Konstanze; they hurry off as Pedrillo climbs up for Blonde. But the mute has seen them. Suspecting thieves and murderers, the bleary-eyed Osmin sends for the guard and dozes. Blonde and Pedrillo spot him too late; all four Europeans are arrested. In a brilliant rondo ('O, wie will ich triumphieren'), with piccolo but without trumpets or Turkish music, which Mozart keeps in reserve, Osmin anticipates the delight of torturing and killing his enemies, his lowest bass notes (to D) filled with ghoulish relish.

The interior of the palace   Osmin claims credit for the arrest. Selim confronts the lovers. Konstanze admits guilt in his eyes, but pleads loyalty to her first lover. She begs to die if only his life can be spared. Belmonte humbles himself; he is worth a fine ransom; his name is Lostados. Selim recognizes the son of the enemy who chased him from his homeland. He bids them prepare for the punishment Belmonte's father would certainly have meted out, and leaves them under guard. Belmonte movingly laments his folly in bringing Konstanze to her doom; she blames herself for his destruction, but death is the path to an eternal union, symbolized by the serenely extended arabesques (recitative and duet, 'Welch ein Geschick! O Qual der Seele!').

Selim asks if they are prepared for judgment. Belmonte says they will die calmly, absolving him from blame. Selim, however, bids him take Konstanze and go. He despises Belmonte's father too much to imitate him; clemency will be his revenge. As he takes dignified leave of them, Pedrillo begs freedom for himself and Blonde. Osmin is overruled; does he not value his eyes? In a vaudeville finale, each sings a verse of suitable sentiment, with a moral sung by the ensemble: those who forget kindness are to be despised. Blonde is interrupted by Osmin whose rage boils over into the litany of torture from his Act 1 aria, complete with 'Turkish' percussion. He rushes off; the others draw the further moral that nothing is so hateful as revenge. A brief chorus in praise of the Pasha, in the principal key, C major, brings back the merry 'Turkish' style of the overture.

*

The viewpoint of *Die Entführung* is decidedly European. Muslim lifestyle is crudely represented as luxurious but immoral; the Enlightenment, through Blonde, makes tart observations about the social position of women. Selim himself, raised to eminence by ability rather than rank, reflects Enlightenment values; he is not moved to clemency by religion, but contrasts his action with the cruelty of Belmonte's Christian father. This ending adds a new dimension to Bretzner's drama in which, implausibly, Belmonte proves to be Selim's son. It is a pity that, unlike the denouement of *Die Zauberflöte*, this scene was not set to music.

The lavish musical invention of *Die Entführung* perhaps exceeds what the dramatic structure is fit to bear; nor is its design immaculate. Apart from the cluster of arias for Konstanze in Act 2, there is surely one aria too many for Belmonte, and the length of the individual numbers (if not their forms) suggests *opera seria* and contrasts starkly with the speed of the dialogue. Was it length or plenitude of instrumentation which induced Joseph II's famous (but probably apocryphal) comment: 'Too many notes, my dear Mozart'? Such problems cannot be overcome by making alterations, still less by cutting the dialogue, for Mozart carefully controlled the flow between speech and music, running some numbers closely together but separating others. His prodigality of invention, however, is also a cause of the opera's enduring fascination. Even as it endangers the dramatic whole, the music, paradoxically through its creation for a specific group of remarkable singers, turns the actors in this serious comedy into humans a little larger than life but of universal appeal.

J.R.

L'oca del Cairo
('The Goose of Cairo')

Opera buffa in two acts, K422, set to a libretto by Giovanni Battista Varesco; the work remained unfinished.

Mozart requested the libretto from Varesco in May 1783, discussed it in Salzburg during the summer, and by December had composed most of the first act. He abandoned work early in 1784 and in a letter to his father (10 February) he offered sharp criticism of detail and design. The libretto involves an amorous intrigue on the island of Ripasecca, ruled by Don Pippo (bass); the Cairo goose was to intervene as a mechanical *deus ex machina*.

Full-length musical drafts survive for two duets (one on a text not in the libretto), two arias, a quartet and a finale; another aria survives complete in the hand of J.S. Mayr. Mozart also set one section of continuo recitative, normally composed last. The scenes nearest completion are between *buffo* servants, Aurelia (soprano) and Chichibeo (bass). The richly expressive quartet is for two more serious pairs of lovers, Celidora and Lavina (sopranos), Biondello and Calandrino (tenors). The finale of 461 bars is packed with action and includes a chorus of police preventing an elopement. Various attempts have been made to 'realize' the fragments, among them a scholarly reconstruction by Nicholas Temperley, staged at Urbana-Champaign, Illinois, in 1991.

J.R.

Lo sposo deluso
('The Deluded Bridegroom')

Opera buffa, K430/424*a*, set to a libretto after *Le donne rivali*; unfinished.

Lo sposo deluso was composed in 1783–4. Its libretto, surviving complete with Mozart's intended casting for the Italian company resident in Vienna, was formerly attributed, without evidence, to Lorenzo da Ponte. Campana (1990) has shown that the libretto is based on a Roman intermezzo, possibly written by Giuseppe Petrosellini.

The first three numbers were drafted and a trio completed. The overture's Allegro begins with a sprightly fanfare; following an Andante, the reprise opens with a quartet, the first number. Pulcherio (tenor, or high baritone, Francesco Bussani) laughs at Bocconio, the title role (bass, Francesco Benucci) for aspiring to a young bride, Eugenia. Bettina (soprano, Catarina Cavalieri), his niece, and Don Asdrubale (tenor, Stefano Mandini) deride the old man's pretensions. Eugenia (soprano, Nancy Storace) arrives; the sketched aria (the second number) reveals a lady of spirit. Pulcherio's aria (the third) is addressed to the ill-matched couple. Eugenia and Asdrubale, former lovers tragically separated, contrast in the trio with the bafflement of Bocconio, expressed in a phrase used again in Bartolo's aria in Act 1 of *Le nozze di Figaro*.

Only the trio suggests the style of the future Da Ponte operas. Some lively invention notwithstanding, the rest, in line with the conventional libretto, represents surprisingly little advance on *La finta giardiniera*.

J.R.

Der Schauspieldirektor
('The Impresario')

Singspiel in one act, K486, set to a libretto by Gottlieb Stephanie the younger; first performed in Schönbrunn, at the Orangery, on 7 February 1786.

Der Schauspieldirektor was performed on 7 February 1786 at Schönbrunn Palace as part of an Imperial entertainment for the Governor-General of the Nether lands. It was played (at the opposite end of the room) before Salieri's *Prima la musica*; three public performances followed.

Frank (spoken role, originally Stephanie), the impresario, and Puf (bass, though no singer; Josef Weidmann) are assembling a company of actors and singers, who squabble over pre-eminence and pay. There are five other spoken roles, including a banker. Besides Mozart's music, extracts from three plays were used for the 'auditions'.

The overture is a sonata allegro with full development. Frank auditions actors, then Mme Herz (soprano, Aloysia Lange): the pathetic style ('Da schlägt des Abschieds Stunde'), yields to a brilliant conclusion. There follows Mlle Silberklang (soprano, Catarina Cavalieri) with an elegant rondò ('Bester Jüngling'). Unfortunately they cannot both be prima donna, and they argue in a hilarious trio ('Ich bin die erste Sängerin'), with Vogelsang, the company's tenor (Johann Valentin Adamberger), keeping the peace (Mme Herz displays her f''' and illustrates the words 'adagio' and 'allegro'). Both ladies are promised large salaries and star billing; quarrels are ended for the sake of art. In the finale, Puf joins in.

Stephanie's *Gelegenheitsstück* ('pièce d'occasion': Mozart called it 'comedy with music', the singers being minor characters) makes a crude contrast with the short opera by Salieri. Nevertheless this silly farce provided the opportunity, which Mozart seized, to write serious arias which could adorn a real opera or concert programme, while the overture is of scintillating ingenuity and charm.

J.R.

Le nozze di Figaro
('The Marriage of Figaro')

Opera buffa in four acts, K492, set to a libretto by Lorenzo Da Ponte after Pierre-Augustin Beaumarchais' play *La folle journée, ou Le mariage de Figaro* (1784, Paris); first performed at Vienna's Burgtheater on 1 May 1786.

The original cast was: Francesco Benucci (Figaro), Nancy Storace (Susanna), Luisa Laschi (Countess), Stefano Mandini (Count), Dorotea Bussani (Cherubino), Maria Mandini (Marcellina), Francesco Bussani (Bartolo and Antonio), Michael Kelly (Basilio and Curzio), and Anna Gottlieb (Barbarina).

Count Almaviva	baritone
Countess Almaviva	soprano
Susanna *her maid, betrothed to Figaro*	soprano
Figaro *valet to Count Almaviva*	bass
Cherubino *the Count's page*	mezzo-soprano
Marcellina *housekeeper to Bartolo*	soprano
Bartolo *a doctor from Seville*	bass
Don Basilio *music master*	tenor
Don Curzio *magistrate*	tenor
Barbarina *daughter of Antonio*	soprano
Antonio *gardener, Susanna's uncle*	bass

Villagers, peasants, servants

Setting Aguasfrescas near Seville, the Almaviva's country house; the action is contemporary with the play and opera

The operatic version of Beaumarchais' *Le mariage de Figaro* may have been a timely notion of Mozart's own. Although the play was banned from the Viennese stage, it was available in print and Paisiello's opera on the earlier play, *Le barbier de Séville*, had triumphed in Vienna in 1783 (and all over Europe). Mozart evidently studied Paisiello's handling of the same personalities and included deliberate references to it. Composition began late in 1785 and the opera may have been drafted in only six weeks. After some opposition attributed to the Italians, and (if Da Ponte is to be believed) after the librettist had overcome the emperor's objections, it was produced in May with an outstanding cast whose character and skills, as well as their performance in Paisiello's Barbiere, contributed to its conception. Michael Kelly discussed the event in his reminiscences. Mozart may have expected Storace to sing the Countess; he rearranged the Act 2 trio and other passages so that Susanna took the upper line.

Contrary to what is often stated, *Figaro* was generally liked, as is indicated by the emperor's ban on excessive encores (only arias were to be repeated). The opera marks the last watershed of Mozart's career; from now on he was a recognized opera composer. There were, however, only nine performances in 1786; the Viennese preferred other works, such as Martìn y Soler's *Una cosa rara*. *Figaro* was next given in Prague, where according to Mozart's report (letter of 15 January 1787) it created a furore and led to the commission for *Don Giovanni*. The successful Vienna revival (26 performances in 1789) preceded the commission for *Così fan tutte*: Susanna was confirmed as the prima donna's role when Mozart wrote two new arias for Adriana Ferrarese del Bene, Da Ponte's mistress and the first Fiordiligi.

By this time *Figaro* had received isolated performances in Italy (Acts 1 and 2, the rest composed by Angelo Tarchi, Monza, autumn 1787; Florence, spring 1788), and had been translated into German for performances in Prague (June 1787), Donaueschingen (1787), Leipzig, Graz and Frankfurt (1788), followed by other German centres over the next few years. These performances used spoken dialogue, as did the first performance in France (Paris Opéra, 1793, using Beaumarchais). The London première took place in 1812, in Italian, following interpolations of numbers into other operas by Storace and Benucci; in 1819 it was given in English, reduced to three acts and arranged by Bishop. In New York the first performances were in 1824, in English, and 1858, in Italian. Numerous translations have been used during the 19th and 20th centuries. *Figaro* is now Mozart's most popular opera, displacing *Don Giovanni*. No major company allows it to fall out of the repetory for long; Glyndebourne opened with it in 1934.

In production, the vein of rococo nostalgia which inspired its epigone, *Der Rosenkavalier*, was displaced by greater realism by Visconti (1963, Rome) and Hall (1973, Glyndebourne); it is now customary to emphasize the socio-political tensions of Beaumarchais which Da Ponte had necessarily suppressed.

In the first part of the Beaumarchais trilogy, *Il barbiere*, Almaviva wooed Bartolo's ward Rosina with the aid of Figaro, now his valet. He has also, despite his Don Juanesque tendencies, abolished the *droit de Seigneur* whereby he had the right to deflower every bride among his feudal dependants.

*

For the overture Mozart abandoned a planned middle section, leaving an electrifying sonata without development which perfectly sets the scene for the 'Crazy Day'.

ACT 1   *An antechamber*   The pacing motif and lyrical response in the opening duet ('Cinque, dieci') belong respectively to Figaro, who is measuring the room, and Susanna, who is trying on a new hat for their forthcoming wedding. She finally entices him from his work to admire her, and to sing her motif, suggesting that she may prove to be the stronger personality. Figaro tells her the Count has offered them this room, conveniently situated between those of the Count and Countess, but she reacts with alarm. In the ensuing duet ('Se a caso madama') she mocks Figaro's imitation of the high and low bells of their employers: the room's convenience will also make it easy for the Count, who has designs on her, to visit Susanna when she is alone. Figaro's confidence is shaken, but if the Count wants to dance, it is he, Figaro, who will call the tune (cavatina, 'Se vuol ballare'), first offering a minuet, then a Presto contredanse.

Figaro has obtained a loan from Marcellina, and, never imagining he will have to keep the bargain, has agreed to marry Marcellina if he defaults. Bartolo offers her his help: in this way he will both avenge himself on Figaro (who thwarted his plans to marry Rosina in *Il barbiere*) and rid himself of an embarrassment (Marcellina). His exit aria ('La vendetta') has a full orchestra with trumpets, in the opera's principal key, D major. His vaunted legal knowledge brings formal counterpoint, but his fury also vents itself in comically undignified patter. Susanna aware of Marcellina's interest in Figaro, hustles her out, the music poised, the exchange of compliments venomous in their duettino, 'Via resti servito'. Cherubino confides in Susanna. In a lyrical arch of melody over a sensuously muted accompaniment, he impulsively babbles of his love for all women ('Non so più'), an enchanting musical image of adolescence. The Count is heard; Susanna hides Cherubino behind a chair. Basilio's voice interrupts the Count, who believing himself alone with Susanna, is making amorous proposals; while he too hides behind the chair, Cherubino nips on to it and Susanna covers him with a dress. Basilio's malicious (but accurate) observation that Cherubino adores the Countess rouses the Count from concealment. Gruffly, in an ascending line, he demands an explanation (trio, 'Cosa sento!'); Basilio, his motif unctuously descending, disclaims knowledge; Susanna, turning to the minor dominant, threatens to faint. The men officiously come to her aid (a new, ardent motif with a chromatic cadence). The Count describes his discovery of Cherubino in Barbarina's room, hidden under a cloth . . . at which he is again revealed, to the Count's self-righteous indignation, Basilio's delight and Susanna's horror. Sonata form perfectly matches the action, the recapitulation fraught with irony (or, from Basilio, sarcasm). Figaro ushers in a rustic chorus praising the Count's magnanimity in renouncing his extra-marital right, but the Count refuses to be trapped into marrying the couple then and there, and banishes Cherubino with an officer's commission. While apparently sending him on his way to a bold march rhythm ('Non più andrai': no more frolicking and flirting; he is off to death or glory), Figaro detains the page for purposes of his own.

ACT 2 *The Countess's chamber* In an achingly tender Larghetto, the neglected Countess prays to the god of love to restore her husband's affections (cavatina, 'Porgi, Amor'). But she listens eagerly to Susanna and Figaro's plotting (Figaro leaves to a snatch of 'Se vuol ballare'). Cherubino is to be dressed as a girl, take Susanna's place, and compromise the Count. His ardour is formalized, in a song of his own composition, 'Voi che sapete', sung to Susanna's 'guitar' accompaniment; in this canzona Mozart miraculously suggests, but evades, the clumsiness of a youth. Susanna tries to dress him but he keeps turning his gaze towards the Countess ('Venite, inginocchiatevi': an action aria replaced in 1789 by the strophic 'Un moto di gioia'). Alone with the Countess, Cherubino is close to winning her heart when the Count demands admittance: he has returned precipitately from the hunt because of an anonymous letter (part of Figaro's ill-laid plot). In confusion the Countess thrusts Cherubino into her closet; the Count asks questions; Susanna enters unseen. The Countess says Susanna is in the closet. The Count's jealous fury, his wife's terror and Susanna's anxious assessment of the situation again outline a sonata form, although the action does not advance (trio, 'Susanna, or via sortite'). When the Count leaves to fetch tools to break down the door, forcing the Countess to go with him and locking the bedroom door behind them, Susanna thrusts Cherubino through the window (duettino, 'Aprite, presto aprite') and enters the closet.

When they return, the Countess confesses that Cherubino is in the closet, half-dressed, but protests his innocence; the Count is ready to kill. Mozart's most consummate comic finale begins by resuming the fury and anxiety of the trio ($E^\flat$, 'Ecci omai, garzon malnato'). But it is Susanna who emerges, to a simple minuet which mocks the nobles' consternation. Explanations and further confusion occupy an extended Allegro which deploys its thematic wealth with marvellous inventiveness. Although puzzled, the Count has to ask forgiveness. At the single abrupt key-change of the finale ($B^\flat$ to G) Figaro enters, again asking for an immediate wedding. Recovering his sang-froid (C major, gavotte tempo), the Count poses questions about the anonymous letter; Figaro prevaricates. Antonio charges in to complain of damage to his garden caused by the page's precipitate exit (Allegro molto, F major). The Count senses more chicanery; Figaro claims it was he who jumped. The tempo slows to Andante (in $B^\flat$) and with measured calm the Count questions Figaro about a paper the page has dropped: the music emerges from an harmonic cloud to a shining recapitulation as Figaro (prompted by the women) identifies it as the page's commission, left with him (he claims) to be sealed. The Count is baffled, but revives when Marcellina, Basilio and Bartolo rush in demanding justice (E$\flat$).

ACT 3 *A large room decorated for the marriage-feast* The Countess urges Susanna to make an assignation with the Count; they will exchange cloaks and compromise him with his own wife. Susanna approaches him, explains her previous reticence as delicacy, and offers to meet him that evening. In a rare outburst in the minor (duet, 'Crudel! perchè finora') the Count reproaches her; changing to major, he sings of his coming happiness with exuberant syncopation. She tries to join in but trips over the right replies ('Yes' for 'No', etc.), correcting herself at a melodic high point. Leaving, she encounters Figaro and carelessly shows her satisfaction: 'without a lawyer we've won the case'. The Count is again suspicious and angry (the first obbligato recitative and aria, 'Vedrò, mentre io sospiro'). Must he sigh in vain while a mere servant wins the prize? The martial orchestration and key, even the contrapuntal language, recall Bartolo's aria, but the music snarls with aristocratic jealousy, not pompous self-importance: within the social structure of this opera it is a truly menacing utterance.

At the trial of Marcellina's case Curzio is finding for the plaintiff. Figaro protests that he cannot marry Marcellina without his parents' consent. On the discovery of a birthmark on his arm, it emerges that he is the lost son of Marcellina, and Bartolo reluctantly admits paternity. Marcellina embraces Figaro and the three express delight while the Count and Curzio mutter their annoyance in a sextet, 'Riconosci in questo amplesso'. Susanna misinterprets the embrace and boxes Figaro's ears. The comical explanation leads to a quartet of satisfaction against which Curzio and the Count fling out a defiant phrase of anger.

The Countess, waiting for Susanna, muses on the past and wonders if there is hope for her marriage. This set piece, an obbligato recitative and rondò, 'Dove sono i bei momenti', which, it has been argued, may originally have been intended to precede the previous scene, shows her as profoundly tender yet impulsive; it reaches a glowing *a"* at the climax. Antonio tells the Count that Cherubino is still in the castle. The Countess dictates a letter from Susanna to the Count confirming their rendezvous (duettino, 'Che soave zeffiretto'), their voices mingling in an expression of the love they feel, each for her own; the honeyed music shows none of the deviousness of their intentions.

During a choral presentation to the Countess, Cherubino is unmasked, but allowed to stay for the wedding as he (and Barbarina) show a tendency to make revelations embarrassing to the Count. Throughout the finale, the necessary action is cunningly woven into the sequence of dances. During the march the two couples (Marcellina and Bartolo have decided to regularize their union) are presented to the Count and Countess. The bridesmaids' duet and chorus (contredanse) precede the alluring fandango, during which Susanna slips the letter to the Count, sealed with a pin (to be returned as a sign of agreement); Figaro notices with amusement that the Count has pricked himself.

ACT 4 *The garden, at night; pavilions on either side* Barbarina, the go-between, has lost the pin (a mock-tragic cavatina, 'L'ho perduta'). Figaro, hearing her tale, concludes that Susanna is unfaithful; an abyss seems to open beneath him. Marcellina is inclined to warn Susanna; she must have a good reason for meeting the Count, and women should stick together ('Il capro e la capretta'). Barbarina is preparing to meet Cherubino in a pavilion. Figaro summons Basilio and Bartolo to witness the betrayal. Basilio moralizes about the wisdom of not resisting one's superiors, adding a tale of his own hot youth ('In quegl'anni'). Figaro's monologue (obbligato recitative and aria, 'Aprite un po' quegl'occhi') uses raw musical gestures to convey the terrors, for a clever but emotionally simple man, of sexual betrayal. Disconnected phrases witness to his anxiety, and horn fanfares mock him without mercy. He overhears but cannot see Susanna, who is disguised as the Countess (obbligato recitative and aria, 'Deh vieni, non tardar'). The floating line and titillating woodwind cadences with which Susanna confides her amorous longing to the night perfectly capture the blended love and mischief with which she deliberately rouses Figaro's passion (in 1789 Mozart replaced the aria with the elaborate rondò, 'Al desio').

From now on all is confusion; the characters mistake identities and blunder into each other in the dark, receiving kisses and blows intended for others, before nearly all of them end up in the pavilions (finale). Cherubino begs Susanna (actually the disguised Countess) for a kiss; Susanna watches anxiously as the Count and Figaro drive the pest away. The Count begins to woo 'Susanna', who responds shyly; Figaro's impotent rage is highlighted in the bass. He contrives a temporary interruption. As the key changes from G to $E^\flat$ a serenade-like melody ironically evokes the peace of the night. Seeing the Countess (actually Susanna), Figaro tells her what is going on; then recognizing her by her voice, he pays 'the Countess' passionate court. Enraged, Susanna boxes his ears again, blows which he greets with rapture. This scene unfolds to a frantic allegro, replaced at the reconciliation by pastoral 6/8. Now they enact Figaro pleading passionate love to the Countess; on cue, with a second abrupt key-change ($B^\flat$ to G), the Count bursts in on them, calling witnesses, dragging everyone including the false Countess from the pavilion, shouting accusations. The entry of the real Countess (in Susanna's clothes) leaves the company breathless. The humbled Count's prayer for forgiveness, and her loving response, build into a radiant hymn before the brilliant conclusion brings down the curtain on the crazy day.

*

Figaro is generally agreed to be the most perfect and least problematic of Mozart's great operas. The libretto, despite its complication (to which any synopsis does scant justice), is founded on a carefully constructed intrigue and Mozart draws musical dividends even from a hat, an anonymous letter and a pin. The advance on the sketched *opere buffe* of the immediately preceding years is astonishing, and must be attributed mainly to the effect on his imagination of the play, ably seconded by Da Ponte's adaptation.

The originality of the ensembles has often and rightly been commented upon. Many of them carry the action forward, not at the 'natural' tempo of recitative but under musical control; this makes such moments as the revelation of Figaro's parents to Susanna (the Act 3 sextet) both touching and funny, and creates palpable tension when the Count comes near to murdering his wife's 'lover' in Act 2, although we know the unseen Susanna will enable the page to escape. The arias are no less original for their brevity and directness. They convey, economically and unforgettably, the essential characterization of Bartolo, Cherubino ('Non so più'), the Countess and the Count. Figaro and Susanna are presented in ensembles and action arias (his Act 1 cavatina, although it is a kind of soliloquy, and 'Non più andrai'; her 'Venite, inginocchiatevi'). Their central place in the intrigue is confirmed when each has an obbligato recitative (normally a sign of high rank) in the last act; these precede the last arias, soliloquies which deepen Figaro's character (although his cynical denunciation of women is not endearing) and reveal the subtlety and tenderness of Susanna. Mozart's replacement of 'Deh vieni' in 1789 by 'Al desio' is a rare case of his damaging his own work by pandering to a singer.

Modern performances often omit Marcellina's Act 4 aria, a stately minuet and melodious Allegro of deliberately old-fashioned cut (with coloratura and strings-only orchestration), and Basilio's, an elaborate and inventively composed narration in three sections (andante, minuet allegro). Despite their virtues these pieces of moralizing by minor characters create a sequence of four arias inappropriate so near the dénouement, and an excess of minuet tempo.

The only other critical reservation about *Le nozze di Figaro* concerns the episodic structure of the third act. It comes precisely where Da Ponte had to depart decisively from Beaumarchais (omitting the extended trial scene). The reordering of scenes has been shown not to represent Mozart's original intention; but the revised sequence avoids two immediately successive entries for the Countess and works well in the theatre. Any non-sequiturs of Act 3, however, count for little in performance and throw into greater relief the ingenious management of its finale. In the great finales of Acts 2 and 4, Mozart reached a level which he could never surpass; indeed, he was hardly to equal the $B^\flat$ Allegro of the second act finale for its mercurial motivic play and the subsequent Andante for the synchronization of dramatic revelation with the demands of musical form.

J.R.

73

Don Giovanni

[Il dissoluto punito, ossia Il Don Giovanni
('The Libertine Punished, or Don Giovanni')]

Opera buffa in two acts, K527, set to a libretto by Lorenzo Da Ponte; first performed at the National Theatre in Prague, on 29 October 1787.

Don Giovanni *a young and extremely licentious nobleman*	baritone
Commendatore	bass
Donna Anna *his daughter*	soprano
Don Ottavio *her betrothed*	tenor
Donna Elvira *a lady from Burgos*	soprano
Leporello *Giovanni's servant*	bass
Masetto *a peasant, betrothed to Zerlina*	bass
Zerlina *a peasant girl*	soprano

Peasants, servants, demons

Setting A Spanish town (traditionally Seville), in the 16th century

Although commissioned by the Prague theatre, Mozart surely had in mind production in Vienna with the personnel of the original *Figaro*. The original and Vienna casts are listed together.

	Prague 1787	*Vienna 1788*
Leporello	Felice Ponziani	Francesco Benucci
Anna	Teresa Saporiti	Aloysia Lange
Giovanni	Luigi Bassi	Francesco Albertarelli
Commendatore/Masetto	Giuseppe Lolli	Francesco Bussani
Ottavio	Antonio Baglioni	Francesco Morella
Elvira	Caterina Micelli	Caterina Cavalieri
Zerlina	Caterina Bondini	Luisa Mombelli/ Theresa Teyber

The commission for *Don Giovanni* followed the triumphant production of *Le nozze di Figaro* in Prague (December 1786). The impresario Guardasoni probably asked Mozart to expand Bertati's one-act *Don Giovanni*, set by Gazzaniga for Venice in February 1787. Da Ponte's memoirs suppressed his indebtedness but he improved Bertati in every respect and drew on other sources, notably Molière's *Dom Juan* and versions from popular theatre. About half the libretto, between the Act 1 quartet and the graveyard scene, is original.

Mozart began work during the summer, leaving for Prague on 1 October. This season in the Bohemian capital has the flavour of legend; but there is no reason to suppose that Mozart's compositional processes were abnormal, even in the late composition of the overture (on the eve of the performance, already twice postponed, or of the final rehearsal). He may have had to resist Bassi's demand for a big aria, and possibly did not know Baglioni when he composed 'Il mio tesoro'.

The new triumph in Prague was not repeated in Vienna, although *Don Giovanni* received more performances than *Figaro* had done in 1786. Mozart wrote a replacement aria for Ottavio, an additional scena for Elvira, so that her role became approximately equal to Anna's, and a buffo duet for Mombelli and Benucci. The final scene, after Giovanni's disappearance, may have been omitted.

Don Giovanni soon acquired a reputation for exceptional difficulty, derived from the superimposed dance metres of the first finale and the unprecedented harmonic richness of the second. Guardasoni gave it in Warsaw in 1789; and it made rapid progress in Germany as a Singspiel, becoming after *Die Entführung* the Mozart opera most performed in his lifetime. At least three translations were made. German was used in Prague in 1791, Vienna in 1792, and outside Germany in Amsterdam (1793) and St Petersburg (1797). *Don Giovanni* became popular in France, often in adapted versions in French, or Italian, 1811. The Italian première was at Bergamo in 1811, followed that year by Rome. In England there is some doubt over the earliest performances, which may have been partly amateur affairs. In 1817 it appeared at rival theatres in Italian and in English; it remained popular in both languages. The first American performances, in 1826, were by Garc'a's company in association with Da Ponte. Nearly every opera singer of note has been associated with one of the main roles.

*

The overture begins with the imposing music for the entrance of the 'stone guest'. Its emergence into the D major Allegro establishes the ambivalence of the opera, its perilous balance of humour and tragedy. The full sonata form has been interpreted as a portrait of Giovanni, or as justice (the heavy five-note figure) pursuing the mercurial seducer. There is no final cadence; the coda modulates to a new key (F major) for the opening scene.

ACT 1 *Courtyard of the Commendatore's house; night* Leporello is always on guard (Introduzione, 'Notte e giorno faticar'), but indulges in fantasy ('Voglio far il gentiluomo'). He hides at the approach of Anna, pursuing Giovanni (who conceals his face); the music is still formal despite its growing intensity (as often hereafter, Leporello comments in the background). Anna's father confronts Giovanni; musical formality yields to disordered gesture as they fight. The old man dies at a rare moment of stillness, even Giovanni being moved (in the short trio in F minor, he has a melody formerly sung by Anna in a faster tempo). Giovanni and Leporello escape. Anna returns and faints over the body (obbligato recitative and duet, 'Fuggi, crudele'); reviving, she responds to Ottavio's tender invitation to take him as husband and father by demanding an oath of vengeance. Their voices unite in powerful D minor cadences which form the first decisive closure of the opera.

A street; dawn Elvira, in travelling clothes, is pursuing her betrayer (aria, 'Ah, chi mi dice mai'); her sincere, slightly ridiculous pose is conveyed by a sweeping melodic line and formal orchestral gestures. Giovanni scents adventure; mutual recognition comes too late to prevent his unctuous advance, which covers the cadence of the aria. He escapes her reproaches, leaving Leporello to show her the catalogue (aria, 'Madamina, il catalogo è questo'). Giovanni's conquests total 640 in Italy, 230 in Germany, 100 in France, 91 in Turkey, but in Spain, 1003. Bubbling patter is succeeded by a luscious minuet as Leporello details the types of women who have yielded; although willing to take anybody, Giovanni prefers the young beginner (an orchestral and tonal shiver underlines this depravity).

[*Mid-morning*]   Peasants invade the stage (a bucolic G major chorus). Attracted to the bride, Zerlina, Giovanni invites them all to his house. He dismisses the jealous Masetto, who upbraids Zerlina in an action aria ('Ho capito, signor, sì') before being dragged away. Giovanni flatters Zerlina with an offer of marriage (duettino, 'La ci darem la mano'). 'Vorrei, e non vorrei': held by the hand, and following his melodic lead, Zerlina still worries about Masetto, but her impending submission is not in doubt, as the music proclaims while their voices join in a pastorale ('Andiam mio bene'). Elvira intervenes with a homily to Zerlina ('Ah fuggi il traditor') is a very short aria of Baroque vigour and formality, ending with strident coloratura. Anna and Ottavio greet Giovanni as a friend, who will help in their quest for vengeance; the devil is frustrating his every plan, but he offers his assistance with exaggerated courtesy. Elvira interrupts again; recognizing a social equal, she tells Anna in measured tones not to trust Giovanni (quartet, 'Non ti fidar, o misera'). Anna and Ottavio are puzzled; Giovanni tries to hush Elvira and explains that the poor girl is mad. In the course of a finely wrought ensemble her denunciation grows more vehement, even shameless. Something about Giovanni's farewell tells Anna, as she explains to Ottavio, that Giovanni was the man who tried to seduce her the previous night. Her harrowing description (obbligato recitative) revives the orchestral turbulence of the music after her father's death; her aria in D major ('Or sai chi l'onore') bespeaks her valiant determination to avenge her father. Ottavio can hardly believe Giovanni's villainy, but his role is to support Anna. (His exquisite aria, 'Della sua pace' K540*a*, was added for Vienna.) Giovanni congratulates Leporello on disposing of Elvira and prepares for a brilliant afternoon's work (aria, 'Fin ch'han dal vino'); wine will warm up the guests, they will mix the minuet, follia and allemande, and ten names will enter the catalogue.

Giovanni's garden [*afternoon*]   In Mozart's most enchanting melodic vein, with cello obbligato, Zerlina wins Masetto back in her aria, 'Batti, batti' (like 'Là ci darem' it begins in 2/4 and ends in a honeyed 6/8). When she hears Giovanni's voice she is too obviously aroused. The finale begins as Giovanni gives orders to his servants; then, espying Zerlina as she tries to hide, he resumes his blandishments. Masetto pops out of hiding; to the sound of a contredanse they go inside. Elvira leads Anna and Ottavio, masked, towards Giovanni's lair. Leporello sees them (the minuet is heard from the window), and they are invited in. Their short prayer for vengeance ('Protegga il giusto ciel') is a moment of stillness at the heart of one of Mozart's most active finales.

The ballroom To music resembling the earlier bucolic chorus, Giovanni and Leporello entertain the peasants. Masetto urges prudence on his bride. The central key-change from E$^\flat$ to C, resplendent with trumpets, greets the masked trio with the acclamation 'Viva la libertà!'. Now in G major, in a tour de force using three small stage bands, the ball resumes. The minuet is danced by Anna and Ottavio; on it is superimposed the contredanse in 2/4 with the same pulse (the 'follia' of Giovanni's aria) danced by Giovanni and Zerlina, and the 'teitsch' (Allemande) with a bar of 3/8 to the prevailing beat, which Leporello forces Masetto to dance. Giovanni drags Zerlina out. She screams; Masetto rushes after them; and as the violently interrupted tonalities return via F to the tonic C, Giovanni complacently blames Leporello and offers to kill him on the spot. The trio, unmasking, and Zerlinda denounce him and he is momentarily nonplussed, but in a whirlwind ensemble he outfaces them all.

ACT 2 *A street* Giovanni scorns Leporello's furious attempts to resign (duet, 'Eh via buffone'). A purse changes hands, but when Leporello tells his master to give up women he claims to need them 'as much as the food I eat and the air I breathe'. His love is universal; faithfulness to one women betrays all the rest. Leporello is forced to change clothes for the seduction of Elvira's maid. It is twilight; Elvira, on a balcony, tries to repress her desire for Giovanni but her fluttering heart betrays her (trio, 'Ah taci, ingiusto core'). Giovanni adopts her melody, but in the more intense dominant (sonata form perfectly matches Mozart's dramatic requirements). In the middle section his ardour is extreme; exploring a remote key (C within the dominant region of A), he anticipates the melody of his serenade. She denounces him; he presses her; she weakens; though he pities her, Leporello is in danger of laughing aloud. She comes down to the disguised servant, who, told to keep her occupied, begins to enjoy the act. Giovanni chases them away and to a mandolin accompaniment serenades the maid with his canzonetta, 'Deh vieni alla finestra'). But Masetto and a group of peasants, bearing crude weapons, are after Giovanni's blood. The false Leporello sympathizes and in an action aria ('Metà di voi quà vadano') gives instructions on how to search the streets and recognize the villain. He keeps Masetto with him and gives him a beating before disappearing. Hearing groans, Zerlina offers the balm only she can provide; a heart-easing melody in a gentle 3/8 invites Masetto to lay his hand on her bosom (aria, 'Vedrai, carino').

A courtyard at Anna's house   Leporello, seeing lights, retreats with Elvira into the dark yard, intent on desertion. She begs him not to leave her; he gropes for the exit (sextet, 'Sola in buio loco'; in E$^\flat$). A moment of magic – soft trumpets and drums mark a key-change from the dominant (B$^\flat$) to D – brings Anna and Ottavio with servants and lights. His renewed plea for marriage, and her prevarication, unfold in long melodic spans which draw the tonality to C minor. Elvira's search for 'Giovanni', and Leporello's for the gate, are interrupted by Zerlina and Masetto. All denounce the betrayer, in a scene of unreality (for the true villain is absent) made pathetic by Elvira's plea for mercy, and comic by Leporello's terror and abject submission when he identifies himself. This movement resembles a short finale, for it ends with a huge ensemble of consternation. Then everybody turns on Leporello, who babbles excuses as he escapes (aria, 'Ah pietà, Signori miei'). Ottavio decides to go to the authorities; he asks the others to watch over Anna while he avenges her. His aria, 'Il mio tesoro', is a full-length virtuoso piece accompanied by muted strings and clarinets.

(In the Vienna version, Leporello escapes in a recitative, using only a motif from the Prague aria; Ottavio decides to go to the authorities.

Then Zerlina drags Leporello back and ties him up, threatening dire punishments (duet, 'Per queste tue manine'); Leporello again escapes. Masetto claims to have prevented another of Giovanni's crimes. Elvira vents her mixed feelings: obbligato recitative, 'In quali eccessi' and aria, 'Mi tradì', a piece of vertiginous emotion embodied in perpetual-motion quavers.)

A graveyard [*night*] Giovanni escapes an adventure by leaping the wall. Leporello joins him complaining that once again he has nearly been killed. Giovanni heartlessly narrates the conquest of Leporello's girl; his heartless laughter is rebuked by the dead Commendatore (an oracular utterance, with trombones). They find the statue and Leporello is forced to read the inscription: 'I await vengeance on the villain who slew me'. Giovanni forces Leporello to invite the statue to supper. This most sinister situation is handled as a *buffo* duet ('O statua gentilissima') mainly reflecting the fear of Leporello as he approaches and retreats. The statue nods, then sings its acceptance; even Giovanni is puzzled and subdued, but he leads Leporello off to prepare the meal.

A darkened room in Anna's house Ottavio is again pressing his suit; he calls Anna cruel. She protests at the word (obbligato recitative, 'Crudele! Ah nò, mio bene'); society would frown on an immediate wedding. The recitative anticipates the Larghetto of the aria ('Non mi dir'), an undulating melody of great sweetness. In the Allegro she hopes that heaven will take pity on her; the blossoming coloratura corresponds to the strength of her resolve. Ottavio is determined to share her martyrdom.

A dining-room in Giovanni's house (finale) Giovanni enjoys a meal without waiting for his guest; Leporello is frankly envious, while astonished at his appetite. A sequence of popular tunes (from Martín y Soler's *Una cosa rara*, Sarti's Fra *i due litiganti* and Mozart's *Figaro*) played by onstage wind band accompanies the farce of Leporello stealing food and being caught with his mouth full. Elvira bursts in, making a last appeal to Giovanni to reform. He laughs at her, invites her join him, and to a newly minted melody drinks a toast to wine and women, 'Sostegno e gloria d'umanità'. Recognizing that she will not change him, Elvira runs off despairingly; then, from outside, utters a piercing scream. Leporello investigates and returns in terror, babbling of a white stone man with earth-shaking strides. When knocking is heard he hides under the table and Giovanni opens the door. The overture music is reinforced by trombones as the statue enters to a crushing diminished 7th. His solemn grandeur, Giovanni's polite, then impatient responses, and Leporello's terrified asides, are musically characterized but subsumed to a harmonic development of unparalleled richness. The statue cannot take mortal food but he invites Giovanni to sup with him. With admirable fearlessness in a phrase of marked dignity, Giovanni accepts; but on grasping the statue's chilling hand he is overcome by his impending fate. Offered a chance to repent, he proudly refuses and is dragged into the engulfing flames. The chorus of demons exactly reflects the cadences of the vengeance duet, at the beginning of Act 1. The others rush on with the police, to find only Leporello, who stammers out enough for them to understand. In an extended Larghetto, Ottavio again pleads with Anna; she tells him to wait a year for their wedding. Elvira will go to a convent, Zerlina and Masetto will marry, Leporello will find another master. All join to point the moral in a bright fugato: 'This is the end of the evil-doer: his death is as bad as his life'.

*

There are two authentic versions of *Don Giovanni*, the differences mainly in the distribution of arias. Each has only one for Ottavio, since when including a new aria for Elvira (Cavalieri) in Act 2, Mozart omitted 'Il mio tesoro' as well as a short aria for Leporello. The concentration of arias in Act 2 which results from the common practice of including in succession those for Leporello, Ottavio and Elvira was never the authors' intention. The additional duet for Zerlina and Leporello, its coarseness perhaps designed to humour the Viennese, is generally omitted, but Elvira's 'In quali eccessi . . . Mi tradì' is too good to lose; some 19th-century performances, including one that may have had Da Ponte's approval, removed it to Act 1.

In musical form and dramatic technique, particularly the proportion and design of arias and ensembles, *Don Giovanni* is largely modelled on *Figaro*. Exceptions include the 'Catalogue' aria, with its fast-slow tempo pattern; the first finale which besides the unique

dance sequence covers a change of location; and the extended introduction, embedded in a vast structure extending from the overture to
the end of the duet 'Fuggi, crudele'. The hammonic language associated with Don Giovanni's fall, including that duet and the second
finale, marks a decisive departure from *buffo* norms (certainly not
anticipated by Gazzaniga, whose setting may have influenced Anna's
first entry). The designation 'dramma giocoso' used by Da Ponte
(though not by Mozart) has no particular significance; the serious
characters are as much embroiled in the intrigue as they are in Figaro.

The tragic elements nevertheless form a new synthesis of buffo
and serious styles, and explain why Don Giovanni has gripped the
imagination of writers and philosophers. In particular they have been
attracted by the daemonic in Giovanni, and by the impossibility of
penetrating a character so mercurial, whose music says so little about
his motivation; even 'Fin ch'han dal vino' is a set of instructions to
Leporello, though also an explosion from his joyous daemon.
Whereas the other characters are remarkably three-dimensional,
Giovanni adapts the style of each of his victims, including the
Commendatore who brings out the heroic in him and Leporello whom
he chaffs in pure buffo style. He woos Anna by courtly flattery,
Zerlina by condescension, Elvira's maid by disguise; Elvira herself
he evades or mocks, but he can also woo her with false ardour (in
the trio at the beginning of Act 2).

Elvira, ignored in the 19th century, now seems the most interesting
because psychologically the most complex of the women. Though the
greatest singers, such as Patti, sometimes sang Zerlina, Anna attracted
most interest; E. T. A. Hoffmann suggested that she had been seduced
by Giovanni and was in love with him rather than Ottavio, a fantasy
which received comic treatment in Shaw's *Man and Superman*.
Stendhal and Kierkegaard used Giovanni to illustrate aspects of
love and the erotic. Significantly Kierkegaard was aware of earlier
dramatic treatments but derived his views from the music, not the
libretto or the historical evolution of the character (B. Williams, in
Rushton 1981).

Don Giovanni is governed by a single idea, Giovanni's flouting of
society in pursuit of sexual pleasure, which binds together a disparate

set of ambivalent or comic incidents. The libretto has been unfairly criticized; its episodic nature is a condition of the subject, in which respect it differs from *Figaro* and *Così*. Divine retribution appears like an act of God, or a different kind of life-force personified in the statue; what in previous treatments had been comic, perfunctory or merely gruesome, is raised to sublimity by Mozart's music.

J.R.

Così fan tutte

[*Così fan tutte, ossia La scuola degli amanti*]

('All Women do the Same, or The School for Lovers')

Opera buffa in two acts, K588, set to a libretto by Lorenzo Da Ponte; first performed at the Vienna Burgtheater on 26 January 1790.

The first cast consisted of Da Ponte's mistress, Adriana Ferrarese del Bene (Fiordiligi), Susanna in the 1789 *Figaro*; Louise Villeneuve (Dorabella); Vincenzo Calvesi (Ferrando); and three stalwarts from the 1786 *Figaro*, Dorotea Bussani (Despina), Francesco Benucci (Guglielmo) and Francesco Bussani (Alfonso).

Fiordiligi ⎱ *ladies from Ferrara, sisters living in Naples*		soprano
Dorabella ⎰		soprano
Guglielmo *an officer, Fordiligi's lover*		bass
Ferrando *an officer, Dorabella's lover*		tenor
Despina *maidservant to the sisters*		soprano
Don Alfonso *an old philosopher*		bass

Soldiers, servants, sailors, wedding guests

Setting Naples, in the 18th century

Così fan tutte was commissioned following the successful revival of *Le nozze di Figaro* in August 1789. The libretto is original; there is no hard evidence for the theory that it was based on a recent Viennese scandal. It has a mythological and literary ancestry in the Procris story, and in Boccaccio, Shakespeare (*Cymbeline*) and Cervantes, all of whom anticipate elements of the plot: the trial of female constancy and the wager.

Così fan tutte was rehearsed at Mozart's apartment on 31 December, and in January with Haydn present. It received five performances before the death of Joseph II on 20 February closed the theatres; five more followed from June to August. There is little information about its genesis or reception.

Performances followed in 1791 in Prague, Leipzig and Dresden, and in German in Frankfurt (as *Liebe und Versuchung*), Mainz and

Amsterdam. At Leipzig in 1794 and in other centres it appeared as *Weibertreue, oder Die Mädchen sind von Flandern*, translated by C. F. Bretzner, author of the source of *Die Entführung aus dem Serail*. No opera of Mozart received such frequent 'improvement' or so many alternative titles besides the standard German *So machen es alle*. The alleged immorality of the libretto encouraged such treatment; some adaptations had the ladies learn of the plot and avenge themselves by turning the tables on their lovers. Critical opinion suggested that it was one of Mozart's weaker pieces, and the music appeared in pasticcios or with a completely different story. Today the opera is given in its original form, even with the restoration of Mozart's own cuts. *Così* was the second opera performed at Glyndebourne (1934) and productions since World War II are too numerous to mention; it is by now as much a repertory piece as the other Mozart-Da Ponte operas.

*

The short introduction to the overture concludes with a motto, a double cadence of striking simplicity (*piano*, interrupted, then *forte*, perfect), later sung to the words of the title. The sonata-form Presto mockingly tosses a figure among the woodwind, its cadence taken from Basilio's line 'Così fan tutte le belle' (*Figaro*, the Act 1 trio, 'Cosa sento!'). The motto reappears just before the end.

ACT 1 *A coffee-house* Ferrando and Guglielmo proclaim the virtues of the sisters Dorabella and Fiordiligi, to whom they are betrothed; Alfonso is sceptical (trio, 'La mia Dorabella'). The young men prepare to defend the ladies' honour with swords, but the diatonic brilliance of music shared by all three argues no great discord. Alfonso declines to fight, but calls them simpletons to trust female constancy: a faithful woman is like a phoenix; all believe in it but none has seen it (his mocking *pianissimo* unison cadence resembles the motto). The others insist that the phoenix is Dorabella/ Fiordiligi (trio, 'È la fede delle femmine'). Alfonso wagers 100 zecchini that fidelity will not endure a day of the lovers' absence; he will prove it if they promise to obey him while wooing each other's betrothed in disguise. Ferrando plans to spend his winnings on a serenade, Guglielmo (the first division between them) on a meal; Alfonso listens politely (trio, 'Una bella serenata'). An extended orchestral coda closes a scene of purely *buffo* electricity.

A garden by the sea [*morning*]   The girls sing rapturously of their lovers (duet, 'Ah guarda sorella'); Dorabella (surprisingly, in view of the sequel) touches a note of melancholy before they launch into voluptuous coloratura in 3rds, united in loving the idea of loving. Alfonso appears, the prolonged F minor cadences of his tiny aria ('Vorrei dir') choking back the awful news: their lovers are to leave for active service. The men take solemn leave with only hints at lyricism (quintet, 'Sento, o Dio'). The girls' agitation is coloured by the dominant minor; Alfonso quells any premature delight at this evidence of love. Ferrando's lyricism (to a motif from the trio, 'Una bella serenata') now matches the girls'; Guglielmo sings with Alfonso (this inevitable consequence of differences in tessitura continually invites differentiation of character). The girls declare they will die; in a prepared speech (duettino, 'Al fato dan legge') the men promise to return. A march is heard (chorus, 'Bella vita militar'). They embrace, promising a daily letter, their rapturous indulgence in misery (particularly intense in the melodic line, taken by Fiordiligi) counterpointed by Alfonso's efforts not to laugh (quintet, 'Di scrivermi ogni giorno'). The men embark (reprise of the chorus); Alfonso joins a moving prayer for their safety (trio, 'Soave sia il vento'), the orchestra evocative yet sensuous. Alfonso prepares for action (arioso); 'He ploughs the waves, sows in sand, traps the wind in a net, who trusts the heart of a woman'.

A furnished room   Despina has prepared the ladies' chocolate and is sampling it when they burst in. Dorabella explains their despair, but her extravagant grief leaves her barely coherent (obbligato recitative and the first real aria, 'Smanie implacabili'). Despina cannot take them seriously; surely they can find other lovers. In the teeth of their protests she inverts Alfonso's creed (aria, 'In uomini'): men, especially soldiers, are not expected to be faithful; women should also use love to enjoy themselves. Alfonso bribes Despina to assist him, without revealing the plot. The men enter as 'Albanians', their bizarre disguise impenetrable even to the sharp-witted Despina (sextet, 'Alla bella Despinetta'). Recovering from laughter, she helps them to plead for a moment's kindness from the ladies; they are rejected in a furious Allegro. Alfonso, emerging, claims them as his friends, but after the men's voices unite, turning recitative towards arioso, Fiordiligi articulates her constancy in a powerful recitative and aria ('Come scoglio'); she stands firm as a rock in tempestuous seas. The three sections grow in brilliance and versatility; near the start, after leaps of a 10th and 12th, she ascends majestically over two octaves (the total range is *a-c'''*); near the end she takes the bass line. Guglielmo's patter-song in praise of his own appearance (especially the moustaches) finds no favour ('Non siate ritrosi'; there is a longer, rejected alternative, 'Rivolgete a lui lo sguardo', к584). As the outraged girls depart, the men bubble with delight (trio, 'E voi ridete?'), brilliantly covering Alfonso's insistence that the more the girls protest, the more sure is their fall. Guglielmo wonders when they can get lunch; Ferrando enjoys the atmosphere of love ('Un' aura amorosa'), muted violins and clarinets supporting his ardently extended line.

The garden [*afternoon*]   At the beginning of the finale, the girls unwittingly share Ferrando's mood of longing, spinning a tender D major melody to a gently ironic rococo decoration of flutes and bassoons. How their fate has changed! Their sighs are displaced by fear when the men rush in drinking poison, to music (in G minor) suddenly suggestive of tragic violence. Alfonso and Despina go for help, instructing the ladies to nurse the men, who are thoroughly enjoying themselves; yet minor modes prevail as never before in Mozart's finales. Despina, to a pompous G major minuet, appears disguised as the doctor, invoking Mesmer as she magnetizes out the poison. The key abruptly changes to B♭: the men profess to believe they are in paradise. In the final Allegro (in D) the men request a kiss and are again rebuffed.

ACT 2   *A room*   Despina tries to persuade her shocked employers that there is no harm in a little flirtation. In Mozart's slyest *buffo* soprano aria ('Una donna a quindici anni'), she explains that a young girl who knows the arts of attracting men can have them at her mercy. The girls agree that there can be nothing wrong in enjoying the men's company, and they select partners (duet, 'Prenderò quel brunettino'). Dorabella will take the brown-haired one (Guglielmo), Fiordiligi the blond (Ferrando; thus they fall in with the men's plan); and they prepare to amuse themselves.

Furnished garden by the sea [*early evening*]   The serenade on wind instruments, repeated by the lovers and chorus ('Secondate, aurette amiche'), is a prayer for success in love. The four meet but are tongue-tied; Alfonso and Despina give a lesson in etiquette (quartet, the ladies silent, 'La mano a me date'), and join their hands. The couples prepare to walk round the garden. Guglielmo is all too successful in winning Dorabella's heart and a mark of her favour, replacing Ferrando's portrait by his own gift, a pendant heart (duet, 'Il core vi dono'). The gently bantering 3/8, in F major, matches Dorabella's innocent flirtatiousness; Gugliemo can hardly believe his success, but falls comfortably in with her mood. Fiordiligi rushes in, pursued by Ferrando: she has seen in him temptation, a serpent, a basilisk; he is stealing her peace. He protests that he wants only her happiness and asks for a kindly glance, noting that she looks at him and sighs. Her lovely soul will not long resist his pleading; otherwise her cruelty will kill him ('Ah lo veggio quell'anima bella'). In this lightly flowing rondo, as in 'Un'aura amorosa', woodwind are added only at the reprise; the ending achieves an unexpected intensity. This aria is traditionally omitted, but without it Ferrando's exit is inexplicable. Fiordiligi wrestles with her conscience, her obbligato recitative ('Ei parte') running a gamut of feeling while traversing tonal space from B♭ to E. In her deeply expressive rondò ('Per pietà, ben mio') the elaborate wind parts (notably the horns) have an *opera seria* formality; sheer musical beauty articulates her cry of despair, as she asks her absent lover's forgiveness. There has been no simple recitative since before the duet for Guglielmo and Dorabella; the symmetry of the couplings breaks down in over 400 bars of continuous music.

The men compare notes: when he learns of Dorabella's fickleness Ferrando is roused to fury (obbligato recitative, 'Il mio ritratto! Ah perfida!'). Guglielmo tries to console him by adopting Alfonso's philosophy (aria, 'Donne mie la fate a tanti'); he is fond of women and defends their honour, but their little habit of deceiving men is reprehensible. The restless perpetual motion conveys Guglielmo's confidence that the tragedy will not befall him. Ferrando's feelings are in turmoil (obbligato recitative, 'In qual fiero contrasto'). An obsessive orchestral figure projects shame ('Alfonso! how you will laugh!') and anger ('I will cut the wretch out of my heart') beyond the decorum of comedy. In a cavatina ('Tradito, schernito') he denounces Dorabella's treachery but admits (clarinets entering as C minor turns to E$^\flat$ major) that he still loves her. Alfonso and Guglielmo overhear the reprise in which the E$^\flat$ melody recurs in C, oboes replacing clarinets: this new instrumental colour (his previous arias used no oboes) may be prophetic. His pride piqued, he agrees to a further attack on Fiordiligi.

A room, with several doors, a mirror, and a table Despina praises Dorabella's good sense; Dorabella answers Fiordiligi's protests in a graceful 6/8 aria ('È amore un ladroncello') which, despite its sophisticated instrumentation, shows her conversion to Despina's easy virtue; love is a thief, a serpent, but if you let him have his way, he brings delight. Alone, Fiordiligi resolves to repel her new suitor; sadistically observed by the men, she prepares to join her lover at the front, and orders Despina to bring his uniform. She launches an aria ('Fra gli amplessi'), but as she quickens the tempo from Adagio Ferrando joins in. Her anguished plea holds a striking allusion to Ferrando's first phrase in the Act 1 trio for the men, 'Una bella serenata'. (The keys and key-scheme parallel the seduction trio of *Don Giovanni*.) Ferrando's lyricism outdoes hers. The note of true ardour is intensified when the acceleration of tempo is halted by a Larghetto (back in A); it is hard not to believe that Ferrando is genuine. Despite a high *a''* on 'crudel', Fiordiligi's responses are tremulous; the solo oboe rises above her, speaks for her, as she admits defeat ('hai vinto'). The fourth (Andante) section of this greatest of Mozart's duets combines their voices in an intimacy never vouchsafed to Dorabella and Guglielmo. The latter is enraged; Ferrando is ironic; Alfonso tells them their only revenge is to marry their 'plucked crows'. Women are always accused of fickleness, but he forgives them; they are not responsible for their own nature ('Tutti accusan le donne'). All three sing the motto from the overture: 'Così fan tutte'.

A reception room prepared for a wedding An Allegro, resembling the opera's opening number, begins the finale, as Despina orders the servants to a prepare a feast (brief choral response) and Alfonso applauds their work. The chorus greets the couples; in their carefree response the accident of casting matches the composer's dramatic insight by bringing Fiordiligi and Ferrando together in expansive coloratura. With Dorabella they sing the toast, a ravishing canon. Guglielmo, whose range prevents him from following on, mutters curses. Alfonso enters in E major, with Despina disguised as a notary. Coughing formally, she reads the marriage contract; the ladies sign it. But then the Act 1 march in D, associated with the officers' departure, is heard. Consternation: their lovers are returning. The Albanians are bundled into hiding, and the men reappear jauntily as their old selves, pretend puzzlement at their reception, drag out the notary, revealed as Despina, and find the marriage contract: indignation, confession, blame (on Alfonso), threats of revenge. Returning half-changed into Albanians, Ferrando greets Fiordiligi (apparently quoting earlier music subsequently abandoned), Guglielmo greets Dorabella (quoting their love duet), and both address the flabbergasted Despina as the doctor (quoting the first finale). Alfonso calms them down; the ladies beg pardon; the men condescend to forgive, and all agree to follow Alfonso's idea of reason: to laugh when there is cause to weep, and so find equilibrium.

*

Only the present century has taken a serious interest in *Così fan tutte*. At first it was considered a heartless farce clothed in miraculous music, a view supported by its obvious artificiality (the lovers' disguises, the 24-hour time-scale). A number of cuts, particularly of Act 2 arias, became customary. Recently directors and critics have sought deeper meanings, and even questioned the restoration of the original pairing of lovers, which it seems legitimate to assume from the conventionality of the conclusion but which is not specified in the libretto or clarified by the music.

Così has been seen as revealing a dark side to the Enlightenment, an anti-feminist sadism. Yet by any showing the most admirable character is Fiordiligi. The girls develop more than the men. Dorabella at least learns to understand her own lightness; and 'Fra gli amplessi' suggests that Fiordiligi has matured through learning the power of sexuality. There is little sign that Guglielmo learns anything in the school for lovers, even that those who set traps deserve to get caught, although his vanity is wounded as deeply as his purse. Ferrando, however, comes to live as intensely as Fiordiligi, and may appear to have fallen in love with her. To suggest that they should marry (leaving Guglielmo for Dorabella) is, however, still less satisfactory than reversion to the original pairings. The conclusion represents not a solution but a way of bringing the action to a close with an artificiality so evident that no happy outcome can be predicted. The music creates this enigma, but cannot solve it.

By standards other than Mozart's, the instrumentation in *Così* would be of novel richness. The invention of B$^\flat$ trumpets allows their substitution for horns in 'Come scoglio' and 'Ah lo veggio', divorced from the timpani; three other numbers also use trumpets without horns. The resourceful use of woodwind, application of string mutes, and exploration of a wider than usual range of keys and key relations, creates an unprecedentedly voluptuous colouring (E major and A$^\flat$ major are juxtaposed in the second finale, the former used in three other numbers, a concentration unusual in Mozart).

Much of the style of *Così* has been attributed to parody, but a stylistic mixture had long been a feature of *opera buffa*. Guglielmo sings pure *buffo* arias, but all Ferrando's strike serious notes reflected in their variety of form. The girls' first arias overplay feelings which will not endure: Dorabella's prolonged cadences in 'Smanie implacabili' recall Alfonso's mock-seriousness in 'Vorrei dir'. 'Come scoglio' is sometimes considered pure parody, Fiordiligi's second aria 'Per pietà' essentially serious; yet the latter has equally wide leaps and even more florid instrumentation, the differences in perception of them being explicable by the fact that one administers a rebuff to the 'Albanian' strangers, and the other, following a disturbing attack on her loyalty to Guglielmo, is an internal monologue.

There are fewer arias in *Così* than in the other Da Ponte operas, but they are correspondingly more important in unfolding the inner drama. The increased number of ensembles is balanced by the brevity of several of them, not only the sparkling *buffo* trios for the men but also 'Soave sia il vento', a gem in which even Alfonso appears moved; it bids farewell to innocence as well as to the lovers. There is a marked increase in the amount of obbligato recitative, which with the tone of some of the arias (notably Fiordiligi's) brings *Così* closer to *opera seria* than the other Da Ponte operas.

Così fan tutte is likely to remain a disturbing experience because of, not despite, its aesthetic attractions. The libretto was originally destined for Salieri; its superb pacing does not mask its potential triviality. Mozart found in it ways to seek out hitherto unplumbed depths in the human psyche, making the uncut whole, for an increasing number of commentators, the profoundest of his Italian comedies.

J.R.

La clemenza di Tito
('The Clemency of Titus')

Opera seria in two acts, K621, set to a libretto by Pietro Metastasio and adapted by Caterino Mazzolà. It was first performed in the National Theatre in Prague on 6 September 1791.

The first cast was Antonio Baglioni (Titus), Maria Marchetti-Fantozzi (Vitellia), Domenico Bedini (Sextus), Carolina Perini (Annius, the travesty role), Gaetano Campi, a well-known *buffo* singer (Publius); with one Signora Antonini singing Servilia.

Tito [Titus Flavius Vespasianus] *Roman Emperor*	tenor
Vitellia *daughter of the deposed Emperor Vitellius*	soprano
Servilia *sister of Sextus, in love with Annius*	soprano
Sesto [Sextus] *friend of Titus, in love with* *Vitellia*	soprano castrato
Annio [Annius] *friend of Sextus, in love with Servilia*	soprano
Publio [Publius] *prefect of the praetorian guard*	bass

Senators, ambassadors, praetorian guards, lictors, people of Rome

Setting Rome, AD *c*80

Although mostly composed after *Die Zauberflöte*, *La clemenza di Tito* was performed first. Its gestation has been dated back to 1789, when Mozart was in contact with the impresario Guardasoni, but the subject cannot have been chosen then. Guardasoni obtained an open commission from the Bohemian Estates only in July, for an opera designed to celebrate Leopold II's coronation as King of Bohemia, and to some degree adapted to his particular taste. Contrary to an opinion often expressed, the commission was far from unwelcome to Mozart; he wanted to show his strength in *opera seria*.

Metastasio's libretto, already set by more than 40 composers, was 'ridotta a vera opera' ('reduced to a proper opera'), as Mozart wrote in his catalogue. Only seven arias and one chorus (designated 'Metastasio' below) were unchanged; Metastasio's aria and recitative

93

texts were manipulated in the ensembles and finales devised by Mazzolà. Reduced by a third, the libretto gains clarity and the musical numbers pertinence, at the expense of dramatic weight.

Mozart probably composed all of *La clemenza* between late July and September 1791. He arrived in Prague on 28 August and despite illness finished work on the eve of the performance. The chief artistic drawback of the short time available was that Mozart sub-contracted the simple recitatives, almost certainly to Süssmayr. The choruses and ensembles were worked out with Mazzolà in Vienna and written there, as were some arias. The singer Mozart knew best was Baglioni, two of whose arias were written in Vienna; the only ensemble composed in Prague (the trio early in Act 2) probably replaced intended arias for Vitellia and Sextus. Problems in these roles are apparent from surviving sketch and autograph material. Mozart began by assuming that Sextus would be a tenor, and Vitellia's 'Non più di fiori', the Act 2 rondò, is distinctly lower in tessitura than the rest of the role.

The reception was modest until a triumphant last night was reported to Mozart (who had left Prague on 15 September) on the day of the première of *Die Zauberflöte* (30 September). Concert performances of extracts and of the whole opera were arranged by Constanze Mozart for her own benefit. In Vienna on 29 December 1791 and in later performances Aloysia Lange sang Sextus. After a further performance in Vienna in 1795 Constanze took the work to Graz, Leipzig and Berlin, herself singing Vitellia. In 1796 the German translation by Rochlitz was performed in Dresden and used in most German centres (including Vienna) within the next 15 years. The first performance outside Germany and Austria was also the first of any Mozart opera in London, on 27 March 1806, for the benefit of Mrs Billington. Performances followed in all the main European centres, usually in Italian (1809, Naples; 1816, Paris and Milan; 1817, in Russian, St Petersburg). Until about 1830 *La clemenza di Tito* was one of Mozart's most popular operas; it then went into eclipse. It has never fully entered the modern repertory and is often described as unworthy of Mozart, hastily assembled for a commission he could not refuse. Critical estimates have risen since World War II, and it is now seen as a positive step towards further reform of *opera seria*.

*

Despite its lack of overt thematic connection with the rest of the opera the overture has been described as a dramatic argument according to Gluck's principles.

ACT 1   *Vitellia's apartments*   Titus is in love with the Jewish queen Berenice; Vitellia denies being jealous, but believes she, an emperor's daughter, should be his consort. Overtly motivated by the need to avenge her father, she induces Sextus to lead an assassination plot. A loyal friend of Titus, he adores her blindly and cannot resist her commands. He begs her to say how he can please her, for she is his destiny (duet, 'Come ti piace, imponi'). She asks why he is delaying; he requests only a tender glance. In the Allegro, both admit to the confusion of their feelings. Annius reports that Titus has dismissed Berenice for reasons of state. Vitellia allows herself to hope, and tells Sextus to suspend the plot. In measured tones (a slow minuet) she declares that to win her he must not exhaust her with suspicions (Metastasio: 'Deh se piacer me vuoi'). The following Allegro returns to the opening words; its principal message, conveyed in a capricious mixture of sturdy rhythms and decorative flourishes, is that doubt encourages deception. Annius asks Sextus for his sister's hand, which he gladly grants in the duettino ('Deh prendi un dolce amplesso'), a winning expression of brotherly affection.

Before the Roman forum   Senators and delegates from the provinces gather at the heart of the Imperial city. Titus enters in state, with lictors, guards and citizens. A march leads directly to a chorus in praise of Titus (Metastasio: 'Serbate, o dei custodi'). After formal expressions of homage from Publius and Annius, Titus replies that his sole aim is to be a good father to his people. The chorus is repeated; Titus calls for Sextus, and the stage is cleared during a repeat of the march. Private conversation (with Annius present) reveals the intimacy of Sextus and Titus. The emperor must publicly deny his love for Berenice by taking a Roman wife; who better than his friend's sister? Annius bravely eulogizes the emperor's choice.

In a mellow Andante (Metastasio: 'Del più sublime soglio') Titus declares that the only happiness afforded by supreme power is to reward virtue. Annius reveals the emperor's decision to Servilia; the exquisite melody of their farewell (duet, 'Ah perdona al primo affetto') touches a nerve of painful tenderness within this severely political opera.

A garden in the Imperial palace on the Palatine To Publius Titus expounds his philosophy of disarming enmity by forgiveness. Servilia dares to confess that she and Annius are in love; he thanks heaven for her frankness, and releases her (Metastasio: 'Ah, se fosse intorno al trono'). The sweep of the melody in this short Allegro conveys his open-hearted nature; if the throne were flanked by such honesty, the cares of office would turn to joy. Vitellia bitterly compliments Servilia who, piqued, does not reveal her refusal. Deaf to reason, Vitellia upbraids Sextus for dilatoriness: Titus must die. Before embarking on his fatal mission he asks again for the loving glance which destroys his loyalty and assures his happiness (Metastasio: 'Parto, parto'). This aria with basset clarinet obbligato is in three sections, accelerating, as sentiment yields to determination, from a nobly extended Adagio through an impassioned Allegro ('Guardami, e tutto obblio') to a brilliant conclusion. Publius and Annius announce to Vitellia that she is the emperor's chosen consort (trio, 'Vengo! aspettate!'); the others mistake her confusion for excess of joy and comment sympathetically, but she is terrified that it is too late to stop the plot (her frantic message recalling Sextus ended Metastasio's first act). This gripping movement is dominated by Vitellia's agitation, expressed in gasping phrases and, when the musical line is more sustained, cruelly high tessitura (touching d''').

A portico before the Capitol Sextus has launched the conspiracy, but is wracked by guilt (obbligato recitative); his weakness has made him a traitor. He cannot turn back; the Capitol is already in flames. The bulk of the finale is an action ensemble. Sextus, in words Metastasio intended as recitative, seems to begin an aria (a prayer for Titus's safety), but to Annius he babbles of his shame and rushes away; Annius is prevented from following by the need to keep Servilia out of danger. Cries of horror are heard from the offstage chorus; Publius appears, fearing for Titus, then Vitellia, frantically searching for Sextus. He returns, looking for a place to hide; all believe Titus dead. Sextus is about to confess when Vitellia silences him. In a concluding Andante all the characters and the distant chorus join in lamenting the murderous treachery.

ACT 2 *Palace gardens* Annius tells Sextus that Titus is alive. Sextus admits that he instigated the plot, refusing to give any reason. Annius gently urges him to throw himself on the emperor's mercy ('Torna di Tito a lato'), his concern enhanced by his repetition, to the end, of 'torna' ('return'). Vitellia warns Sextus too late; Publius comes with guards to arrest him (trio, 'Se a volto mai ti senti'). The principal melodic ideas belong to Sextus, bidding Vitellia a lingering farewell; the music darkens suddenly as her admiration for his devotion conflicts with her fear that he will implicate her. In the Allegretto, Sextus asks Vitellia to remember his love; she is gripped with remorse; Publius, though touched, remains firm (Metastasio's second act ends here).

A large room, with a writing-table The chorus (patricians, praetorian guards and people) thank Fate for sparing Titus ('Ah grazie si rendano'). In the middle section of this ironically serene Andante, Titus thanks them for their loyalty. He tries to understand the conspirators; Lentulus (who led the attack) is clearly guilty; perhaps he has accused Sextus to protect himself. In a short aria (Metastasio: 'Tardi, s'avvede') Publius bluffly comments that the good-natured find it hard to believe others capable of betrayal. A moment later he returns with Sextus's confession and news of his condemnation by the Senate. Annius pleads for mercy ('Tu fosti tradito'): Titus has been betrayed, but hope remains if he consults his heart (an episode in Metastasio in which Annius is accused is omitted). Bitterly hurt, Titus condemns his own hesitation in signing the death warrant, but the word 'death' stops him short (obbligato recitative, 'Che orror! che tradimento!'). He sends for Sextus; incisive orchestral gestures yield to sustained harmonies as he persuades himself that he cannot refuse the hearing which justice offers the meanest citizen. Publius brings in Sextus. The first speeches are sung aside (trio, 'Quello di Tito è il volto'). Sextus's fear appears in string tremolandos, his desperation in wide intervals and an anguished turn to the minor: can this be the face of Titus? Titus can barely recognize his guilt-ridden friend; Publius witnesses the emperor's tangled emotions. Titus commands Sextus to approach, but he is rooted to the spot. The ensemble freezes in the Allegro, Sextus's angular line again dominating while the others comment on his evident terror. Titus reduces Sextus to tears of contrition by addressing him kindly. But Sextus, protecting Vitellia, cannot justify his treachery. Titus dismisses him coldly. Gathering his feelings into a nobly arching melody, Sextus asks Titus to remember their earlier friendship (rondò, 'Deh, per questo istante solo'). In the Allegro the boundaries of the tonic (A major) are twice burst by cries of despair (in C and F majors); its gentler principal melody ('Tanto affanno soffre un core') becomes hectic in the faster coda. Titus signs the fatal paper, then tears it up; he is no Brutus, and cannot begin a career of tyranny by executing a friend. He tells Publius only that Sextus's fate is settled (Metastasio: 'Se all' impero, amici dei'); if the noble gods require an emperor to be cruel, they must deprive him of empire or give him another heart. This is the only aria in the modern equivalent of da capo form; its weight, balanced by considerable floridity, prepares fully for Titus's renunciation of revenge, while underlining his strength of purpose in a march-like coda.

Publius tells Vitellia he has heard nothing of the emperor's conversation with Sextus. Annius and Servilia ask the empress-designate to help. Servilia's lightly-scored minuet (Metastasio: 'S'altro che lagrime') is a gentle but penetrating plea; weeping is not enough to save Sextus. Moved by Sextus's constancy, Vitellia is at the point of decision (obbligato recitative, 'Ecco il punto, o Vitellia'); can she betray him to die alone? No chains of flowers will accompany the descent of Hymen (rondò, 'Non più di fiori'); the music, with bassethorn obbligato, paints the serene image which she must renounce. Her despair breaks out in the Allegro ('Infelice! qual orrore!'); she cannot live knowing the horror of what she has done. The aria merges into a transition with the character of a slow march.

A public place, before a temple The chorus acclaims the godlike emperor ('Che del ciel'). Annius and Servilia ask for mercy, but

Titus addresses Sextus with severity. Before he can pronounce sentence (which all assume will be death) Vitellia intervenes, claiming sole responsibility for the conspiracy. Titus is bewildered; he was about to absolve one criminal, and another appears (obbligato recitative, 'Ma, che giorno'). But he defies the stars to deter him; all must be forgiven. In the finale they praise him and he rewards them with his confidence; may he die when Rome's good is not his chief concern. Chorus and principals together ask the gods to grant him long life.

*

La clemenza di Tito, like several of its predecessors, ends in forgiveness, here predicated in the title. The goodness of Titus (in contrast to his counterparts in *Lucio Silla* and *Die Entführung*) is so strongly presented in his arias that the outcome of his struggle in Act 2 is inevitable; his role is close to Metastasio's conception and his music has a correspondingly old-fashioned cut. Vitellia is capricious in the opening scenes, selfish but perplexed about her own motivation in the Act 1 trio, yet capable of noble renunciation ('Non più di fiori'). Sextus is an equally rewarding role, with two large arias and the dominant part in several ensembles.

As in *Così fan tutte*, several of the musical numbers are very brief, allowing the expansion of crucial arias and the first-act finale within a short opera. The use of accompanied recitative is traditional, but the arias range from *buffo* simplicity for Servilia and Publius, through the more developed but still direct style of Annius, to the fully elaborated arias of the three main characters: of these two are rondòs, and two were given obbligatos for the clarinettist and basset-horn player Anton Stadler. In the context of *opera seria*, however, the highest originality lies in the ensembles. There is a strong predilection for movements with two tempos (the usual slow-fast reversed in the first finale). While the folklike duets of the first act approach the style of *Die Zauberflöte*, the trios show that *buffo* textures are equally suited to tragic situations. The first finale is unique in Mozart's output, bridging the gap between Gluck and the 19th century in the realism of its opening, its stark modulation from $E^\flat$ to $G^\flat$ (by implied C and G minors and $B^\flat$, bars 17–24), and its offstage chorus and tremolando; compared to *Idomeneo*, the sparing use of such effects corresponds to the absence of a supernatural dimension to the plot.

Had he lived to prepare further performances, Mozart would surely have replaced the simple recitatives (which do not always end in an appropriate key). He might have increased the orchestrated recitative to a quantity approaching that in *Così* and, as he had planned for *Idomeneo*, rearranged the vocal forces, with a tenor Sextus. Now that performances and recordings, and a general revival of 18th-century repertory, encourage reassessment of its virtues, *La clemenza di Tito* clearly appears a conception not fully realized, but still masterly and amply rewarding study and performance.

J.R.

Die Zauberflöte
('The Magic Flute')

Singspiel in two acts, K620, set to a libretto by Emanuel Schikaneder; first performed in Vienna, at the Theater auf der Wieden, on 30 September 1791.

Schikaneder himself sang Papageno at the première; Benedikt Schack was Tamino; the Queen was Mozart's sister-in-law Josepha Hofer; Pamina was Anna Gottlieb (the first Barbarina, still only 17); Monostatos was Johann Joseph Nouseul; Sarastro, Franz Gerl.

Sarastro *Priest of the Sun*	bass
Tamino *a Javanese Prince*	tenor
An Elderly Priest ['Sprecher'; Orator, Speaker]	bass
Three priests	bass, tenor, spoken role
The Queen of the Night	coloratura soprano
Pamina *her daughter*	soprano
Three Boys	2 sopranos, mezzo-soprano
Papagena	soprano
Papageno *a birdcatcher, employed by the Queen*	baritone
Monostatos *a Moor, overseer of the Temple*	tenor
Two Men in Armour	tenor, bass
Three Slaves	spoken roles

Priests, Attendants, Acolytes, Slaves

Die Zauberflöte is an allegory set in no real locality or historical period. Ancient Egypt is evoked by the mysteries, but early productions also showed Islamic influence on costumes and neo-classical architecture appropriate to the Enlightenment. The exotic costumes and setting (and Tamino's nationality) are a mask; Mozart and Schikaneder intended a coded representation of Freemasonry.

Carl Ludwig Gieseke (who originally played the First Slave) said many years later that he had contributed as much as Schikaneder to the libretto, but his claims are now generally discredited. The sources of the libretto are diverse. Christoph Martin Wieland provided the

101

title (*Lulu, oder Die Zauberflöte* from *Dschinnistan*) and the source of Gieseke and Wranitzky's opera *Oberon* (both 1789). Egyptological sources include Gebler's *Thamos, König in Agypten*, for which Mozart had written incidental music anticipating the style of *Die Zauberflöte*. But in the main the libretto is original and contemporary in its significance.

It has been suggested that the Queen represents Maria Theresa, Sarastro Ignaz von Born (formerly Master of a masonic lodge) and Tamino Joseph II. Fortunately there is no reason for different significations not to coexist. The masonic allegory (evident in the Egyptian/mystic devices which illustrate the printed libretto) is transparent except for the role of Pamina (see below), and in the rapidity of Tamino's rise from initiate to ruler-designate. *Die Zauberflöte* was mostly composed before *La clemenza di Tito* which, however, was performed first. Mozart entered the 'Introduction' [*sic*] in his catalogue in July, but the March of Priests and Overture are dated 28 September, two days before the première. Schikaneder had successfully presented popular 'machine-comedies' at the out-of-town Theater an der Wieden since 1789. Although it was not a fashionable venue, audiences were good and included all ranks; Salieri attended a performance and complimented Mozart warmly. Mozart tested Schikaneder's nerve and improvisatory powers by fooling with the glockenspiel part in his Act 2 aria. Schack himself played the flute in the finales. Minor parts were taken by members of the theatre company including Schikaneder's brother and the wives of Schack and Gerl.

In Vienna, there were 20 performances in the first month, and publication of extracts began in November; Schikaneder had given over 200 performances by 1800. The first Hoftheater performance was in 1801. Soon after Mozart's death *Die Zauberflöte* was given in Prague and in all other centres of German opera (including Warsaw and St Petersburg) before 1798. Goethe projected a sequel; one by Schikaneder, *Das Labyrinth*, was set by Peter Winter (1798). The first British performances were in Italian (1811), and it was frequently played as *Il flauto magico*. English versions reached London and New York in 1833. No major operatic centre was without a production in the 19th century and, while understanding of it may alter, the popularity of *Die Zauberflöte* has never waned. Among recent presentations Ingmar Bergman's sensitive film, sung in Swedish, has reached an international audience.

*

Overture: three chords (a masonic number: five if the short upbeats are counted) establish and question the tonic $E^\flat$, before a deliberate but mysterious progression to the dominant. The Allegro is monothematic, its principal idea (taken from a piano sonata by Clementi) presented in fugue and (in the dominant) as a counter-point to smoother wind phrases. The $B^\flat$ cadence is marked by three times three tutti chords, the 'dreimalige Akkord'. The development is a tour de force and the recapitulation miraculously transforms elements by new dynamics and counterpoint.

ACT 1   *Rocky country, with trees and mountains; in the foreground a temple*   Tamino is pursued by a monstrous serpent, his terror evoked by *Sturm und Drang* gestures (Introduction, 'Zu hilfe! sonst bin ich verloren'. Three Ladies arrive; they kill the monster and triumph in the first of many delectable multi-sectioned ensembles. They take stock of the unconscious Prince and quarrel over which will guard him while the others tell the Queen. Spitefully (a skipping 6/8) they all decide to go, and make a lingering farewell.

Papageno punctuates a folk-like song about his métier with high-pitched piping ('Der Vogelfänger bin ich ja', in three strophes). In the first extended dialogue Tamino asks who he is. His answer hints at one of the work's themes: 'a man, like you'. He lives by eating and drinking; he catches birds for the starry Queen. Papageno happily accepts responsibility for killing the serpent, whereupon the Ladies bring water and a stone instead of wine and bread, and padlock his mouth. They give Tamino a portrait of Pamina, the Queen's daughter. He contemplates its beauty and falls in love, can he be destined for her (aria, 'Dies Bildnis ist bezaubernd schön')? The tender appoggiaturas and pulsations bespeak his wonder and his racing heart. He learns that Pamina has been kidnapped by the tyrant Sarastro. The mountains are sundered, revealing a sumptuous chamber; the Queen is discovered on a starry throne ('O zitt're nicht, mein lieber Sohn!'; 'Do not fear, dear son'). Her aria is a melting G minor Larghetto, the first music in triple time ('Zum Leiden bin ich auserkoren': her daughter's loss torments her), and a fiery Allegro ending in giddy coloratura ascending to f''' ('Du, du, du wirst sie zu befreien gehen'). It forms Tamino's commission to rescue her daughter; its passion and brilliance leave him no room to suspect ulterior motives. The finale to the first scene is a quintet ('Hm hm hm hm'), another blend of comedy and numinous beauty. Papageno can only grunt until the Ladies unlock his mouth. All sing the moral: if liars were gagged brotherly love would prevail. Tamino receives a magic flute, which protects him and can change sorrow to joy. Papageno instructed to accompany Tamino, in whom he has no confidence, is horrified at the thought; Sarastro will surely eat them. He is given a chime of silver bells for his protection. To a final Andante of transcendent simplicity, they are told that three wise and lovely boys will guide them.

A fine Egyptian-style chamber in Sarastro's apartment   Slaves discuss Pamina's escape from the lust of Monostatos; but he has caught her (trio, 'Du feines Täubchen, nur herein!'). In the brisk *buffo* style which characterizes him throughout, the Moor has the protesting maiden bound. As she faints, Papageno appears; he and Monostatos terrify each other and run away. Papageno recovers (if birds are black, why not a man?), identifies and frees Pamina, and tells her of the Prince who loves her. He, for his part, alas, has no mate. Princess and birdcatcher reflect on the mutual dependence of wife and man: united by love, they approach the divine (duet, 'Bei Männern, welche Liebe'). This duet epitomizes the opera's moral, as well as its musical directness. With the simplest accompaniment, it consists of no more than two almost identical 16-bar strophes (each lightly touching on the dominant) and a coda of the same length. The pastoral 6/8 nevertheless brings $E^\flat$, the 'Masonic' tonic, also the key of love (compare Tamino's first aria). Only Pamina's serene ornamentation differentiates the voices: it is a vision of classless, as well as domestic and sexual, harmony.

A grove, with three beautiful temples: at the back, 'Wisdom'; on the right, 'Reason'; on the left, 'Nature'   The holiness of the place is evoked by the sturdy rhythms of the trombones, silent since the overture, at the opening of the finale. The Three Boys leave Tamino, urging him to be steadfast, patient and silent – the first clear hint of masonic practice. Tamino, in a recitative, assimilates his surroundings: surely a place of virtue. His purpose is honest; let the tyrant tremble! But his approaches to Reason and Nature (to music reminiscent of the Priest's speech in *Idomeneo*) are rebuffed by unseen voices. The old Priest (Orator, sometimes rendered as 'Speaker') emerges from the temple of Wisdom and in an awe-inspiring dialogue finds Tamino's sentiments worthy but his mind clouded by prejudice; he should not trust a woman's tears. He can say nothing of Pamina 'Sobald dich führt der Freundschaft Hand/Ins Heiligtum zum ew'gen Band' ('Until sacred friendship leads you by the hand to join the eternal Order'). Tamino asks when light will come to him; the unseen chorus, while the cellos repeat the Orator's arioso cadence, replies: 'Soon, or never'. But Pamina is alive. In an outburst of gratitude he plays the magic flute: wild animals come to listen, but not Pamina. Then he hears Papageno's pipe, answers it, and runs after the sound. Pamina and Papageno are caught by Monostatos as he sarcastically comples their cadences. As the slaves bring chains, Papageno is inspired to set them dancing with his bells, and they celebrate freedom with the folk-like 'Könnte jeder brave Mann' (remembered by Schubert in 'Heidenröslein'). Trumpets announce Sarastro, in a chariot drawn by lions, acclaimed in the first substantial chorus. Papageno trembles but Pamina tells the truth: her flight was not from him but from the Moor. Sarastro reassures her, but her mother's pride is beyond forgiveness, and Pamina must stay to learn the ways of virtue from men. Monostatos brings in Tamino, he and Pamina embrace, to the chorus's surprise and Monostatos's fury. Sarastro rewards the Moor with a beating (the chorus again sings Sarastro's praise, but *sotto voce*) and orders the strangers to be veiled and led to the temple for purification. The act ends with a masonic chorus ('Wenn Tugend und Gerechtigkeit') which anticipates the end of *Fidelio*: virtue and justice will make a paradise on earth.

ACT 2   *A palm grove, with 18 seats: on each, a pyramid and a horn*
The priests enter bearing palm-fronds, to strains of a solemn march,

105

coloured by flutes, basset horns and trombones. Punctuated by the 'dreimalige Akkord', Sarastro tells the Priests that Tamino awaits their consent to undergo the ordeals. Pamina is his destined bride and their union a defence against the malice of Night. The Orator inquires whether Tamino will endure the trial: he is, after all, a prince. More, replies Sarastro: he is a man. The scene closes with a noble invocation by Sarastro of the Egyptian gods ('O Isis und Osiris, schenket der Weisheit Geist').

A small forecourt, in darkness: thunder The Orator tells Tamino he can still withdraw, but he is determined to seek the light. Papageno, terrified of the dark, is told he will find no wife without undergoing the trials ('I'll stay single'). But he agrees to try when he learns that he will have his reward in Papagena, whom he has not yet seen. The piquant contrast of Tamino's quest through obedience to priestly instruction, and the popular-theatre gags of Schikaneder as Papageno, continues throughout the trials. They are warned by the two priests to mistrust women's arts, and meet them with silence ('Bewahret euch vor Weibertücken'). The Three Ladies ask why they are in this place of death; they are lost if they disobey the Queen, who is already within the sacred precinct (quintet, 'Wie? wie? wie? Ihr an diesem Schreckensort?'). Papageno believes everything, but Tamino silences him. The Ladies try a softer approach, but admit defeat and vanish (thunder and offstage chorus), leaving Papageno fainting to a minor-mode cadence. After the threefold chords they are led to new trials.

A garden The Moor prepares to rape the sleeping Pamina (aria, 'Alles fühlt der Liebe Freuden'). Mozart asked the orchestra to sound remote; the piccolo and lightning tempo suggest Turkish music. Why cannot a black slave share the delights of love? but the moon can close its eyes. The Queen's arrival sees him off, but now to her daughter she exposes her true motivation. She wants the power conferred by the sevenfold circle of the Sun, which her dying husband confided to the initiates. Tamino and Pamina will both be cursed unless hell's fury is assuaged by Sarastro's blood (aria, 'Der Hölle Rache'). Surpassing her Act 1 aria in brilliance (though not in difficulty), this Allegro reaches f''' four times, and adds a flood of triplet figuration; yet in addition to agility it demands the passion of a Donna Anna, with similar chromatic harmony in a vengeful D minor. Monostatos has overheard, and offers Pamina death or submission; but Sarastro intervenes. Pamina begs mercy for her mother who, he says, is punished by her own actions. His aria ('In diesen heil'gen Hallen') expresses his humanistic creed; the two verses, in E major, have the purity of folksong, the authority of wisdom. In these sacred halls, they govern not by vengeance but by love, which alone can overcome tyranny.

A large hall The candidates are left alone, bound to silence. Papageno grumbles; his desire for a drink is answered by a very old lady bringing water. She is 18 (not 80) and her boyfriend is ... Papageno! A thunderclap covers the sound of her own name as she hurries off. The Three Boys bring real refreshments ('Seid uns zum zweiten Mal will-kommen'). Their exquisite E major trio is a warning of imminent crisis. Tamino plays the flute, leaving Papageno to eat. Pamina enters joyful at finding them; Tamino, mindful of instructions, turns away. Her hurt is palpable in Mozart's most haunting G minor aria ('Ach, ich fühl's'), its ornate melody arched over the simplest accompaniment so that every note bears its weight of pathos. The threefold chord summons them; Papageno remains behind to continue eating.

The vault of a pyramid. Two priests carry an illuminated pyramid; others hold pyramidal lamps The happy outcome of Tamino's trials is anticipated in radiant D major chorus ('O Isis und Osiris, welche Wonne!'). Sarastro brings Pamina to him; they must say a last farewell before the greater trials (trio, 'Soll ich dich, Teurer, nicht mehr sehn?'). Sarastro is reassuring; Tamino expresses confidence, but Pamina is full of fears, for him rather than herself. Papageno comes running but the Orator tells him he will never reach enlightenment; he would settle for a drink, and is given wine. Ringing the bells (their part more elaborate with each of the three verses), he sings his second Volkslied: all he wants is a little wife ('Ein Mädchen oder Weibchen'). The power of the bells brings her dancing in, still looking 80, but when, somewhat reluctantly he promises to be true she is revealed as the lovely Papagena and whisked away.

A small garden   The finale is preceded by an introduction for wind band. The Three Boys evoke sunrise, which banishes darkness and death; without change of tempo, the homophonic trio develops into a dramatic quartet. The boys watch the grief-stricken Pamina greet her mother's dagger as bridegroom. At the last moment they intervene (Allegro, 3/4), restoring $E^\flat$, and with affectionate assurances lead her to Tamino.

Rocky landscape with two mountains, one gushing forth water, the other fire   After a solemn introduction two Men in Armour sing a penitential chorale melody ('Ach Gott, vom Himmel sieh' darein') over nervous counterpoint, but the text foretells the triumph of the brave. Tamino, in ritual garb (shoeless), declares himself ready. Pamina calls; they respond with rapture; even death cannot separate them now. The tonality having settled into $A^\flat$, F major has the luminosity of a much sharper key, and it brings Pamina ('Tamino mein! o welch'ein Glück') with the rising major 6th which seems especially significant in Mozart (as at the Count's plea for forgiveness in *Figaro*). She takes Tamino's hand: he must play the flute, which her father carved in a magic hour of violent storm, deep in an ancient wood. The disarmingly simple C major of the slow march for flute, brass, and timpani forms a complement to what should be magnificent scenic effects. Tamino plays them through fire and water; the chorus acclaims their triumph.

The small garden   Papageno blows his pipe but cannot bring back Papagena. His agitated rondo seizes the attention despite the preceding sublimity. He is about to hang himself in true pantomime style, enlisting the aid of the audience to delay the event, when the boys remind him of the bells; their magic brings Papagena in feathered youthfulness, and their stammering duet becomes an excited hymn to domesticity and children. Monostatos leads the Queen and Ladies beneath the temple ('Nur stille, stille', a sinister little march). The Queen, bereft of high notes, stoops to offering the defector her daughter. But the sun beams forth, Sarastro appears on high with Tamino and Pamina in priestly robes. At this transfiguration the demons are exorcised. The Armed Men's introduction recurs, radiant in the $E^\flat$ major Andante 'Heil sei euch Geweihten!': 'Hail chosen ones, who have overcome Night . . . [Allegro] Steadfastness conquers and grants the crown to beauty and wisdom'.

*

For the allegory, the end is strikingly unorthodox. Masons left their wives at home, whereas Pamina undergoes tests of constancy (the Queen's temptation; Tamino's rejection) equal to the man's, before joining him in trials by fire and water. Like *Così*, *Die Zauberflöte* has been accused of hostility to women. This is to confuse the attitudes of characters, including the absurdly misogynist priests in their duet at the beginning of Act 2 (itself a stage in Tamino's trials rather than dogma), with the meaning of the drama. If the Queen is the source of evil, Pamina is the strongest force for good and a necessary complement to Tamino: their union is divinely ordained. However alien to Freemasonry, the implication that women should become initiates is the opera's title to true Enlightenment.

There is no evidence to support the often-reiterated claim that the authors changed the plot, and that the Queen was originally good and Sarastro evil. If even Mozart's music cannot unequivocally distinguish hypocrisy from sincerity it is a condition (not a deficiency) of the art. That the flute and bells come from the Queen is a problem more apparent than real. By tradition such objects are neutral, or can only help the righteous; but the Queen believes in the justice of her cause. She takes a greater risk in offering the guidance of the wise Boys, but it is the Orator who begins the process of enlightenment. Monostatos, the untrustworthy servant, represents ordinary nature going bad; as cowardly as Papageno, the other representative of Everyman, he chooses evil and seeks power (over Pamina, by misused sexuality and by joining the Queen). He is punished, whereas Papageno, falling short of enlightenment, is good-hearted and achieves domestic contentment.

Die Zauberflöte possesses attributes of pantomime, but is not ramshackle. It unfolds in many short scenes, a Shakespearian dramaturgy which effectively contrasts the grave with the comical, the austerely hieratic with the earthily improvisational. The only possible weakness is Tamino's second rejection of Pamina. This scene may be an addition to the original plan, and was perhaps misplaced from earlier in Act 2; even disguised as a formal farewell ('Soil ich dich, Teurer') it appears redundant, coming between 'Ach, ich fühl's' and Pamina's attempted suicide.

The full dialogue should be retained; even the slaves' scene adds to our understanding, and the priestly debates are indispensable (Mozart snubbed a booby who seemed to find them funny). The musical numbers function by contrast, employing an unprecedented stylistic range. Yet interconnections exist (such as the echo of the Queen's 'O zitt're nicht' in Tamino's 'O ew'ge Nacht', first finale) as does architecture through distinctive instrumentation (emblematic flute, bells, trombones) and tonality (the $E^\flat$/C axis which gives unusual prominence to C minor). Diversity and discontinuity do not deprive the score of the right to be considered as an entity, the masterpiece of Mozart's late style.

J.R.

Librettists

Pierre-Augustin Beaumarchais

Pierre-Augustin (Caron de) Beaumarchais, was born in Paris, on 24 January 1732; he died there on 18 May 1799. He is remembered today as the author of two genial stage comedies, *Le barbier de Séville, ou La précaution inutile* and *La folle journée, ou Le mariage de Figaro*, both destined for immortality also as opera librettos. To his contemporaries his notoriety had many other sources besides: he began his career in 1753 as a watchmaker, the king, Mme de Pompadour and other nobility at Versailles soon becoming his clients; then he served as harp teacher to Louis XV's four daughters (1757). He bought his way into the nobility (1761), became a judge (1763), later an occasional diplomat and even a spy. He was an eternal litigant, and the popularity of his witty – if unscrupulous – pamphlets pillorying his legal opponents rivalled that of the *Provincial Letters* of Pascal. He was also a supplier, or would-be supplier, of arms to both the American and the French Revolutions. In 1794, while he was abroad, mishaps caused his name to be inscribed on the list of criminal émigrés and his family placed under arrest. Returning to Paris in 1796, his finances and his health in disarray, he spent the remaining three years of his life recuperating his losses.

Beaumarchais also emerged as an important literary personality, indeed the last great writer of comedy of the *ancien régime*. His earliest surviving theatrical efforts were written (starting in about 1757 or 1758) for private performance at Etiolles, the estate of Mme de Pompadour's husband, and were never published during his lifetime. These pieces included vaudevilles and *comédies mêlées d'ariettes*. His first publicly staged plays were both 'drames', inspired mainly by Diderot: *Eugénie* (first performed 1767) and *Les deux amis* (1770). Beaumarchais' own *Essai sur le genre dramatique sérieux* (published with *Eugénie* in 1767), also owing much to Diderot, remains one of the clearest expositions of the 'drame' written during the century. Neither of these plays is performed today.

Le barbier de Séville, ou La précaution inutile, though belonging to the classical Molière tradition, was designed to be the first episode

113

in a cycle that would finally include two more plays: *Le mariage de Figaro* and *La mère coupable* (the author had hoped to add still others). Apparently modelled after the Oedipus cycle of antiquity, this was a daringly original conception; it was unheard of before Beaumarchais to invent stage characters who, play by play, would grow older and change, and who were to be imagined as leading lives outside the texts the author wrote for them.

Both Figaro comedies, *Le barbier* and *Le mariage de Figaro*, lent themselves exceptionally well to musical setting. *Le barbier* was turned into opera at least four times, by F. L. Benda, Paisiello, Isouard and Rossini. The play in its original version (1772) had been intended as an *opéra comique* for the Comédie-Italienne. Even when it was revised as a stage play for the Comédie-Française, the plot featured various twists that were perfectly designed for the incidental music which Antoine-Laurent Baudron, principal violinist of the threatre orchestra, composed and orchestrated for it. Some of this music made its mark: Baudron's musical 'storm' between Acts 3 and 4 made a hit with the audience, a unique example of incidental music being remarked on at that theatre. 'Je suis Lindor' from Act 1 scene vi was used by Mozart for a theme and variations for piano (κ354/299*a*).

Le mariage, the longest stage comedy of the century, overflowed with incidental songs, dances and musical ceremonies composed mainly by Baudron. It came closer to an *opéra comique* than any previous French play, a feature upon which Mozart and Da Ponte capitalized in *Le nozze di Figaro*. The structure of Beaumarchais' comedy largely survived the transformation into an opera libretto, and one of the enduring elements was Beaumarchais' innovatory strategy (part of his long-standing feminism) in giving the lead to women – the Countess and Suzanne – to devise the deceptions of the plot, rather than to males as was the more usual theatrical practice. Conservative Vienna demanded certain *adoucissements*, mainly political but also sexual. Figaro's enormous monologue, with its daring thrusts against the nobility, disappeared almost entirely. The sexual overtones of the relationship between the Countess and the young page, Chérubin, considered almost shocking in the original comedy, were played down, as were Marceline's feminist outbursts;

PLATE 1

A scene from *Die Zauberflöte* at the Bregenz Festival, 1985 [Bregenzer Festspiel]

PLATE 2

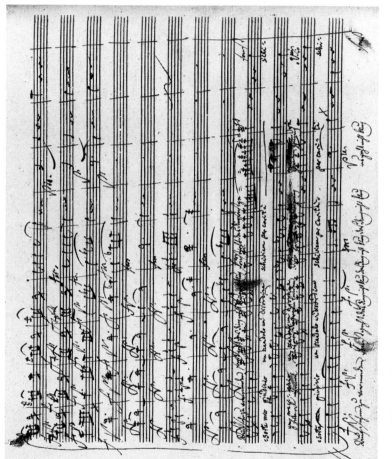

Autograph score of 'Le nozze di Figaro' (1786): part of the Act 2 trio, showing the upper line (extended to c') assigned initially to the Countess; as elsewhere in the opera, the upper line may eventually have been taken by the Susanna (Nancy Storace). A German text is written into the score. [Deutsche Staatsbibliothek]

PLATE 3

Il re pastore, Act 1 scene i (the countryside beyond the walls of Sidon, as described in the libretto); engraving from the *Opere* of Pietro Metastasio (Venice, 1758) [Fototeca dell'Istituto per le Lettere, il Teatro e il Melodramma, Fondazione Giorgio Cini]

PLATE 4

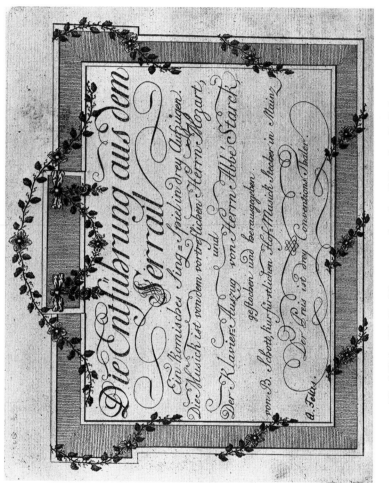

Playbill for *Die Entführung aus dem Serail* [Stanley Sadie]

PLATE 5

'*Le mariage di Figaro*': engraving by J.-P.-J. de Saint-Quentin showing the final denouement, from the first authentic edition of Beaumarchais' 'La folle journée, ou Le mariage de Figaro' (Paris, 1785) [Bibliothèque Nationale de France]

PLATE 6

Angelica Catalani as Susanna and Giuseppe Naldi as Figaro in *Le nozze di Figaro* at the King's Theatre, London 1812: anonymous drawing [Theatre Museum/Board of Trustees of the Victoria & Albert Museum]

PLATE 7

Wolfgang Amadeus Mozart: unfinished portrait (probably 1789) by Joseph Lange [Internationale Stiftung Mozarteum; in the Mozart Museum, Salzburg]

PLATE 8

R. BONG. X. A.

Luigi Bassi in the title role of *Don Giovanni*: engraving by Médard Thoenert (1787) [Mary Evans Picture Library, London]

the trial scene, unsuitable for opera, was excised completely. Though in Beaumarchais' play the Countess's final gesture of forgiveness was touching enough, it could never have had the sublimity it achieved in the Mozart-Da Ponte opera: his Countess was not so innocent as theirs.

In 1793 a heavily revised version of the Mozart-Da Ponte opera was produced at the Paris Opéra, in French translation. As in an *opéra comique*, extensive parts of Beaumarchais' original spoken dialogue were reinserted in place of the recitatives. The production had no success.

The last instalment of the Figaro trilogy, a 'drame' whose full title is *L'autre Tartuffe, ou La mère coupable*, was staged during the Revolution (1792), and in its painful emotions and dark-coloured settings intensely reflected the new spirit of the times. The 'guilty mother' is the Countess, who has had an illegitimate son by Chérubin, following a moment of *égarement* in which he forced his will upon her. Later Chérubin was killed in a far-off land, and his death seems to have drained the life and gaiety from the remaining characters. Just as in Molière's *Tartuffe*, the entire family in the last act faces financial disaster, but this time there is a hair's breadth escape thanks to Figaro's wits, while the Count is called upon to make a dramatic gesture of forgiveness towards the guilty mother, even as the Countess had earlier done for him. Although praised by connoisseurs such as Victor Hugo and Charles Péguy, the play is all but forgotten today. Grétry apparently offered to provide music for parts of the text, but the work became an opera only with Milhaud's setting (1966, Geneva). John Corigliano borrowed characters from the play for the plot of his opera *The Ghosts of Versailles* (1992).

In 1782 Beaumarchais submitted a revision of Voltaire's libretto *Samson* (music by Rameau, unperformed) to the Opéra. Although Voltaire's text was shortened from five acts to three, the action tightened, more emphasis placed on the love interest, and a new composer chosen for the music, the revised version was never put into rehearsal. Five years later Beaumarchais produced an opera libretto of his own making, *Tarare*, with music by Salieri; generally considered this composer's masterpiece, it was performed at the Opéra in 1787 and frequently revived there until 1826. Much influenced by Gluck, Beaumarchais' preface, 'Aux abonnés de l'Opéra qui voudraient aimer l'opéra', set forth a challenging conception of the relationships between plot, words and music – a theory that seems to prefigure the reforms of Wagner. In the opera proper, the semi-allegorical plot, based on a *conte arabe*, featured perilous escapes and grandiose scenic effects. Tarare's effort to liberate his imprisoned wife recalls, in a more sombre mode, the plot of *Le barbier*, while the moral lesson of the piece, that success depends on character rather than rank, looks back to Figaro and probably also to the materialism of Diderot.

W.E.R.

Christoph Friedrich Bretzner

Christoph Friedrich Bretzner was born in Leipzig, on 10 December 1748; he died there on 31 August 1807. He spent his entire life as a businessman in Leipzig, and began writing plays in 1771. A set of four comic opera texts printed in 1779 quickly established him as a fashionable librettist in Germany. More colourful and exotic than those of C. F. Weisse, they also offer somewhat greater scope for music. Viennese as well as northern composers greeted them warmly. Bretzner is best remembered as the author of *Belmont und Constanze*, written for the Berlin composer Johann André in 1780 and subsequently adapted by Stephanie the younger for Mozart as *Die Entführung aus dem Serail*. (The much-quoted 'protest' against Mozart of 1782 is a fabrication, although in 1783 Bretzner did publicly denigrate Stephanie's poetic additions.) A second set of librettos, issued in 1796, shows Bretzner's facility at imitating *opera buffa* in German. In addition to writing original opera texts and one melodrama, he translated several Italian texts for the German stage, including Mozart's *Così fan tutte* (as *Weibertreu, oder Die Mädchen sind von Flandern*, 1794) and Salieri's *La scuola de' gelosi* (*Die Schule der Eifersüchtigen*, 1794).

T.B.

Vittorio Amedeo Cigna-Santi

Vittorio Amedeo Cigna-Santi was born in Poirino, near Turin, around 1730; he died sometime after 1795. Very little is known about his life and activities. Conflicting accounts report his birth as early as 1725, but this is contradicted by later reports of his age. He published only a few known celebratory poems before being appointed principal librettist in the Teatro Regio, Turin, from 1754–5, a post he was to keep for nearly 30 years. A volume of poetry published in 1760 ascribes his education to the Accademia dei Trasformati of Milan. Most of the original librettos he wrote for Turin achieved at least modest success outside the city as well, such as *Mitridate re di Ponto*, later set by Mozart for Milan in 1770. His most successful libretto, *Motezuma*, is typical of his dramaturgical style and was adapted and set, after its première in a version by G. F. Majo for Turin in 1765, by Mysliveèek, Paisiello, Galuppi, Sacchini, Anfossi, Insanguine and Zingarelli over the next 16 years (the Zingarelli version was revised and restaged by Haydn in 1785). Cigna-Santi's poetry is clearly less polished and elegant than that of either Zeno or Metastasio, whom he imitates. The choice of Montezuma as a subject is itself telling; influenced by the wave of exotic settings popular in the 1760s and 70s, it concerns a warrior (Cortez) who, by deception and with financial motives, seeks to destroy the kingdom of Montezuma – not a very appropriate Arcadian idea. The usual balance among five to seven roles is also strained, with the three main characters almost entirely dominant. Arias are sometimes overplayed in the drama for simple effects, and motivation for the characters' actions is not always clear. Metastasio found Cigna-Santi's poetry worthy of public praise, as he reported in a letter to Tommaso Filipponi on 27 February 1760. *Alcina e Ruggero*, his last *dramma per musica*, was staged primarily for visual display, with spectacular effects and intricate machines, a kind of production Cigna-Santi later defended. By his own account he spent much of his energy adapting other librettos for local performance. In 1777 he was nominated a 'poeta della società' of the Cavalieri. Outside the theatre his interests were wide-ranging; he produced a translation of Seneca, and for his studies in history and genealogy was named by the king in 1785 as 'istoriografo del supremo Ordine della Sma Annunziata'.

D.E.M.

Lorenzo Da Ponte

Lorenzo [Conegliano, Emmanuele] Da Ponte was born in Ceneda [now Vittorio Veneto], on 10 March 1749; he died in New York, 17 August 1838. His involvement in the remarkable flowering of *opera buffa* in Vienna from 1783 to 1790 and his collaborations with Martín y Soler, Salieri and, above all, Mozart make him arguably the most significant librettist of his generation: his three librettos for Mozart (*Le nozze di Figaro*, *Don Giovanni* and *Così fan tutte*) are justifiably regarded as peaks of the genre.

LIFE   Da Ponte's biographers rely largely on his *Memorie*. Written from the age of 60 onwards as an apologia for a life plagued by (often self-induced) misfortune, they present a carefully constructed image of the man and his work. Accounts of raffish adventures in the manner of his friend Casanova mix with vainglorious statements of achievement and accusations of treachery by friend and foe; sometimes fact can only with difficulty be separated from fiction.

Born Emmanuele Conegliano, Da Ponte adopted the name of the Bishop of Ceneda, Lorenzo da Ponte, when his father, a Jewish tanner, converted to Christianity in 1763. Da Ponte's early training in Ceneda and Portogruaro prepared him for the priesthood (he was ordained in 1773) and for teaching (at seminaries in Portogruaro, 1770–73, and Treviso, 1774–6). However, his penchant for liberal politics and married women led to a ban on his teaching in the Veneto and, on 17 December 1779, a 15-year exile from Venice. He went first to Gorizia and then to Dresden, believing that his friend, the poet and librettist Caterino Mazzolà, would secure him a court post: in Dresden he worked with Mazzolà translating and arranging plays and librettos (including Quinault's *Atys*; Da Ponte had already collaborated with his brother, Girolamo, on a translation of J.-F. de La Harpe's *Le comte de Warwick* in 1780). Mazzolà then provided Da Ponte with a recommendation to Salieri in Vienna: he arrived there in late 1781, meeting Metastasio just before his death. Da Ponte attracted the favour of Joseph II, and when Joseph abandoned his pursuit of German opera and revived the Italian company (in 1783), Da Ponte was appointed poet to the court theatre.

Da Ponte's facility for versifying, his ready wit and sound knowledge of languages made him an ideal theatre poet. His work included translating texts from French to Italian, reworking old librettos for revivals and providing new works (themselves often adaptations) for Viennese composers. His first new libretto for Salieri as musical director of the company, *Il ricco d'un giorno*, was a failure (Da Ponte blamed the music). But in 1786 his position was assured by the success of his *Il burbero di buon cuore* for Martín y Soler. That year saw a remarkable output of six librettos, including *Le nozze di Figaro* for Mozart and the hugely popular *Una cosa rara* (again set by Martín y Soler).

Da Ponte had an uneasy relationship with Count Rosenberg, director of the theatre, and his rivalry with the poet Giambattista Casti found expression in satirical poems (notably the *Epistola nell'Abate Casti*, Vienna, 1786) and even on the stage. Nor did Da Ponte's arrogance (see Michael Kelly's *Reminiscences*, 1826) help matters. He managed to regain Salieri's favour, providing *Axur, re d'Ormus* (based, like *Figaro*, on Beaumarchais) at the same time as writing *L'arbore di Diana* for Martín y Soler and *Don Giovanni* for Mozart; he later produced three other librettos for Salieri. He also published a volume of *Saggi poetici* (Vienna, 1788). In 1789 Da Ponte was involved in the revival of *Figaro*, probably providing the new texts for arias to be sung by his mistress, Adriana Ferrarese (the new Susanna), and he also wrote *Così fan tutte* in that year (Ferrarese was Fiordiligi). In addition, he claims to have saved the Italian opera in Vienna from threatened closure. However, the death of his patron Joseph II on 20 February 1790 and court intrigue on the succession of Leopold II led to his dismissal (for which he blamed Salieri, among others) in 1791.

The poet was denied permission to return to Venice, and although a reported meeting (in Trieste) with the short-lived Leopold II and the support of Leopold's successor Francis II went some way towards healing the rift, he never re-established himself in Vienna. Instead, having 'married' an Englishwoman, Ann (Nancy) Grahl, on 12 August

1792, he set off for Paris and then, discouraged by the unstable political situation there, headed for London. Doubtless he hoped to join forces with his former colleagues in Vienna, the singer Michael Kelly and the composer Stephen Storace. After a futile year attempting to establish Italian opera in Brussels, Rotterdam and The Hague, he was appointed to the King's Theatre, Haymarket, by the new manager, William Taylor. While there Da Ponte arranged operas by Cimarosa and others, collaborated again with Martín y Soler on two operas during the composer's stay in London from 1794 to 1796, and also provided librettos for Francesco Bianchi. A trip to Italy in 1798 to recruit singers for the theatre reunited him with his family and his beloved Venice, although his old enemies forced a quick departure. His return to London saw his position blocked by intrigue – he was dismissed in 1799 – and the King's Theatre in financial disarray: his unwise involvement in Taylor's dubious dealings led to Da Ponte's declaring himself bankrupt in February 1800. He was reinstated at the theatre in 1801 and collaborated with Peter Winter on three new operas, but, pursued by creditors, he followed Nancy to America in 1805.

Da Ponte became a grocer and general merchant in New York, then Sunbury (Pennsylvania) and Philadelphia, supplementing his income with private teaching and dealing in Italian books (an activity begun in London). He also produced an early version (1807) of what was to become a compendious autobiography. Returning to New York in 1819, he determined to bring Italian culture to his newly adopted country (he took American citizenship) through teaching and book-dealing; he also occupied the (largely honorary) post of Professor of Italian at Columbia College in 1825 and from 1827 until his death. The publication both of a complete version of the *Memorie* (1823–7) and of a volume of *Poesie varie* (New York, 1830) seems to have formed part of this endeavour; he also issued other translations (e.g. of Byron), catalogues and miscellaneous prose (including a *Storia della lingua e della letteratura italiana in New York*, 1827). His interest in opera revived in his later years; he saw *Don Giovanni* performed by Manuel García's visiting company in 1826, and a new edition of *Figaro, Don Giovanni, Axur* and his tragedy *Il Mezenzio*, reportedly the only dramatic works from his European period that he had with him in America, was published that year. Notwithstanding his grief at Nancy's death (he issued a volume of commemorative verse in 1832), Da Ponte became financially involved in the ill-fated tour of the Montresor company in 1832–3 (he published an account in 1833) and acted briefly as manager of the newly built Italian Opera House. The initiative brought financial loss, and also a sense that his life's work had been for nothing – a projected final volume of the *Memorie* was never completed – although by all accounts his elaborate funeral offered significant recognition of his achievement.

WORKS   Accounts of Da Ponte's working methods rely heavily on the *Memorie*, and one need not set much store by his claim of writing *Axur, re d'Ormus*, *L'arbore di Diana* and *Don Giovanni* concurrently, sustained by his snuff-box, a bottle of Tokay and the ministrations of a 16-year-old Calliope ('whom I would have liked to love simply as a daughter, but . . .'). However, the *Memorie* offer intriguing insights into theatre life in Vienna, London and New York, as well as into Da Ponte's own perception of his art: 'poetry is the door to music, which can be very handsome, and much admired for its exterior, but nobody else can see its internal beauties if the door is wanting'. He also made comments on contemporary librettists (whom he generally derided) and on the composers with whom he worked. Da Ponte was well aware of the different talents of his collaborators and carefully crafted his librettos to suit their needs. Although an obvious admirer of Mozart, he was less enthusiastic than one might expect (which may reflect Mozart's mixed critical reception in the early 19th century), while he praised Salieri (with only a little irony) as an educated and worthy *maestro di cappella*. But his favourite composer seems to have been Martín y Soler: Da Ponte viewed *L'arbore di Diana* as his best libretto. Other composers such as Vincenzo Righini and Francesco Piticchio are roundly dismissed.

The prodigiousness of Da Ponte's output was doubtless due to his facility as a poet: significantly, he was a skilled improviser. But it also reflects his reliance on existing works: nearly all his librettos involve some adaptation, and he appears less happy when inventing original dramatic situations. However, adaptation was common in the period, and Da Ponte's skill lay in his precise knowledge of the dynamics of opera: he condensed situations, pinpointed characters and focussed the action in a manner allowing the composer freedom to create drama through music. Beaumarchais, Da Ponte reported, admired the libretto of *Le nozze di Figaro* for 'contracting so many *colpi di scena* in so short a time, without the one destroying the other'. Even if the remark is apocryphal, it reflects Da Ponte's perception of his achievement.

Da Ponte had a profound sense of the literary and dramatic traditions within which he was working. He claimed to have admired Metastasio from childhood; echoes of and quotations from Metastasio abound in his librettos. But Da Ponte took his heritage further back still to the Renaissance. His linking of *Axur* with Tasso, *L'arbore di Diana* with Petrarch and *Don Giovanni* with Dante is no coincidence: as his later teaching proved, he was intimately familiar with Italian Renaissance poetry. Again, references and quotations in his librettos emphasize the point: Dante, Petrarch, Boccaccio, Ariosto, Sannazaro, Tasso and Guarini all make appearances (and Da Ponte arranged Guarini's celebrated pastoral play *Il pastor fido* for Salieri in 1789). Moreover, Da Ponte made careful use of rhyme and metre as well as complex syntactical and rhetorical patterns. The rich resonances and subtle structures give his librettos a literary emphasis that sets them apart from the workaday efforts of his contemporaries. He was well aware of his skill: his texts often refer to, as they deliberately surpass, verse by Bertati, Casti and Mazzolà.

Two dramatists rarely mentioned in the *Memorie* are Goldoni and Carlo Gozzi, perhaps because they were too close to home. Da Ponte's first success, *Il burbero di buon cuore*, was an adaptation of Goldoni, and from him Da Ponte learnt the secret of comic pacing, of lexical manipulation (in particular, witty '-ino' and '-etto' diminutives) and of taut poetic structures. The debt is particularly apparent in *Don Giovanni*, notwithstanding its more immediate borrowings from Giovanni Bertati's recent 'Don Giovanni' libretto (set by Gazzaniga; Da Ponte later reworked this version in London). Da Ponte's 'dramma giocoso' (the term itself derives from Goldoni) owes much to Goldoni's play *Don Giovanni Tenorio*, as well as to Molière, and Leporello's opening solo has clear echoes of *Il servitore di due padroni*. Da Ponte claimed that the mixture of comedy and seriousness in the opera was his idea, not Mozart's, and it relates directly to Goldoni's notion of a new kind of drama for the 18th century.

As for Gozzi (whom he knew in Venice in the late 1770s), Da Ponte entered his fantasy world in *L'arbore di Diana*, while Gozzi's *Le droghe d'amore* (1777) may have influenced *Così fan tutte*. In *Così* (which the librettist always called *La scuola degli amanti*), Da Ponte's sense of literary play reaches its peak. It is perhaps best viewed as an opera about opera – failure to do so accounts for the oft-perceived 'problems' of the work – in the vein of Casti's *Prima la musica e poi le parole* (there are echoes in the text). Da Ponte ranked the libretto below *Figaro* and *Don Giovanni*, probably because of the opera's poor critical reception, but, as Dent realized, it contains his best work. Attempts to find a single source for the story have largely failed (but there are roots in Ovid, Boccaccio and particularly Ariosto). However, Da Ponte clearly placed the drama in the time-honoured tradition of the pastoral (in Act 1 Don Alfonso quotes directly from Sannazaro: 'Nel mare solca e nell'arena semina'). He also revelled in the allegorical play of essentially abstract characters and situations. Whether or not Mozart fully grasped this aspect of the libretto is another matter; moreover, opera was soon to move in very different directions. But *Così* marks an eloquent testament both to Da Ponte's literary heritage and to opera in the Age of Enlightenment.

T.C.

Giovanni De Gamerra

Giovanni De Gamerra was born in Livorno, in 1743; he died in Vicenza, on 29 August 1803. A cleric, he served in the Austrian army (1765–70) after studying law at Pisa and produced many plays and poems, including a *poema eroicomico* in seven volumes. After 1771, when he was appointed poet to the Regio Ducal Teatro in Milan, his literary output was dominated by librettos. Some of his early serious librettos – *Lucio Silla*, *Erifile* and *Medonte re d'Epiro* – were set repeatedly by leading composers. De Gamerra's flirtation, during the French Revolution, with revolutionary politics nearly cost him his career: in 1791 Emperor Leopold II urged his brother Ferdinand, governor of Milan, not to engage him as librettist for La Scala, describing him as 'fanatic to excess, hot-headed, imprudent concerning . . . liberty, very dangerous' (letter, Vienna, Haus-, Hof- und Staatsarchiv). In 1793, however, he was appointed house librettist for the court theatres in Vienna, and during the next decade he collaborated with Salieri and Weigl as well as providing librettos for Winter, Paer and Mayr. He is also said to have made the first Italian translation of *Die Zauberflöte*.

De Gamerra's librettos are in many ways typical of late 18th-century developments in Italian musical drama. They are the product of a poet steeped in the traditions of Metastasian opera but eager to incorporate ideas of the kind proposed by Calzabigi, Verazi and other innovators. In 'Osservazioni sull'opera in musica', published in 1771 in his *Armida* libretto (of which no setting is known), he argued in favour of more 'spectacle' in *dramma per musica* in the form of chorus, ballet and elaborate scenery, and he put those ideas into practice with tableaux like the dimly lit *ombra* scene among the funeral urns in Act 1 of *Lucio Silla* and, in *Pirro*, with large-scale action ensembles including an assassination attempt on stage. In his late librettos De Gamerra adapted to Viennese taste by combining comic and serious elements.

J.A.R.

Carlo Goldoni

Carlo [Fegejo, Polisseno] Goldoni was born in Venice, on 25 February 1707; he died in Paris, on 6 or 7 February 1793. His best comedies, distinguished by a seemingly effortless dramatic technique and an acute observation of character and manners, place him in the front rank of Italy's dramatic authors. In a career that began slowly but at its peak made uncommon demands on his creative energies (in 1750–51 he promised, and delivered, 16 new comedies), Goldoni also found time to write some 80 librettos, most of them comic, although he also wrote *opere serie*, cantatas and oratorios.

LIFE   Goldoni's evinced a literary bent while still at school but wrote poetry of no special distinction. He studied law at Padua and was admitted to the bar in Venice in 1732. Meanwhile he had written some comic intermezzos (1729/30, 1732) and a *dramma per musica*, which he himself destroyed (1733). Finding his legal profession unprofitable, he attached himself to a *commedia dell'arte* troupe in 1734, furnishing them with spoken tragicomedies and sung inter-mezzos, the latter set to music by mostly unknown composers and performed between the acts of the spoken plays. At the same time he was hired to assist Domenico Lalli, the poet-in-residence at the chief opera house in Venice, San Giovanni Grisostomo; this involved helping to stage *opere serie* and adapting or rewriting their librettos. The experience thus gained in two very different branches of theatre was to stand him in good stead; meanwhile, he appears to have aspired to the dignity of tragic poet *à la* Metastasio, for the years 1736 to 1741 saw the modestly successful production of five (if not all six) of his serious operas at the Giovanni Grisostomo.

In 1743 he left Venice, settling in Tuscany to practice law. When he returned, in 1748, he was under contract to another *commedia dell'arte* troupe. Abandoning traditional scenarios in favour of wholly written-out comedies, Goldoni at the age of 40 embarked at last on the career that gained him his place in Italian literature. At the same time, he launched upon the long series of *opera buffa* librettos, working at first with Ciampi but soon (from 1749) with Galuppi, in a collaboration that over the next seven years produced some of the century's most successful comic operas. Goldoni worked fast; a comic opera libretto took him four days, as he testified in a letter of 1762. He was then on his way to Paris, where he arrived that August. There he settled never to return to Italy; his productivity as both playwright and librettist continued for a while but then abated.

WORKS   In his various autobiographical writings, Goldoni studiously belittled his librettos; indeed, once he had become famous he signed them with his Arcadian sobriquet, Polisseno Fegejo, as if to distinguish them from the works on which he wished to rest his reputation. To him they were a lucrative sideline. Yet he permitted, and probably supervised, at least the first collection of his comic librettos, in four volumes (1753), and very probably approved the ten-volume set (Venice, 1794–5) published by Zatta shortly after his death. At least three other collected editions appeared during his lifetime. Goldoni was no Zeno or Metastasio: his librettos do not stand up as literature. Yet they worked remarkably well in the theatre and were repeatedly set to new music. Indeed, it was through his librettos that Goldoni's work first reached St Petersburg and Moscow, Warsaw, Prague, Brussels, London, Madrid and Barcelona; and Haydn and Mozart were among the many foreign composers who set them to new music.

Goldoni's flair for the living stage prevented any of his productions (whether for the spoken theatre or for the opera house) from ever smacking of literature; they were meant to be seen rather than read. The same genius that produced vignettes of everyday life in the spoken plays provided talented composers with the most variegated materials, drawn mostly from fantasy and rich in spectacle and twists of plot, for the realization of the very different requirements of the *opera buffa*. An opening ensemble (eventually to be termed 'introduzione'), providing a colourful tableau and some inkling of the action to follow, plentiful ensembles sprinkled throughout the rest of the three-act work, a duet between the two principals just before the concluding scene of Act 3: these are some of the hallmarks of the typical

Goldoni *opera buffa* libretto. His principal contribution, however, and one recognized as such by his contemporaries, was the lengthy, action-studded finale, designed for continuous musical setting, that invariably concluded each of the first two acts. It is here that composers learnt to deal musically with one element in opera (action or incident) that had traditionally been beyond their purview, having been relegated until then to recitative.

Before extensive comparative studies have been made of the librettos of less eminent contemporary authors, it is not possible to state categorically that every single aspect of this new, mid-18th-century *opera buffa* type originated with Goldoni. There is no doubt, however, as to the sheer quantity and immense popularity of his librettos. His *Il filosofo di campagna*, set by Galuppi in 1754, and *La buona figliuola*, in the 1760 resetting by Piccinni, were possibly the most influential, certainly the most successful operas of the period. His, it is safe to say, was a pivotal role in the history of the genre; at the very least he helped to give *opera buffa* the shape in which, in the mid-18th century, it gained the ascendancy on the stages of Italy and Europe.

P.W.

Caterino Mazzolà

Caterino Mazzolà was born in Longarone on 18 January 1745; he died in Venice on 16 July 1806. About 1767–8 his family moved to Venice, where Caterino's firm grounding in Latin and the classics began at a Jesuit school before he moved on to a Somaschi institution in Treviso. By the time he married, in 1780, his career as a librettist had already begun. He had also become a known figure in the houses of men of letters in Venice, where he met Casanova in 1774 and Lorenzo da Ponte in 1777. The following year the composer Joseph Schuster helped to secure his appointment as court poet at Dresden, a position Mazzolà held from 1780 to 1796. For six months in 1780 Mazzolà was joined in Dresden by Da Ponte who, in addition to gaining insight into the work of a librettist, received from his host a letter of introduction to Salieri which led to his first appointment in Vienna as librettist to the newly revived Italian opera. That the inaugural performance (1783) was a production of the Salieri Mazzolà opera *La scuola de' gelosi* was probably no mere coincidence. From 1790 Da Ponte began to fall from favour in Vienna, and it is likely that both he and Salieri were instrumental in gaining the position of court poet for Mazzolà for a brief period early in 1791 through their influence with Count Rosenberg, the court theatre director. Rosenberg was replaced, however, and Giovanni Bertati was subsequently named to the position. Mazzolà is described as a generous and gracious man who seems to have been much appreciated by his employer in Saxony. When he left Dresden in 1796, Friedrich August III obtained diplomatic work in Venice for him and also requested that some of his writings be sent back to the Saxon court each year.

Most of Mazzolà's librettos are of the *opera buffa* type, set mainly by the Dresden composers Naumann, Schuster and Seydelmann. Salieri's interest in his friend's texts was to be expected, but Mazzolà librettos were also set by other important composers of the time. Da Ponte described him as 'possibly the first to know how to write a comic libretto', and *La scuola de' gelosi* bears a striking resemblance to *Le nozze di Figaro*, not only in its similarities of plot and characters but also because of its rapid pace, clear delineation of characters and sectional Act 1 finale. Mazzolà's masonic opera *Osiride* was known to Mozart, with whom Mazzolà may have discussed *Die Zauberflöte* while in Vienna from May to July 1791. His collaboration with Mozart in adapting Metastasio's *La clemenza di Tito* for Prague in 1791 produced a libretto that vividly reflects contemporary trends in the content and structure of Italian serious opera. These trends, often originating in *opera buffa*, include the two-act structure, opening duet, medial ensembles, rapid pace and directness of emotional expression, characteristics to be found in Mazzolà's earlier librettos. *Il mostro*, a text that antedates *Tito* by six years, provides a particularly clear example.

D.N.

Pietro Metastasio

Pietro (Antonio Domenico Bonaventura) Metastasio [Trapassi] was born in Rome on 3 January 1698; he died in Vienna on 12 April 1782. His fame rests chiefly with his 27 *opera seria* librettos written between 1723 and 1771. In settings by over 300 composers, adapted versions of these texts span a period of over a hundred years that stretches well into the 19th century.

LIFE   Metastasio's family was poor, and his early education was arranged by his godfather, Cardinal Pietro Ottoboni. In 1708, it was taken over by Gian Vincenzo Gravina, a jurist and a man of letters who, impressed by the boy's intelligence and ability at verse impro-visation, adopted him and directed his studies in the classics, projecting for him a career in law. He also encouraged him to recite at social gatherings and to participate in improvisation contests. In 1712 he wrote his only tragedy, *Giustino*, in strict imitation of ancient models; it was published five years later with a collection of poems under the title *Poesie di Pietro Metastasio* (the name change from 'Trapassi' to 'Metastasio', the hellenized equivalent, was engineered by Gravina in 1715). That year he went to Scalea in Calabria where he studied with Gravina's cousin, Gregorio Caloprese, a noted scholar of Cartesian philosophy. Upon his return to Rome, Metastasio studied jurisprudence while maintaining his interest in poetry. He took minor orders at the Lateran Basilica in 1714.

When Gravina died in January 1718, Metastasio was left well educated, well connected and well provided for. Free from tutelage and unprepared for the responsibility of financial independence, Metastasio squandered most of the 15,000 scudi left him by Gravina and had to find employment. He was disappointed at the papal court and at the University of Turin, and also disappointed in love when the daughter of a musician at the Lateran Basilica, passed him over for another early in 1719. Metastasio moved to Naples where he found work in a law office. He also found recognition in aristocratic circles as a poet. Over the next two years he fulfilled various aristocratic commissions with odes and *azioni*, two of which were performed in Naples as birthday celebrations to honour the Empress Elizabeth.

In 1723 his first opera libretto, *Siface re di Numidia*, came to the stage in a setting by Feo. This was a reworking and his first original libretto, *Didone abbandonata*, launched his career in Naples the following year in a setting by Sarro. While writing this work Metastasio lived in the home of Giuseppe Bulgarelli and his wife, the singer-actress Maria Anna Benti ('La Romanina'), who probably influenced the shape of the work. In her salon he met the composers who first set his early works and began his lifelong friendship with the castrato Farinelli (Carlo Broschi). The Romanina and the first Aeneas, the castrato Nicolini (Nicolo Grimaldi), subsequently appeared in settings of *Didone abbandonata* in both Reggio and Venice in 1725. They were thus in Venice to take the leading roles in Metastasio's second original drama, *Siroe re di Persia* (1726), with music by Vinci. When *Catone in Utica* opened in Rome two years later, again in a setting by Vinci, Metastasio had the satisfaction of seeing his first three original texts given successively in the three major opera centres in Italy. Following the première of *Ezio* (1728, Venice), three more dramas opened in Rome during the period 1729–30, all in settings by Vinci: *Semiramide riconosciuta* in February and, for the following carnival season, the two librettos that were to gain the greatest popularity of all Metastasio's works, *Alessandro nell'Indie* and *Artaserse*.

When, in 1729, Metastasio received an invitation to take up the position of Caesarian court poet in Vienna, he was already known to the imperial household, and his reputation as a poet and dramatist was fully established. He moved in April 1730 to Vienna, where over the next ten years he wrote, in addition to other smaller works, another 11 dramas, including *L'olimpiade*, *Demofoonte* and *La clemenza di Tito*, seven oratorios and 11 texts for occasional pieces. In general, the oratorios were performed at Easter and the operas and occasional pieces were given to celebrate royal birthdays or name-days.

In 1740 Maria Theresa succeeded as empress. In 1764 Joseph was crowned as successor to the empire. Changes in Austrian affairs of state and theatre policy worked against Metastasio. Maria Theresa's reign was beset by wars with Prussia; this, together with concerns over internal politics and the debt inherited from her predecessors, relegated new opera commissions to a low priority. From 1740 to 1746 Metastasian operas in Vienna were mainly first stagings of works already written, followed by a preponderance of new settings of existing texts over the next four years. From the early 1750s to the mid-1760s, Metastasian opera representations at the court theatres dwindled almost to nothing.

Between 1740 and 1782 several of Metastasio's best works had premières outside Vienna, while at home the imperial court's demands of him were for in-house entertainments and works to honour only the most special royal events. In addition to smaller works, he produced, during this 42-year period, texts for 16 occasional pieces and only eight designated dramas for the *opera seria*. *Antigono* (1743) and *Nitteti* (1756), his most successful opera librettos from this time, had their premières at the courts of Dresden and Madrid respectively. Metastasio's renown, after 1750, was chiefly proclaimed by the number of editions of his works produced, the continued settings and imitations of his texts, and the literary commentaries with Metastasio as subject that proliferated outside the imperial capital. Metastasio died in 1782, at the age of 84, from a cold that turned to a fever.

As with all stage texts designated for musical settings at the time, each of Metastasio's librettos for the *opera seria* is labelled 'dramma' or 'dramma musicale', and together they exhibit certain fundamental characteristics. Generally, the plots concern six or seven characters of royal or noble birth, their interrelationships and their complex dilemmas, which are intensified as the action proceeds and finally resolved in a *lieto fine*. The dramas divide into three acts, and each act into an average of 12 scenes, defined according to the entry or exit of a character. A series of scenes will often be linked by a character common to all of them (the *liaison de scène* technique), and a change of location will often follow at the end of such a series. Apart from the occasional duet, almost always for the principal couple, the usual set musical piece is the aria which, if included in a scene, has its expected place at the end. Opening scenes usually begin with a situation already in progress; each of the first two acts will generally conclude with a climactic scene for a principal character or a duet; and the third will normally end with a united 'coro' for all the *dramatis personae*.

Half of Metastasio's dramas received over 30 different musical settings during the 18th and early 19th centuries: *Artaserse*, his most popular, close to 90. Whatever the number, only the first composer to set any given text actually did so as Metastasio wrote it, and a setting by any one composer given in a different location could also be subject to further changes.

PURPOSE, PHILOSOPHY   Metastasio once stated that he had 'wasted his entire life in order to instruct mankind in a pleasing way'. He held that 'pleasures that do not succeed in making impressions on the mind and on the heart are of short duration'. Thus emerges his aim, which was to instruct under the guise of giving pleasure, and to reinforce the moral issue by arousing the emotions for the sake of the moral purpose. This principle of 'pleasurable instruction' stretches back to Horace and Plato, less directly to Aristotle, and leads to a clear division between poetry as pleasurable in itself and poetry as a means of instruction.

The creation of pleasure in poetry for its own sake meant exercising care over the basic construction of a dramatic work as well as its poetic style. Aristotle and Horace had advice to offer on the first of these considerations, which included the choice of events and the interest created in them, the conduct of the characters and the probability of their actions, and the exploitation of the dramatic elements of conflict, contrast and accumulated intensity. Arcadia had much to say about the manipulation of poetic elements. For example, such matters as choice of words, versification, figures of speech and eloquence of style that are topics of discussion in several of Metastasio's letters are discussed as items of 'external' beauty by Giovanni Crescimbeni, the first president of the Accademia degli Arcadi, and as elements of 'corporeal' beauty by Lodovico Muratori, a friend of Zeno and an associate of the Accademia degli Accesi in Bologna.

Metastasio's verses are concise, economical and mellifluous, and, for all his claims towards literary drama, his musical education allowed him to hear his verses mentally as operatic vocal lines as he wrote them. He possessed an unmatched facility to express the subtle nuances of a vast range of human emotions while conveying the meaning vividly and in a few words which, in combination, could exploit the consonance, assonance and rhythm appropriate to the emotion of the moment. In addition, in writing arias for da capo settings, he generally supplied two stanzas (mostly quatrains), mindful of the appropriate vowel placement for coloratura extensions.

Poetry as a means of instruction meant, to Metastasio, the process of 'inducing, by way of pleasure, the love of virtue so necessary for general happiness'. For Crescimbeni this was the area of 'internal' beauty, for Muratori that of 'incorporeal' beauty, and it included matters of profundity, hidden mysteries, philosophy and theology. Metastasio's poetry, however, was to prove the example *par excellence* of what Crescimbeni called 'mixed' beauty, the highest achievement of all, with its emphasis on internal matters without losing sight of 'external' considerations. His leanings towards 'internal' beauty established his texts as moral dramas that realized on stage the principles set out in René Descartes' treatise on moral philosophy, *Les passions de l'âme*.

In 1649, the year in which *Les passions de l'âme* was published, Descartes went to Stockholm as tutor to Christina of Sweden. Her abdication and removal to Rome thus provided a direct link from Descartes to the Arcadian movement and hence to Metastasio. Further contacts with Cartesian philosophy came from his studies and from his knowledge of French 17th-century drama. Burney acknowledged Metastasio a master at unfolding and displaying 'all the passions of the human heart', and it is upon this subject that Descartes' philosophy focusses. Metastasio saw passions as 'the necessary winds by which one navigates through the sea of life', and was at one with Descartes in the belief that all the passions are 'good in themselves' and that 'we have nothing to avoid but their evil uses or excesses'. Indeed, morality was seen to exist, above all, in the power of the individual to gain control over the desires that arise from human

136

passions and so prevent the actions to which these passion-incited desires may lead. In demonstrating such a process, Metastasian drama became a drama of moral forces personified by specified characters who are differentiated by emotionally charged actions and reactions that drive them towards either personal moral victory or moral self-defeat. At the centre is a moral hero or heroine, like Titus or Semiramide, who must not only triumph over his or her own spontaneous desires but also uphold a moral vision against the onslaughts of the morally weak who fall victim to their personal desires. For the sake of the veiled exhortation to moral endurance, the moral crusader must succeed in the *lieto fine*, and the power of the achievement will be marred if the antagonists are not brought to moral truth (along with the audience) by the example; and at court performances, the moral hero served to set before the monarch the ideal of the morally inspired ruler.

D.N.

Emanuel Schikaneder

Emanuel (Johann Joseph [Baptist]) Schikaneder [Schickaneder] was born in Straubing, on 1 September 1751; he died in Vienna, on 21 September 1812. He was a dramatist, theatre director, actor, singer and composer of German origin. Educated at the Jesuit Gymnasium at Regensburg, where he was a cathedral chorister, Schikaneder may briefly have been a town musician before he became an actor with F. J. Moser's troupe in 1773 or 1774. In 1774 he danced in a court ballet at Innsbruck, where his Singspiel *Die Lyranten* (of which he wrote both words and music) was performed in 1775 or 1776. The Innsbruck company, then under Andreas Schopf and Theresia Schimann, moved in 1776 to Augsburg, where on 9 February 1777 he married Maria Magdalena (known as Eleonore) Arth (born Hermannstadt, 1751; died Vienna, 22 June 1821), an actress in the company. In 1777–8 they were in Nuremberg with Moser's company, and in December 1777 Schikaneder made a famous guest appearance as Hamlet at the Munich court theatre, where he was obliged to repeat the final scene as an encore. From January 1778 he was director of the troupe, appearing at Ulm, Stuttgart, Augsburg, Nuremberg, Rothenburg and elsewhere. In 1780 they went to Laibach (now Ljubljana), Klagenfurt and Linz before beginning a lengthy season at Salzburg in September, during which Schikaneder became friendly with the Mozarts. Further travels through Austria included summer seasons at Graz in 1781 and 1782, the winter of 1782–3 in Pressburg (now Bratislava), and a guest appearance in summer 1783 at the Kärntnertortheater, Vienna.

After further visits to Pest and Pressburg, where Joseph II saw him perform in October 1874, Schikaneder was invited to play in Vienna. He and Hubert Kumpf began a three-month season of operas and Singspiels at the Kärntnertor on 5 November. Thereafter, Schikaneder was a member of the Nationaltheater, performing in plays and operas, from 1 March 1785 until 28 February 1786. During this time his own troupe was run by his wife and Johann Friedel and touring in southern Austria until it moved into the Freihaus-Theater auf der Wieden,

Vienna, in November 1788. Schikaneder himself, in February 1786, had been granted an imperial licence for the building of a suburban theatre but did not make use of it for 15 years, forming instead a new company specializing in Singspiels and operas, which he took to Salzburg, Augsburg and Memmingen. In February 1787 he took over the Prince of Thurn and Taxis's court theatre at Regensburg. When Johann Friedel died at the end of March 1789 Schikaneder and his wife took over the Freihaus-Theater, bringing from Regensburg the singer-composers Schack and Gerl. Schikaneder's reign at the Freihaus began on 12 July 1789 with the first performance of his 'Anton' opera *Der dumme Gärtner*, and from this time dates the beginning of his steady series of plays, opera and Singspiel librettos which were the backbone of the repertory of his theatre (but which were also performed in other theatres, sometimes with new musical scores).

Schikaneder's years of travel had seen the production of more straight plays than operas; in Vienna he placed the emphasis firmly on opera, and commissioned settings of his own texts from Mozart (*Die Zauberflöte*), Süssmayr (*Der Spiegel von Arkadien*), Wölfl (*Der Höllenberg*), Mederitsch and Winter (one act each of *Babylons Pyramiden*; Winter also set *Das Labyrinth*, a sequel to *Die Zauberflöte*). He also received scores from his theatre Kapellmeister, Henneberg (*Die Waldmänner*), Haibel (*Der Tiroler Wastel*) and Seyfried (*Der Löwenbrunnen* and *Der Wundermann am Rheinfall*). As the 1790s advanced, Schikaneder began to suffer from increasing financial difficulties as he strove to surpass the achievements of his rivals and of his own greatest successes. In 1799 he handed over the management of the theatre to Bartholomäus Zitterbarth while continuing his artistic direction. Of the 12 greatest successes at the Freihaus, which closed on 12 June 1801, eight – including the first five – were written by Schikaneder himself.

On 13 June 1801 Schikaneder opened the new Theater an der Wien, using the licence he had previously been granted; it was the most lavishly equipped and one of the largest theatres of its age, and has continued in almost unbroken use. It opened with Teyber's setting of Schikaneder's libretto *Alexander*, but a change in public taste and a decline in Schikaneder's standards and powers of judgment were influential in the decision to sell the licence to Zitterbarth after less than a year. Schikaneder continued to supply plays and librettos, and to act, but despite two further periods as artistic director his fortunes were waning. After the sale of the theatre in 1806 Schikaneder left Vienna and took over the Brno Theatre. At Easter 1809 he was back in Vienna, but financial ruin and failing mental health darkened his last years. On his way to Budapest to take up an appointment as director of a new German theatre company in 1812 he became mad, returned to Vienna, and died in penury shortly after; a performance of his play *Die Schweden vor Brünn* was given for his benefit at the Theater in der Leopoldstadt on 18 July 1812 – an uncommon tribute from a rival theatre, albeit one that had successfully staged his plays since the early 1780s and would continue to do so until the 1850s.

Schikaneder was one of the most talented and influential theatre men of his age. Although it is fashionable to decry his plays (of which there are nearly 50) and librettos, they more than satisfied the demands of their day. Goethe praised his skill at creating strong dramatic situations, and though the verse is often trite the libretto of *Die Zauberflöte* (Gieseke's claims to the authorship of which were proved false by Komorzynski and more scientifically by Rommel) is by no means unworthy of Mozart's music. Some of Schikaneder's comedies (the 'Anton' plays, *Der Tiroler Wastel*, *Das abgebrannte Haus*, *Der Fleischhauer von Ödenburg*, *Die Fiaker in Wien*) continued to be much performed for many years and strongly influenced the later development of the Viennese *Lokalstück* ('local play'). Early in his career Schikaneder composed two, and perhaps several more, theatre scores: it has long been known that the music as well as the text of *Die Lyranten* was his work; and for the production of his Singspiel *Das Urianische Schloss* (1786, Salzburg) at the Theater in der Leopoldstadt in November 1787 a score by him is specifically mentioned by Wenzel Müller in his diary ('Opera by Em: Schikaneder, music, and book').

Schikaneder's brother, Urban (1746–1818), was an actor and singer; he sang First Priest in the première of *Die Zauberflöte* in 1791 and took a part in the administration of his brother's travelling company. Urban's daughter Anna (or Nanny or Nanette; 1767–1862) sang First Boy in the *Zauberflöte* première and was later a member of the Theater in der Leopoldstadt company, singing the Queen of Night when that company first gave *Die Zauberflöte* in 1811. Her brother Karl Schikaneder was also a man of the theatre.

P.B.

Gottlieb Stephanie

Gottlieb Stephanie was born in Breslau, on 19 February 1741, he died in Vienna, on 23 January 1800. He was an actor, playwright and librettist and was mainly active in Vienna. Called Stephanie der Jüngere (the younger) to distinguish him from his elder brother, the actor Christian Gottlob, Stephanie was prevented from studying law by his conscription into the army of Frederick the Great. He was captured at Landshut and later joined the Austrian forces; after serving as a recruiter, he began a career in 1769 as an actor in Vienna but soon turned to writing plays (40 in all, 29 of them written before 1780). He involved himself actively in theatrical affairs, ingratiated himself at court, and was named one of the five inspectors of the Nationaltheater, established by Joseph II in 1776. He also participated in the National-Singspiel, created in 1778, as a translator and adapter of French and Italian comic operas. In 1781 its direction was placed in his hands.

Stephanie earned a dark reputation as an inveterate intriguer, but he remained a warm supporter and friend of Mozart's, facilitating the commissioning of *Die Entführung aus dem Serail* in 1781 as well as choosing and adapting the text. After the demise of the National-Singspiel in 1783, he continued to provide texts for the German companies at the Kärntnertortheater, including several of Dittersdorf's most successful operas.

As a playwright Stephanie enjoyed sustained popularity in Vienna but scant critical acclaim. His librettos vary considerably in tone, plot and characterization, depending on the stage for which they were intended. Those for the National-Singspiel are more refined than his later texts for the Kärntnertor. As a translator of foreign operas for the National-Singspiel, he showed uncommon skill in placing new German texts beneath the original music. In his own operas his verses gained little esteem and he often resorted to pilfering from or adapting other poets for this purpose. He frequently adapted German texts for new settings by local composers, although the extent of his revisions of C. F. Bretzner's *Belmont und Constanze* for Mozart is unusual.

Bretzner publicly ridiculed the new musical numbers Stephanie wrote for *Die Entführung*. In 1792 Stephanie published his original librettos and included an informative preface on many of the conventions that governed German comic opera at Vienna during the 1780s.

T.B.

Giovanni Battista Varesco

(Girolamo) Giovanni Battista [Gianbattista] Varesco was baptized in Trent, on 26 November 1735; he died in Salzburg, on 25 August 1805. A cleric, poet and musician, he was educated at the Jesuit college in his home town from 1753 to 1756. In 1766 he became a chaplain to the Archbishop of Salzburg, serving also as a musician in the archbishop's orchestra. When Mozart received the commission for *Idomeneo* (1781) from the Munich court, he turned not to an established theatrical poet but to Varesco, who, as an Italian educated by the Jesuits in the liberal arts, was as capable as more prolific librettists. Furthermore, his presence in Salzburg allowed Mozart to work closely with him during the preparation of the libretto and the early stages of composition. Varesco translated and reworked Danchet's *tragédie lyrique Idoménée* (1712) under Mozart's supervision, producing a libretto in which the grand choruses, spectacular effects and supernatural elements reflect its French origins and probably the influence of Gluck's *Alceste*. Varesco's work is fluent and theatrical, with moments of great beauty, both poetic and dramatic.

Although Varesco was offended by Mozart's persistent attempts to alter the libretto of *Idomeneo*, that did not keep him from a second collaboration with Mozart. When Joseph II organized an *opera buffa* troupe in Vienna in 1783, Mozart, eager to display his abilities as a composer of Italian comic opera, set to work with Varesco on *L'oca del Cairo*. Most of the first act had been completed when, in early 1784, they abandoned the project, possibly because Mozart was dissatisfied with Varesco's work. After *L'oca del Cairo*, Varesco collaborated with Michael Haydn on the *opera seria Andromeda e Perseo* (1787). Having survived Mozart by 14 years, Varesco died in poverty in his adopted city.

J.A.R.

Interpreters

Valentin Adamberger

Valentin Josef Adamberger was born in Munich, on 6 July 1743; he died in Vienna, on 24 August 1804. In 1755 he studied singing with J. E. Walleshauser (Giovanni Valesi) while at the Domus Gregoriana, a Jesuit institution in Munich. In 1760 he joined the Kapelle of Duke Clemens and on Clemens's death in 1770 was taken into the elector's Hofkapelle. He sang leading tenor roles in *opere serie* at Modena, Venice, Florence, Pisa and Rome from 1775 to 1777, then at the King's Theatre in London until 1779, and again in Italy until he joined the National Singspiel at Vienna, where he made his début on 21 August 1780. In 1781 he married the Viennese actress Marie Anne Jacquet (1753–1804). On the demise of the National Singspiel in 1783 Adamberger joined the Italian company that replaced it at the Burgtheater, then in 1785 the new German troupe under imperial subvention at the Kärntnertortheater, and on its dissolution in 1789 the Italian company at the Burgtheater once again. He retired from the stage in 1793 but continued as a member of the imperial Hofkapelle and as an eminent singing teacher.

Adamberger's voice was universally admired for its pliancy, agility and precision, although Schubart and Mount Edgcumbe also remarked on its nasal quality. Mozart wrote the part of Belmonte in *Die Entführung* (1782) and Vogelsang in *Der Schauspieldirektor* (1786) for him, as well as several arias (κ420 and κ431) and the cantata *Die Maurerfreude* (κ471).

Before coming to Vienna, Adamberger created leading tenor parts in serious operas by J. C. Bach, Sarti, Pietro Guglielmi, Sacchini, Bertoni and others. The arias they wrote for his voice reveal a fondness for moderate tempos, B♭ major, obbligato clarinets and expressive chromatic inflections. At Vienna Mozart (*Die Entführung*), Umlauf (*Das Irrlicht*) and Dittersdorf (*Doktor und Apotheker*) perpetuated these features, which made Adamberger 'the favourite singer of softer hearts', according to a local journalist.

T.B.

147

Francesco Albertarelli

Francesco Albertarelli, an Italian bass, flouished in the late 18th century. From 1788 until 1790 he was a member of the *opera buffa* company in Vienna. He made his début as Biscroma in Salieri's *Axur, rè d'Ormus*, appeared in Paisiello's *La modista raggiratrice*, sang the title role in the first Vienna performance of Mozart's *Don Giovanni*, and created the role of the Marchese in Weigl's *Il pazzo per forza*. Mozart contributed an aria for him in his role of Don Pompeo for the 1788 version of Anfossi's *Le gelosie fortunate*. Albertarelli sang Brunetto in Da Ponte's 1789 pasticcio *L'ape musicale*. In 1790 he sang Rusticone in Salieri's *La cifra* in Milan, and in 1791 he appeared at the King's Theatre in London.

D.L.

Antonio Baglioni

Antonio Baglioni was an Italian tenor and singing teacher who flourished in the 1780s and 90s. He may have been related to Francesco Baglioni. He sang in productions of comic opera, particularly in Venice during the late 1780s and early 1790s, and of serious opera. Two of his most important roles were Don Ottavio in the first production of Mozart's Don Giovanni (1787, Prague) and Titus in La clemenza di Tito (1791, Prague). His range encompassed e to $b^{\flat\prime}$. He was said to have had a well-trained, pure and expressive voice. As a singing teacher, he taught, among others, Giulietta da Ponte, the niece of Mozart's librettist, Lorenzo da Ponte, who claimed that Baglioni was 'a man of perfect taste and great musical knowledge who had trained the most celebrated singers in Italy'. Baglioni also wrote music, including a set of vocal exercises.

B.D.M.

148

Luigi Bassi

Luigi Bassi was born in Pesaro, on 4 September 1766; he probably died in Dresden, in 1825. He studied in Senigallia with Pietro Morandi and appeared on the stage at the age of 13. He completed his studies with Laschi in Florence, where he appeared at the Pergola Theatre. In 1784 he joined Bondini's company in Prague and in 1786 sang Count Almaviva in the first Prague performance of *Le nozze di Figaro*; the next year he created the name part in *Don Giovanni* (1787). He is said to have asked Mozart to write him another air in place of 'Fin ch'han dal vino' and to have induced Mozart to rewrite 'Là ci darem' five times. In later years he stressed that no two performances were the same and that Mozart had specifically wished that he should improvise as long as he paid attention to the orchestra.

Bassi was praised in the *Gothaer Taschenkalendar* (1793):

This rewarding singer was from the start the ornament of the company and he still is. His voice is as melodious as his acting is masterly. Immediately he comes on, joy and cheerfulness pervade the whole audience and he never leaves the theatre without unequivocal and loud applause.

In 1793 Bassi sang Papageno in Italian at Leipzig. But by 1800 his voice had deteriorated, although his histrionic ability remained unimpaired. According to the *Allgemeine musikalische Zeitung* (1800):

Bassi was an excellent singer before he lost his voice, and he still knows very well how to use what remains. It lies between tenor and bass, and though it sounds somewhat hollow, it is still very flexible, full and pleasant. Herr Bassi is furthermore a very skilled actor in tragedy with no trace of burlesque, and with no vulgarity or tastelessness in comedy. In his truly artful and droll way he can parody the faults of the other singers so subtly that only the audience notices and they themselves are unaware of it. His best roles are Axur, Don Giovanni, Teodoro, the Notary in *La molinara*, the Count in *Figaro* and others.

In 1806 Bassi left Prague because of the war and relied on the patronage of Prince Lobkowitz, making occasional appearances in Vienna. In 1814 he returned to Prague, where Weber consulted him about *Don Giovanni*. In the autumn he was engaged for the Italian company in Dresden; and in 1815 he was made director. He still appeared in Mozart's operas; in 1816 he sang Count Almaviva, although he could no longer encompass the role vocally, but in 1817 he was well received as Guglielmo. He no longer performed Don Giovanni but sang Masetto, for which he was criticized because his figure was unsuited to the part. His contract with the Dresden company continued until his death.

C.R.

Domenico Bedini

Domenico Bedini was probably born in Fossombrone, circa 1745; he died sometime after 1795. His career as a soprano castrato began intermittently in comic opera at Pesaro (1762) and Rome (1764), and as secondo uomo in *opera seria* at Venice (1768). In 1770–71 he was secondo uomo in five Italian houses and then entered the service of the Munich court, resuming his career in Italy in 1776 and soon becoming primo uomo in leading houses. He is mostly remembered as the first Sextus in Mozart's *La clemenza di Tito* (1791, Prague). He retired after singing at Florence in Carnival 1792 and by 1795 was in the *cappella* of the San Casa of Loreto in his native region.

D.L.

Francesco Benucci

The bass Francesco Benucci was born around 1745; he died in Florence on 5 April 1824. He sang at Pistoia in 1769, then more widely in Italy, appearing as the leading character *buffo* in Venice (1778–9), and singing in Milan (1779–82) with great success and in Rome (1783–4). He first appeared in Vienna in 1783 and became the leading member of the celebrated company there, creating Tita in Martín y Soler's *Una cosa rara* and four Salieri roles including Trofonio and Axur. Described by Mozart as 'particularly good' (letter of 7 May 1783), he sang Figaro at the première of *Le nozze di Figaro* (1786), Leporello in the first Vienna performance of *Don Giovanni* (1788), when Mozart composed an extra duet for him, and Guglielmo in the première of *Così fan tutte* (1790). In 1789 he went to London where he sang Bartolo in Paisiello's *Il barbiere di Siviglia* and appeared in Gazzaniga's *La vendemmia* opposite Nancy Storace, with whom he had sung in Vienna. They introduced the first piece from any Mozart opera to be heard on the London stage, the duet 'Crudel! perchè finora' from *Figaro*. Benucci returned to Vienna later in 1789, remaining until 1795. His last great triumph was to create Count Robinson in Cimarosa's *Il matrimonio segreto* in 1792. He had a round, beautifully full voice, more bass than baritone; probably he was the finest artist for whom Mozart wrote, and as a *buffo* outshone his contemporaries as a singer and actor.

C.R., D.L.

Pasquale Bondini

Pasquale Bondini was probably born in Bonn around 1737; he died in Bruneck, in the Tyrol, on 30 or 31 October 1789. He is first mentioned as a *buffo* bass in Cajetan Molinari's opera company at Prague in the 1762–3 season. He was later a prominent member of Bustelli's company in Prague and Dresden. In 1777 he became director of the Elector of Saxony's new company at Dresden; he also assumed responsibility for Leipzig. The company's repertory also included plays by Shakespeare, Lessing and Schiller. Operas performed included works by virtually all the leading Italian composers of the day. In 1781 Bondini also took over direction of the theatre at Count Thun's palace in Prague and shortly afterwards Count Nostitz's theatre. His company performed at Leipzig mainly in the summer and gave *Die Entführung* there at Michaelmas 1783 and at Dresden on 12 January 1785. But because he and his personnel were so heavily extended by his many activities Bondini was obliged to engage other troupes and managers. His most important assistant was Domenico Guardasoni, who in 1787 became his co-director and in 1788 or 1789 his successor as impresario of the operatic side of his companies. Johann Joseph Strobach became musical director in 1785, and though the opera ensemble was small, it was highly regarded and very popular.

In December 1786 Bondini mounted *Figaro*, and in January he invited Mozart and his wife to Prague to share in the triumph the opera was enjoying; during his stay Mozart conducted a performance. Before returning to Vienna in February he had been commissioned by Bondini to write *Don Giovanni*; after delays due to illness in the company, the work was first performed on 29 October 1787 with Mozart conducting. His letter to Gottfried von Jacquin of 15–25 October contains valuable but tantalizingly brief comments on Bondini's ensemble and on the preparations for the work. Within a year of the première Bondini's fortunes had waned; ill-health led him to make Franz Seconda responsible for the drama company, and in the summer of 1789 he handed over his remaining assets before setting off for a visit to Italy. He died at Bruneck on the way.

Bondini's wife Caterina was a popular soprano in her husband's company in the mid 1780s. She sang Susanna in the first Prague production of *Figaro* in early December 1786, and on 14 December a performance was given for her benefit; her praises were sung in poems distributed in the theatre. She created the role of Zerlina in *Don Giovanni*; from the rehearsals dates the anecdote that Mozart taught her to scream effectively during the abduction scene in the finale of Act 1 by grabbing her unexpectedly round the waist.

The Bondinis' daughter Marianna (1780–1813) sang Susanna in the French première of *Figaro* and often appeared with her husband, the bass Luigi Barilli, who was later manager of the Théâtre de l'Odéon in Paris.

P.B.

Dorothea Bussani

Born Dorothea Sardi in Vienna in 1763, she died sometime after 1810. On 20 March 1786 she married the Italian bass Francesco Bussani. She specialized in *opera buffa* and made her début creating Cherubino in *Le nozze di Figaro* (1786); she also created Ghita in Martín y Soler's *Una cosa rara* (1786), Despina in *Così fan tutte* (1790) and Fidalma in Cimarosa's *Il matrimonio segreto* (1792). She always pleased the public, and a contemporary wrote that he had never heard such a beautiful and charming chest voice nor one used with such humour and so mischievously (*Grundsätze zur Theaterkritik*, 1790). Lorenzo Da Ponte, on the other hand, wrote: 'though awkward and of little merit, by dint of grimaces and clowning and perhaps by means even more theatrical, she built up a large following among cooks, grooms, servants, lackeys and wigmakers, and in consequence was considered a gem' (*Memorie*, 1823–7).

In 1795 she went to Florence and sang in Italy during the next decade. She appeared in Lisbon, 1807–9, and at the King's Theatre, London; Parke later described her as having 'plenty of voice, but whose person and age were not calculated to fascinate an English audience' (*Musical Memoirs*, 1830).

C.R.

Francesco Bussani

Francesco Bussani was born in Rome in 1743; he died sometime after 1807. He started his career as a tenor, appearing in Rome in 1763 in Guglielmi's *Le contadine bizzare*. He sang in Venice, Milan and Rome for the next 15 years and first appeared in Vienna in 1771. In 1777 he was described in Florence as singing *primo buffo* and *mezzo carattere* roles; by this time his voice was a bass-baritone. He appeared in Venice from 1779 and in 1783 was invited to Vienna where he remained until 1794. With 20 years' experience of the theatre, he was engaged not only as a singer but also as manager of scenery and costumes, he also arranged pieces and in 1784 adapted Goldoni's *Il mercato di Malmantile* as a libretto for music by Barta. He appeared regularly in the Italian repertory and sang Pippo in Bianchi's *La villanella rapita*, for which Mozart wrote the quartet 'Dite almeno' K479 (28 November 1785), he doubled the roles of Bartolo and Antonio in the première of *Le nozze di Figaro* (1 May 1786). He was an active member of the Italian faction in Vienna during the 1780s and according to Da Ponte (*Memorie*, 1823–7) intrigued against him and Mozart when *Figaro* was in rehearsal. Lorenzo Da Ponte described Bussani as knowing something of every profession except that of a gentleman.

Bussani sang the Commendatore and Masetto in the first Vienna performance of *Don Giovanni* (1788) and created Don Alfonso in *Così fan tutte* (26 January 1790). According to Da Ponte, Bussani found little favour with the new emperor, Leopold II. He achieved only moderate success as he was always in the shadow of Benucci, who had the stronger stage personality and was the public's favourite. In 1795 he sang in Florence in 1799 in Rome, and in 1800–1 in Naples and Palermo. He remained active in Italy and went with his wife, Dorothea, to Lisbon in 1807.

C.R.

155

Vincenzo Calvesi

Vincenzo Calvesi [Caldesi] was an Italian tenor who was probably born in Faenza and whose career flourished between 1780 and 1794. After successful appearances in Verona (as Count Bandiera in Salieri's *La scuola de' gelosi*, 1780) and Venice, he made his Vienna début in 1785 as Sandrino in Paisiello's *Il re Teodoro* and remained there until 1788. He went to Naples but returned to Vienna in 1789 and stayed until 1794 with occasional absences (he sang in Moscow in 1790). As the leading Italian lyric tenor in Vienna, he created Prince Giovanni in *Una cosa rara* (1786) and Endymion in *L'arbore di Diana* (1787), both by Martín y Soler, as well as roles in operas by Storace (*Gli sposi malcontenti* and *Gli equivoci*) and Salieri (*La grotta di Trofonio* and *Axur, re d'Ormus*). In 1785 he sang the Count in the quartet 'Dite almeno, in che mancai' K479 and the trio 'Mandina amabile' K480 written by Mozart for Bianchi's *La villanella rapita*. He created Eufemio of Syracuse in Storace's *Gli equivoci* (1786), and Ferrando in *Così fan tutte* (1790). He was described in Grundsätze zur Theaterkritik (1790) as 'one of the best tenors from Italy ... with a voice naturally sweet, pleasant and sonorous'. Calvesi also acted as impresario, at Faenza (apparently his native city) in 1788, and later in Rome (circa 1800–4).

C.R., D.L.

Caterina Cavalieri

Caterina [Kavalier, Franziska Helena Appolonia] Cavalieri [Cavallieri] was born in Vienna, on 19 February 1760; she died there on 30 June 1801. During a versatile career, confined almost exclusively to Vienna, she appeared with equal success in comic and serious roles in both the Italian and German repertories. In her early career Cavalieri possessed an impressive upper range, to *d'''*. An extraordinary stamina and flexibility are reflected in consistently large-scale bravura arias. Of her début in Vienna (19 June 1775 at the Kärntnertortheater), as Sandrina in Anfossi's *La finta giardiniera*, Count Khevenhüller wrote that she possessed a very strong chest voice and met with 'well-deserved approbation'. In 1776–7 she belonged to a troupe of Italian singers. In 1778 she sang Sophie in Umlauf's *Die Bergknappen*, the inaugural production of the National Singspiel, and went on to sing 18 leading roles in the company including Nannette in Salieri's *Der Rauchfangkehrer* (1781) and Konstanze in Mozart's *Die Entführung* (1782). Of the challenging *fioriture* in 'Ach ich liebte', Mozart wrote to his father (26 September 1781): 'I have sacrificed Konstanze's aria a little to the flexible throat of Mlle Cavallieri'; this and another bravura showcase in the same act, 'Martern aller Arten', came willingly from the astute Mozart, eager to ingratiate himself with Cavalieri and her protector, the court composer Salieri. When Joseph II inaugurated *opera buffa* at the Burgtheater, Cavalieri was put to use both as a serious and comic lead. Her hard-hitting bravura is evident in rewritten or new solo numbers in works by Salieri and Cimarosa.

Cavalieri is best known through Mozart's music for her. Her aria as Mme Silberklang in *Der Schauspieldirektor* (1786) has muscular tunes, with driving, vigorous two-note phrases and quaver scales. For her appearance as Donna Elvira in the first Vienna production of *Don Giovanni* (1788), Mozart composed a large-scale aria ('Mi tradì') for her; she clearly no longer commanded her earlier high notes. For the revival of *Le nozze di Figaro* (1789), in which Cavalieri sang the Countess, Mozart rewrote 'Dove sono', eliminating the repeat of the intimate, restrained initial material and adding *fioriture* in the faster section.

Early in her career, Cavalieri was said to want 'animation and accuracy, and a firmer assurance', and criticized for almost 'unintelligible' speech (M. A. Schmitt, *Meine Empfindungen im Theater*, 1781). The Viennese dramatist Gebler, writing in 1780–81, said she had 'eine starke und angenehme Stimme, mit tiefen und hohen Tönen, die man selten beysammen antrift, singt ebenfalls die schwehrsten Passagen' ('a strong and pleasant voice, in both the high and the low notes, a combination which one seldom encounters, [she] sings equally well the most difficult passages'). Zinzendorf noted that in a duet in Sarti's *Giulio Sabino* 'Cavalieri drowned Marchesini's voice with her shouts' (4 August 1785), but two days later recorded that 'she screamed less'.

P.L.G.

Vincenzo Dal Prato

Vioncenzo Dal Prato [Del Prato], an Italian castrato, was born in Imola, on 5 May 1756; he died in Munich, in 1828. He studied with Lorenzo Gibelli and made his début at the opera house in Fano in 1772. After touring extensively in Germany and the Netherlands, he sang at Stuttgart in 1779 for the future Russian Tsar Paul I. In 1780 Dal Prato was appointed to the court of Carl Theodor, the Elector of Bavaria, in Munich, where he spent the rest of his career. His voice was apparently a high mezzo. His most famous role was Idamantes in Mozart's *Idomeneo* (1781), and he also sang in Salieri's *Semiramide* (1782), Holzbauer's *Tancredi* (1783) and Vogler's *Castore e Polluce* (1787). Mozart complained about the inexperienced singer's poor stage presence and had to teach Dal Prato his music. But Dal Prato was apparently eager to learn, and Mozart referred to him as his 'molto amato castrato Dal Prato'. His singing was admired more for its grace and polished execution than its power or dramatic qualities.

P.C.

Ernst Dauer

Johann [Joseph] Ernst Dauer was born in Hildburghausen, in 1746; he died in Vienna, on 12 September 1812. He began his career in 1768, and in 1771 was engaged in Hamburg, where he sang in Singspiels. In 1775 he went to Gotha and in 1777 to Frankfurt and Mannheim. In 1779 he was engaged at the court theatre in Vienna, initially singing in the Singspiel company (making his début as Alexis in Monsigny's *Le déserteur*) and, the following year, also acting in the spoken theatre company. He created Pedrillo in Mozart's *Die Entführung aus dem Serail* (1782) and Sturmwald in Dittersdorf's *Der Apotheker und der Doktor* (1786). He was a useful though uninspired performer: according to the actor F.L. Schröder, 'He touched the heart in neither serious nor comic roles. His manner was a little cold and remote; his movement somewhat wooden' He played secondary lovers, character roles and sturdy, unpolished lads.

C.R., D.L.

Anna Lucia De Amicis

Anna Lucia De Amicis [De Amicis-Buonsollazzi], was born in Naples, circa 1733; she died in Naples, in 1816. Italian soprano. She began performing in comic operas with her family in the 1750s in Italy, Paris and Brussels, then in 1762 made her London début at the King's Theatre. Following her début as a serious singer in J. C. Bach's *Orione* (1763), she left comic opera. As prima donna in Milan (1764–5), Venice (1764), Innsbruck (1765) and Naples (1766), she became involved in theatrical disputes and wished to retire. But after marriage (1768) to a Florentine physician she resumed her career, singing in Venice (1768–9, 1770–71) and Naples (1769–70, 1771–2, in Jommelli's *Armida abbandonata* and *Ifigenia in Tauride*). Mozart praised her highly, and in the role of Junia she ensured the success of his *Lucio Silla* in Milan (1772). Engagements in Naples (1773–6), Turin (1776–9) and the Italian première of Gluck's *Alceste* (1778, Bologna) concluded her brilliant career, though she sang for at least another ten years in private Neapolitan productions.

De Amicis amazed listeners with her vocal agility. Burney described her as the first to sing staccato divisions, and the first to 'go up to E(in altissimo, with true, clear, and powerful *real* voice'. She was equally impressive as an actress: Metastasio wrote that 'among the dramatic heroines . . . there was absolutely no one but the signora De Amicis suited to portray the character . . . with the fire, the boldness, the frankness, and the expression necessary'.

K.K.H.

Guglielmo Ettore

Guglielmo Ettore [d'Ettore] was born on Sicily, around 1740; he died in Ludwigsburg, in the winter of 1771–2. He sang in Hasse's *Achille in Sciro* in Naples in 1759 and he later moved to Bologna. In 1761 he was engaged in Munich, remaining in service there to 1771. He appeared in several Italian centres in the 1760s, among them Venice and Verona in 1765, in operas by Sarti, and Turin, where in 1767 he sang in Bertoni's *Tancredi* and Quirino Gasparini's *Mitridate, rè di Ponto*. By then he was a *cavaliere* ('d'Ettore'). He sang the title role in Bernasconi's *La clemenza di Tito* at Munich in 1768 and Admetus in Guglielmi's *Alceste* the next year in Milan. Burney reported that he was the most applauded of the singers in Sacchini's *Scipio in Cartagena* in Padua in 1770; elsewhere he referred to him as reckoned 'the best singer of his kind on the serious opera stage'. Schubart wrote that he had 'never heard anyone sing with the feeling of a d'Ettore' (*Schubart's Leben und Gesinnungen*, Stuttgart, 1791–3, i, p.94). Later that year he sang the title role in Mozart's *Mitridate* in Milan; the young composer had to rewrite one aria four times for him, and Ettore ultimately included an aria by Gasparini (displaying his splendid top c'') in place of another of Mozart's. Relations were so strained that eight years later the mention of Ettore's name evoked unpleasant memories for Mozart. Ettore was engaged at the Württemberg court on 28 January 1771 but died the next winter. His compositions include arias and many vocal duets, in a fluent melodic style.

H.J.-W.

Adriana Ferrarese

Adriana [Andreanna, Andriana] Ferrarese [Ferraresi, Ferrarese del Bene] was born around 1760; she died sometime after 1800. She studied at the Mendicanti in Venice from 1780 to 1782, and has long been identified with a Francesca Gabrielli, '*detta* la Ferrarese', whom Burney heard at the Ospedaletto in Venice in 1770; Gerber may have been the first to assume that Burney's Gabrielli and Adriana Ferrarese were one and the same, but no solid evidence links them. She eloped with Luigi del Bene in 1783 and appeared at the Teatro Pergola, Florence, on 8 May 1784.

In 1785–6 Ferrarese sang in London, at first in serious opera and then comic (though her roles were in *seria* style), and was generally well received. She returned to Florence, where her roles included Tarchi's Iphigenia and Gluck's Alcestis. In 1788 she settled in Vienna. Her background in *opera seria* made her particularly effective in heroic roles, such as Diana in Martín y Soler's *L'arbore di Diana* (her début role there), Eurilla in Salieri's *La cifra* (1789) and her most famous role, Mozart's Fiordiligi (26 January 1790). Her tenure of 30 months coincided with the peak of Lorenzo da Ponte's influence; she was dismissed with Da Ponte, with whom she was romantically involved, in early 1791, and continued her career throughout Italy until the late 1790s, after which further records of her performances disappear.

Music written for Ferrarese tends to emphasize *fioriture, cantar di sbalzo* (large leaps) and the low end of her range. She appears to have been unsuited for the comic style; every adaptation of existing music for revivals and new music written for her tends to enhance the serious style at the expense of the comic. Weigl (*Il pazzo per forza*) and Salieri (*La cifra*) in particular met her vocal requirements successfully within roles that made limited demands on her modest acting ability. Her singing won much praise, notably from Count Johann Karl Zinzendorf, who wrote that 'La Ferrarese chanta à merveille' (27 February 1789). The casting of Ferrarese as Susanna for the 1789 revival of *Le nozze di Figaro* met with only qualified enthusiasm from Mozart, who wrote that 'the little aria [K577] I have made for Ferrarese I believe will please, if she is capable of singing it in an artless manner, which I very much doubt' (19 August 1789); he also composed a large-scale rondò in *opera seria* style, K579, to replace 'Deh, vieni, non tardar'. As Fiordiligi in *Così fan tutte* her vain temperament and formidable vocal resources were exploited to perfection by Mozart, creating a rigid *seria* character who is the object of comic intrigue.

J.A.R.

Ludwig Fischer

Johann Ignaz [Karl] Ludwig Fischer was born in Mainz on 18 August 1745; he died in Berlin on 10 July 1825. He studied the violin and cello, then singing with Anton Raaff from about 1769, in Mannheim where he became *virtuoso da camera* at the court in 1772. He moved with the court to Munich (1778), where he married the singer Barbara Strasser (born 1758; died after 1825). From 1780 to 1783 the couple worked in Vienna, where Fischer sang Osmin in the first performance of *Die Entführung aus dem Serail*, much to the satisfaction of Mozart, who frequently wrote about him in his letters and gave him an introduction for Paris. He then secured his reputation with a tour of Italy and visited Vienna, Prague and Dresden. After serving in Regensburg from 1785 he received a lifelong appointment in Berlin in 1789. Guest appearances in London (1794, 1798), Leipzig (1798), Hamburg (1801–2) and elsewhere added to his fame. He gave up public performance in 1812.

Fischer was regarded as Germany's leading serious bass. His voice, said to range from D to a', was praised by Reichardt as having 'the depth of a cello and the natural height of a tenor'. He also composed. His autobiography, covering up to 1790, is in manuscript in the Berlin Staatsbibliothek. His son (?Anton) Joseph Fischer (born Berlin, 1780; died Mannheim, 1862) was a bass and composer and his daughters Josepha Fischer-Vernier (born 1782) and Wilhelmine (born 1785) were also distinguished singers.

R.W.

Franz Xaver Gerl

Franz Xaver Gerl [Görl], Austrian bass and composer, was born in Andorf, Upper Austria, on 30 November 1764; he died in Mannheim, on 9 March 1827. The son of a village schoolmaster and organist, by 1777 he was an alto chorister at Salzburg, where he must have been a pupil of Leopold Mozart. He was at the Salzburg Gymnasium, 1778–82, and then studied logic and physics at the university. In autumn 1785 he went to Erlangen as a bass, joining the theatrical company of Ludwig Schmidt, who had earlier been at Salzburg. In 1786 he joined G. F. W. Grossmann's company, performing in the Rhineland, and specialized in 'comic roles in comedies and Singspiels'. By 1787 he was a member of Schikaneder's company at Regensburg, making his début in Sarti's *Wenn zwei sich streiten* (*Fra i due litiganti*) and appearing as Osmin in *Die Entführung*. From summer 1789 he was a member of Schikaneder's company at the Freihaus-Theater auf der Wieden, Vienna. On 2 September 1789 he married the soprano Barbara Reisinger. His name first appears as one of the composers of *Der dumme Gärtner aus dem Gebirge* (*Der dumme Anton*), Schikaneder's first new production at his new theatre, on 12 July 1789; it is unlikely that this was Gerl's first theatre score since Schikaneder would hardly have entrusted such an important task to a novice. *Der dumme Anton* proved so successful that it had no fewer than six sequels; Gerl certainly performed in two of these, though he and Schack may not have written all the scores. Between 1789 and 1793 Gerl wrote music for several more plays and Singspiels.

Gerl played a wide variety of parts in plays and operas (including Don Giovanni and Figaro in German) during his Vienna years, though he is most often associated with the role of Sarastro in *Die Zauberflöte*, which he created on 30 September 1791 and continued to sing at least until November 1792 (the 83rd performance, announced by Schikaneder as the 100th). The Gerls appear to have left the Freihaus-Theater in 1793; they were at Brünn (Brno), 1794–1801, and from 1802 Gerl was a member of the Mannheim Hoftheater. Apart from operatic roles he also appeared frequently in plays; he retired in 1826. That year he married Magdalena Dengler (née Reisinger – his first wife's elder sister), the widow of Georg Dengler, director of the Mainz theatre.

Although the paucity of the surviving material and the difficulty of identifying Gerl's contribution to joint scores make it impossible to evaluate him as a composer, the works he wrote were popular in their day. His career as a singer is better documented. When Schröder, the greatest actor-manager of his age, went to Vienna in 1791 he was told not to miss hearing Schack and Gerl at Schikaneder's theatre. At the end of May he heard Wranitzky's *Oberon*, in which both were singing, and thought Gerl's singing of the Oracle 'very good'. Mozart's high regard for his qualities is evident in the aria 'Per questa bella mano' (K612), written for Gerl in March 1791, and above all in Sarastro's music. Mozart's friendly relationship with Gerl is attested by the fact that Gerl was one of the singers who is said, on Mozart's last afternoon, to have joined the dying composer in an impromptu sing-through of the Requiem (the others were Schack and Mozart's brother-in-law Franz Hofer).

P.B.

Anna Gottlieb

Maria Anna Josepha Francisca [Nanette] Gottlieb, was born in Vienna, on 29 April 1774; she died there on 1 February 1856. She was a daughter of two members of the German theatre company of the Nationaltheater. At the age of five she started appearing there in small acting and singing roles. When she was 12 she created Barbarina in Mozart's *Le nozze di Figaro* (1786). In 1789 she was engaged by Emanuel Schikaneder for the Freihaustheater, where Mozart wrote Pamina for her in *Die Zauberflöte* (1791). That role represented the artistic peak of her career (although she was not yet 18).

In 1792 she was engaged at the Leopoldstädter Theater, at that time under the direction of Marinelli. During her 36 years there she gradually moved from a youthful singer to a character actress playing comic old women. Her best years saw her singing in Gluck's *Die Pilgrime von Mekka* (*La rencontre imprévue*) and works by Dalayrac. Her greatest successes were in the roles she created in Singspiels and travesties to words by Perinet and C. F. Hensler (Marinelli's successor at the Leopoldstädter Theater, 1803–17), set by Wenzel Müller and Ferdinand Kauer: in *Das Neusonntagskind* (1793, Perinet and Müller), as Hulda in *Das Donauweibchen* (1798, Hensler and Kauer), a role she performed over a thousand times, as Evakathel in *Evakathel und Schnudi, oder Die Belagerung von Ypsilon* (1804, Parinet and Müller) and in the title role of *Die neue Alceste* (1806, Perinet and Müller). She was absent from the stage in 1808–11 and returned with diminishing success, finally singing mainly secondary roles. She was dismissed without a pension in 1828 and sank into poverty. In 1842 she introduced herself to L. V. Frankl, editor of the *Sonntagsblätter*, as 'the first Pamina' and the last living friend of Mozart; his emotional appeal on her behalf raised enough money to send her to Salzburg for the unveiling of the Mozart monument. She died in the year of Mozart's centenary and, like Mozart, was buried in St Mark's cemetery.

C.H.

Josepha Hofer

Josepha Hofer was born Maria Josepha Weber in Zell, in 1758 and died as Josepha Mayer in Vienna, on 29 December 1819. A soprano, she was the sister of Aloysia Lange. She was the eldest daughter of the singer and violinist Fridolin Weber (1733–79). After her father's death she moved to Vienna, and was then engaged as a soprano at Graz, 1785–7. On 21 July 1788 she married the court musician Franz de Paula Hofer (1755–96), and began performing at the suburban Theater auf der Wieden the next January. According to contemporary reports, she commanded a very high tessitura but had a rough edge to her voice and lacked stage presence. In September 1789 Mozart wrote for her the bravura insertion aria 'Schon lacht der holde Frühling' (K580, for a German version of Paisiello's *Il barbiere di Siviglia*). Two years later he composed the role of the Queen of Night in *Die Zauberflöte* for her; she finally ceded the part to Antonia Campi in 1801. Josepha's second husband, from 1797, was (Friedrich) Sebastian Mayer (1773–1835), who created Pizarro in Beethoven's *Fidelio* (*Leonore*) in 1805. In that year Josepha retired from the stage, to be replaced by her daughter Josefa Hofer.

T.B.

Michael Kelly

Michael Kelly was born in Dublin on 25 December 1762; he died in Margate, on 9 October 1826. He was a tenor, composer, theatre manager and music publisher. The eldest of the 14 children of Thomas Kelly (Master of the Ceremonies at Dublin Castle, and a wine merchant), Michael Kelly grew up amid the rich musical life of Dublin, and received singing lessons from various immigrant Italians, notably Passerini and Rauzzini. His piano teachers included Michael Arne. Having made his earliest operatic appearances in Piccinni's *La buona figliuola*, Dibdin's *Lionel and Clarissa* and Michael Arne's *Cymon*, Kelly left Dublin in 1779, on Rauzzini's advice, to study in Naples.

His most influential teachers were Finaroli and Aprile. Equally important, perhaps, was the patronage of Sir William Hamilton. Kelly made his way northwards, obtaining engagements in many opera houses. In Venice his fortunes took a decisive turn. Early in 1783 the Austrian Emperor Joseph II intended to build up an Italian opera company at his court and instructed Count Durazzo, his ambassador in Venice, to recruit singers, and he offered engagements to Kelly, Nancy Storace, Benucci and Mandini. The four years that Kelly spent in Vienna were to prove the climax of his musical career. Not only did he create the parts of Don Curzio and Don Basilio in *Le nozze di Figaro*, but he also met most of the great composers and singers of the day. Kelly and Storace were the only singers from the British Isles to sing in any first performance of a Mozart opera.

In his *Reminiscences* he left a vivid picture of his acquaintance with Mozart, both socially and in the opera house. Although Kelly's comments on musical life in Vienna are often superficial, he saw humanity in the round with keen observation and humorous detachment. It is these qualities which make the book so attractive: its first volume, particularly, is a valuable source of information about the music and manners of the time. Even if written with the aid of a rough diary or notes, the *Reminiscences*, which run to some 170,000 words, are a remarkable testimony to Kelly's memory. They were ghosted, not long before Kelly's death, by Theodore Hook, who was described by his great-great-nephew, the English music critic Martin Cooper (1910–86), as 'a man of the theatre, professional writer, almost a professional wag and something of a crook'. Perhaps some of Hook's character colours Kelly's narrative.

In February 1787, with the Storaces and Attwood, Kelly left Vienna for London, visiting Mozart's father in Salzburg en route. Kelly quickly established himself, and his services as a singer were in continual demand throughout the British Isles during the next 30 years. He won greater approval for his technique than for the quality of his voice. In his *Memoirs of the Life of John Philip Kemble* (1825), James Boaden wrote:

His voice had amazing power and steadiness, his compass was extraordinary. In vigorous passages he never cheated the ear with the feeble wailings of falsetto, but sprung upon the ascending fifth with a sustaining energy that often electrified an audience.

Lord Mount Edgcumbe, however, no mean judge, expressed a less favourable view in his *Musical Reminiscences* (1825):

Though he was a good musician and not a bad singer, having been long in Italy, yet he had retained, or regained, so much of the English vulgarity of manner that he was never greatly liked at this theatre [Drury Lane].

As a composer, Kelly claimed to have written over 60 theatre pieces between 1797 and 1821. But for many of these he contributed just a few songs; at other times he wrote in collaboration. He commanded a limited but prolific vein of melodic invention and seems to have relied on others for harmony and orchestration. In 1801, Thomas Moore wrote: 'Poor Mick is rather an imposer than a composer. He cannot mark the time in writing three bars of music: his understrappers, however, do all that for him'. Kelly himself says (i, 133–4) that the German bandmaster R.T. Eley provided the wind accompaniment for the march in *Blue Beard*. He caught the current taste so well that his music became widely popular: it was extensively pirated in America, resulting in some 200 separate issues. *Blue Beard* remained in the repertory for 26 years. In 1801 Kelly set up as a publisher, in premises so close to the King's Theatre that he could offer patrons a private entrance through the shop, directly on to the stage. His publications included operas in vocal score and a considerable number of single songs. But the business seems to have needed more time than he could spare and was declared bankrupt in 1811. Kelly also engaged in the wine trade which, added to the suspicion that some of his compositions came from abroad, induced Sheridan to suggest that his shop-sign should read 'Michael Kelly, composer of wines and importer of music'.

Much of Kelly's time and energy was devoted to the King's Theatre in the Haymarket; he became its stage manager in 1793 and served it with little intermission for nearly 31 years. Thus as singer, publisher and manager, he lived in the heart of London's musical life. He never married, though he lived with Anna Maria Crouch for some years in what seems to have been a platonic relationship. Kelly was buried in the churchyard of St Paul's, Covent Garden. His niece, Frances Maria Kelly (1790–1882), was an actress and singer of considerable distinction.

The Garrick Club possesses two portraits of Kelly, one by De Wild, showing him in costume as Cymon, the other a half-length by James Lonsdale. The frontispiece to the *Reminiscences* was engraved by H. Meyer from a drawing by A. Wivell, which cannot now be traced. The Garrick Club also has two letters in Kelly's autograph.

A.H.K.

Aloysia Lange

Born Maria Aloysia [Aloisia, Aloysia Louise] Antonia Weber in Zell or Mannheim, circa 1761, she died Aloysia Lange in Salzburg, on 8 June 1839. She was the sister of Josepha Hofer, and sister-in-law of Mozart, who married her sister Constanze in 1782. She studied in Mannheim with Vogler and with Mozart, her association with whom produced seven concert arias and a role in *Der Schauspieldirektor* (as well as a series of letters by Mozart notable for their elucidation of his views on vocal performance and training). Their first encounter, during Mozart's stay in Mannheim in 1777–8 (when he fell in love with her) resulted in the concert arias K294, 316/300*b* and probably 538. She moved from Mannheim to Munich in 1778, where she made her début as Parthenia in Schweitzer's *Alceste* (Carnival 1779); she was then engaged for the new National Singspiel in Vienna, where she made her début on 9 September 1779 as Hännchen in a German adaptation of Philidor's *Le rosière de Salency*. She married the court actor and painter Joseph Lange on 31 October 1780.

When in 1782 Joseph II removed German opera to the neighbouring Kärntnertortheater and reinstated Italian comic opera at the Burgtheater, she was retained as a leading singer of the Italian troupe. For her début, as Clorinda in Anfossi's *Il curioso indiscreto* (1783), Mozart composed two substitute arias, K418 and 419. Lange participated regularly in Italian opera for only eight months; probably she fell out of favour because of disagreements over salary and roles as well as missed performances. In 1785 she was among the German singers transferred to the less prestigious Kärntnertortheater, where she revived many roles of her early career with the important addition of Konstanze in Mozart's *Die Entführung* (1785–8). Lange continued to appear occasionally at the Burgtheater, notably for a German revival in 1785 of Gluck's *La rencontre imprévue*, for the Vienna première of Mozart's *Don Giovanni* (as Donna Anna) and for Cimarosa's *Il fanatico burlato*, both in 1788. She was retained by Leopold II for his *opera seria* venture in Vienna in 1790, as a seconda donna. In 1795 Aloysia undertook a concert tour with her sister Constanze, continuing her successes as Mozart's Sextus, a role she had performed in Vienna.

A report in the *Deutsches Museum* (1781) states that she 'has a very pleasing voice, though it is too weak for the theatre', and Gerber pronounced her voice 'more suited for an ordinary room than the theatre'. Leopold Mozart corroborates this view in a letter to his daughter of 25 March 1785:

It can scarcely be denied that she sings with the greatest expression: only now I understand why some persons I frequently asked would say that she has a very weak voice, while others said she has a very loud voice. Both are true. The held notes and all expressive notes are astonishingly loud; the tender moments, the passage work and embellishments, and high notes are very delicate, so that for my taste the one contrasts too strongly with the other. In an ordinary room the loud notes assault the ear, while in the theatre the delicate passages demand a great attentiveness and stillness on the part of the audience.

Mozart's compositions give the clearest picture of her voice. His sensitivity to Lange's small instrument may be seen in the light orchestration and relatively high tessitura. Her music exploits expressive, cantabile delivery and gives ample opportunity for portamento and the addition of ornaments. Her *fioriture* consist primarily of scale work and *abbellimenti* spun out in varied, flexible rhythmic configurations, and there is an almost casual assaying of her remarkable upper range, extending to g''' (as Blanka in Umlauf's *Das Irrlicht*, 1782, she sang to a'''). Gebler regarded her as 'a splendid singer, [with] a tone and an expression that goes to the heart [and] an extraordinary upper range; she correctly performs the most difficult passages and blends them with the song as it should be done'.

P.L.G.

Luisa Laschi

Luisa Laschi [Mombelli] was born in Florence in the 1760s; she died in 1789. When she made her Viennese début, in 1784 in Cimarosa's *Giannina e Bernardone*, the *Wiener Kronik* said: 'she has a beautiful clear voice, which in time will become rounder and fuller; she is very musical, sings with more expression than the usual opera singers and has a beautiful figure'. In 1785 she sang Rosina in Paisiello's *Il barbiere di Siviglia* 'very well, and was much applauded' (Zinzendorf). Joseph II grudgingly released her for the 1785 season in Naples, but she returned in 1786 and sang at the Viennese court opera during its finest period. On 1 May 1786 she created Countess Almaviva in *Le nozze di Figaro*. She had a further success on 15 May as Barbarina in Anfossi's *Il trionfo delle donne*, and in August appeared, probably for the first time in Vienna, with her future husband, the tenor Domenico Mombelli, in Sarti's *I finti eredi*. In November she created the role of Queen Isabella in Martín y Soler's *Una cosa rara*, and in 1787 created Cupid in his *L'arbore di Diana*, a role that required her to appear alternately as a shepherdess and as Cupid. A contemporary reviewer described her portrayal: 'Grace personified . . .; ah, who is not enchanted by it, what painter could better depict the arch smile, what sculptor the grace in all her gestures, what singer could match the singing, so melting and sighing, with the same naturalness and true, warm expression?'

In January 1788 she appeared in the première of Salieri's *Axur, rè d'Ormus* and in May sang Zerlina in the first Vienna performance of Mozart's *Don Giovanni*; Mozart composed a new duet to be sung by her and Benucci. She was already seven months pregnant but continued singing until the day before her confinement and reappeared four weeks later. But there were difficulties between the Italian company and the management and the emperor gave the Mombellis notice. In September Luisa created the role of Carolina in Salieri's *Il talismano* and in February 1789 she made her farewell appearance as Donna Farinella in *L'ape musicale*; nothing further seems to be known about her, but in 1791 Domenico, apparently a widower, married the ballerina Vincenza Vigano, by whom he had 12 children.

C.R.

Maria Mandini

A French soprano, and the wife of Stefano Mandini, Maria Mandini's career flourished between 1783 and 1787. The daughter of a Versailles court official, she was engaged with her husband in the Italian opera company in Vienna; she made her début there in 1783 as Madama Brillante in Cimarosa's *L'italiana in Londra* and then sang Countess Belfiore in Sarti's *Fra i due litiganti*. She is known to have created three roles, all small parts: Marina in Martín y Soler's *Il burbero di buon cuore* (1786), Marcellina in *Le nozze di Figaro* (1786) and Britomarte in Martín y Soler's *L'arbore di Diana*. In 1787 she appeared in Cimarosa's *Le trame deluse* and sang Livietta in Paisiello's *Le due contesse*. Nothing is known of her later career. She was apparently an attractive but poor singer. Zinzendorf wrote of her performance as Marina: 'La Mandini let us see her beautiful hair'. As Britomarte she was said to sound 'like an enraged cat' and the performing score contains a pencilled comment at the head of her only aria: 'canta male'.

C.R.

Stefano Mandini

Stefano Mandini was born in 1750; he died circa 1810. He appeared at Venice in 1775–6 and at Parma in 1776, described as 'primo buffo mezzo carattere'. In 1783 he and his wife were engaged by Joseph II for his new Italian opera company in Vienna; Stefano was a leading member during its finest period. There is some confusion between Stefano and his younger brother Paolo. Stefano made his Vienna début on 5 May 1783 as Milord Arespingh in Cimarosa's *L'italiana in Londra*; that season he appeared as Mingone in Sarti's *Fra i due litiganti*, Don Fabio in Cimarosa's *Il falegname* and Count Almaviva in Paisiello's *Il barbiere di Siviglia*; in the last, Zinzendorf noted, he excelled in all four disguises in Almaviva's role. The following season he sang in *Le vicende d'amore* (P. A. Guglielmi), *La finta amante* and *Il re Teodoro in Venezia* (Paisiello) in which he created the title role, and *La vendemmia* (Gazzaniga). In 1785 he created Artidoro m Storace's *Gli sposi mal contenti* and Plistene in Salieri's *La grotta di Trofonio*.

Mandini created three roles in 1786: the Poet in Salieri's *Prima la musica e poi le parole*, Count Almaviva in Mozart's *Le nozze di Figaro* (on 1 May) and Lubino in Martín y Soler's *Una cosa rara*. He also sang in Sarti's *I finti eredi* and Paisiello's *Le gare generose*. In 1787–8 he appeared as Leandro in Paisiello's *Le due contesse* and created Doristo in Martín y Sojer's *L'arbore di Diana* and Biscroma in Salieri's *Axur, re d'Ormus*. He was then released to go to Naples. Later he sang at the Théâtre de Monsieur in Paris, having considerable success in *Il barbiere di Siviglia*, *Una cosa rara* and *La villanella rapita*, and in Venice (1794–5), then returned to Vienna for Piccinni's *La Griselda* and Paisiello's *La molinara*; he then went to St Petersburg, where the painter Elisabeth Vigée Le Brun remarked that he was an excellent performer and sang wonderfully. Nothing is known for certain of his later career, though it was probably he rather than Paolo who appeared in Berlin in 1804. An extremely versatile singer, he acquitted himself well both as the comic servant (e.g. Doristo) and as the serious lover (e.g. Lubino). His wide range permitted him to create Count Almaviva as a tenor for Paisiello and as a baritone for Mozart.

C.R.

Giovanni Manzuoli

Giovanni Manzuoli was born in Florence around 1720; he died in Florence in 1782. He was first a soprano castrato and later a contralto. After appearances in operas in Florence (1731) and Verona (1735) he settled in Naples until late 1748, occasionally performing in Rome and Venice. By the mid-1740s he was singing leading parts at San Carlo. After the 1749 at Milan he performed in ten productions in Madrid (1749–52). He left after an incident occasioned by his arrogant temperament, and sang in Parma in the 1754 Carnival, but was in Lisbon for the opening of the Teatro de los Paços Ribeira in 1755 and briefly back in Madrid. He returned to Italy and remained there until 1764 except for a trip to Vienna, where his performance in Hasse's *Alcide al bivio* (1760) made him the idol of the city, according to Metastasio. In the 1764–5 season Manzuoli, a fine actor whose voice was 'the most powerful and voluminous soprano that had been heard ... since the time of Farinelli' (Burney), drew 'a universal thunder' of applause at the King's Theatre, London; there he became acquainted with the Mozart family and sang in the première of J.C. Bach's *Adriano in Siria*. He retired to Florence in 1768 after three successful seasons in Italy (Verona, Turin, Venice and Milan), but sang again in Rome in 1770 and in Milan the next year in Hasse's *Ruggiero* and Mozart's *Ascanio in Alba*.

K.K.H.

Maria Marchetti Fabtozzi

Maria (?Vincenza) Marchetti Fantozzi [née Marchetti], was born circa 1760; she died probably sometime after 1800. She was one of the leading singers of *opera seria* during the 1780s and 90s. Around 1783 (earlier than 1788, the date given by Abert) she married the tenor Angelo Fantozzi and thereafter usually identified herself as Maria Marchetti Fantozzi. She was praised throughout Italy for her acting as well as her singing, particularly in Naples, where she performed in at least seven different operas in 1785–6. Marchetti was a specialist in the portrayal of passionate, tragic heroines like Semiramide and Cleopatra; she was thus ideally suited to create the role of Vitellia in Mozart's *La clemenza di Tito*. The music that she sang in that opera shows her to have been an extraordinary virtuoso, with a large range and a capacity for difficult coloratura.

J.A.R.

Domenico Panzacchi

Domenico Panzacchi [Pansacchi] was born in Bologna around 1730; he died in Bologna in 1805. He is said to have been a pupil of Bernacchi and sang in *opera seria* from 1746, in 1748–9 in Vienna, where he first worked with Raaff, who was to overshadow him in parts of his later career. In 1751–7 he was at Madrid (Raaff arriving at a higher salary in 1755) and from 1760 until his pensioning in 1782 in the service of the Munich court (which Raaff joined after 1778), with occasional operatic engagements in Italy. He is remembered for creating Arbaces in *Idomeneo* (1781), Mozart finding his singing and acting still worthy of respect in spite of his age.

D.L.

179

Anton Raaff

Anton Raaff [Raff] was born in Gelsdorf, near Bonn, and was baptized on 6 May 1714; he died in Munich, on 28 May 1797. After being appointed to the service of Clement Augustus, Elector of Cologne, Raaff was sent in 1736 to Munich, where he studied with Ferrandini and sang in one of his operas. The following year he studied with Bernacchi in Bologna, remaining in Italy until 1741–2, when he returned to electoral service in Bonn. In 1749 he left for Vienna where he sang in several operas composed and directed by Jommelli. He was in Italy in 1751–2, when he was called to the court of Lisbon; from there he went in 1755 to Madrid and, in 1759, he travelled with Farinellito Naples.

For the next decade Raaff was the principal tenor on the Neapolitan and Florentine stages, appearing in operas by Hasse, Majo and J. C. Bach, as well as Sacchini, Piccinni, and Mysliveèek. In August 1770 he arrived at Mannheim, Carl Theodor's seat, where he sang the title roles in Piccinni's *Catone in Utica* (1770) and Bach's *Temistocle* (1772) and *Lucio Silla*(1775). Mozart was severely critical of his singing and acting in the title role of Holzbauer's *Günther von Schwarzburg* (1777), but was more sympathetic after hearing him sing Bach's 'Non so d'onde viene' from *Alessandro nell'Indie* at the Concert Spirituel in Paris during June 1778; Mozart tried to win his favour by composing a setting of one of the tenor's favourite texts, 'Se al labbro mio' (K295). Raaff's last role was the title part in *Idomeneo* (1781), composed for Munich where Carl Theodor had transferred his court. Though Raaff's voice was praised by Schubart as having an unusually large range from bass to alto, with flexible coloratura throughout, Mozart found it small in range and limited in technique. Yet Raaff sang well enough in 1787 to impress Michael Kelly, who wrote that 'he still retained his fine *voce di petto* and sostenuto notes, and pure style of singing'. He was one of the last and greatest representatives of the legato technique and portamento, brought to perfection by Bernacchi and his school.

D.H. (with P.C.)

Venanzio Rauzzini

Venanzio Rauzzini was born in Camerino, near Rome, and was baptized on 19 December 1746; he died in Bath, on 8 April 1810. He was an Italian soprano castrato and composer. After early studies in Rome and possibly also in Naples with Porpora, he made his début at the Teatro della Valle in Rome in Piccinni's *Il finto astrologo* (7 February 1765). His first major role was in Guglielmi's *Sesostri* at Venice during Ascension Fair 1766. In the same year he entered the service of the Elector Maximilian III Joseph at Munich, where he remained until 1772. He first appeared there in Traetta's *Siroe* (Carnival 1767) and later that year was given leave to perform at Venice and at Vienna, where Mozart and his father heard him in Hasse's *Partenope*. Burney, visiting Rauzzini in August 1772, praised his virtuosity and the quality of his voice, but was most impressed by his abilities as a composer and harpsichordist. His last known operatic performance in Munich was in Bernasconi's *Demetrio* (Carnival 1772). According to Michael Kelly he was forced to leave because of difficulties with noblewomen engendered by his good looks.

Rauzzini performed for two more years in Italy before moving permanently to England. Engaged for Carnival 1773 at Milan, he was primo uomo in Mozart's *Lucio Silla* (26 December 1772) and in Paisiello's *Sismano nel Mogol* (30 January 1773). In January Mozart wrote for him the brilliant motet *Exsultate, jubilate* K165/158a. Later that year he sang at Venice and Padua, and in 1774 at Turin (Carnival) and Venice (Ascension Fair).

From November 1774 to July 1777 Rauzzini sang regularly at the King's Theatre in London, making his simultaneous début as singer and composer in the pasticcio *Armida*. Bingley reported that his acting in Sacchini's *Montezuma* (7 February 1775) greatly impressed Garrick. Both Burney and Lord Mount Edgcumbe, however, deemed his voice sweet but too feeble, a defect Burney ascribed to Rauzzini's devoting too much time to composition. Indeed, Rauzzini contributed arias to four other pasticcios in the season 1775–6 and wrote a comic opera, *L'ali d'amore*. *Piramo e Tisbe*, his best-loved opera, was first staged in London on 16 March 1775 (and probably not in Munich, 1769, as claimed in many biographical sketches); it was revived there in three other seasons and performed at many continental theatres. In the following years many of his works, both vocal and instrumental, were published in London.

In autumn 1777 Rauzzini took up residence in Bath, where he managed concerts by many renowned performers, among them his pupils John Braham, Nancy Storace, Charles Incledon, Mrs Billington and Mme Mara. At Dublin in 1778 he met and taught Michael Kelly and promoted his career with advice to study in Naples. In spring 1781, again in London, Rauzzini sang in concerts with Tenducci and others and wrote the second act of the opera *L'omaggio di paesani al signore del contado*. He was intermittently in London during the next three seasons to stage his operas *L'eroe cinese*, *Creusa in Delfo* and *Alina, o sia La regina di Golconda*, which was heavily criticized by the *Public Advertiser* (10 May 1784). Ballets with music by him were performed at the King's Theatre in the season 1783–4, and he also directed the production of Sarti's *Le gelosie villane* (15 April 1784). During this period a scandal arose over his claim that certain arias in Sacchini's operas were his own. The London première of his opera *La vestale* (1 May 1787) was unsuccessful, and thereafter he remained permanently at Bath. Near the end of his life Rauzzini published a set of 12 vocal exercises with an introduction summing up his ideas on the art of singing and reflecting his own tasteful execution.

K.K.H.

Teresa Saporiti

Teresa Saporiti [Codecasa] was born in 1763; she died in Milan, on 17 March 1869. As a member of Pasquale Bondini's company she sang, with her sister Antonia (who died 1787) in Leipzig, Dresden and Prague. A report in the *Litteratur und Theater Zeitung* (summer 1782) refers to 'both Demoiselles Saporiti' being engaged for Bondini's company:

The elder, Antonia, had been a concert singer in Leipzig. She sings the most difficult passages with considerable ease; it is a pity that her voice is somewhat small and that she neglects expression in recitatives. Her younger sister is half a beginner as an actress and singer, and is acclaimed only because of her figure . . . the younger Demoiselle Saporiti often appears in man's costume and takes over the role of a castrato, which she does poorly and with a bad grace.

Mozart thought well enough of Saporiti, however, to write elaborate and demanding music for her as Donna Anna in *Don Giovanni* (1787, Prague). She appeared in Venice in P. A. Guglielmi's *Arsace* (1788) and his *Rinaldo* (1789), and in Francesco Bianchi's *Nitteti* at La Scala (1789), and she sang in Bologna, Parma and Modena. In 1795 she was designated *prima buffa assoluta* in a company at St Petersburg, where she achieved a personal success in Cimarosa's *L'italiana in Londra* and Paisiello's *Il barbiere di Siviglia* (1796).

C.R.

Benedikt Schack

Benedikt Emanuel Schack [Cziak, Schak, Žák, Ziak], Austrian composer and tenor of Bohemian origin, was born in Mirotice, on 7 February 1758; he died in Munich, on 10 December 1826. After early musical training from his father, a schoolteacher, he became a pupil and singer at the Jesuit monastery in Przbram-Birkenberg at the age of 11. He later studied at Staré Sedlo and Svatá Hora and, from 1773, in Prague, where he was also a chorister at St Vitus's Cathedral. In 1775 he moved to Vienna to study medicine and took singing lessons with Karl Frieberth. After several years as Kapellmeister to Prince Heinrich von Schönaich-Carolath in Silesia (from 1780), he joined Emanuel Schikaneder's travelling troupe in 1786 as a tenor and composer. The company made visits to Augsburg and Regensburg and shorter stops in other southern cities, including Salzburg. Leopold Mozart commented in a letter to his daughter (26 May 1786) that Schack 'sings excellently, has a beautiful voice, an effortlessly smooth throat and a beautiful method'. Schikaneder and his troupe settled in Vienna, in the Freihaus-Theater auf der Wieden, in 1789. During his four-year stay in Vienna, Schack composed numerous operas for the Wieden stage and sang principal tenor roles in many of the theatre's productions. He became well acquainted with Mozart, who composed the role of Tamino for him (Schack perhaps played the flute parts himself) and also wrote the duet 'Nun liebes Weibchen' (K625/592a) for Schack's opera Der Stein der Weisen. In 1793 Schack secured an appointment in Graz. Three years later, in 1796, he moved to Munich to become a member of the ensemble of the Hoftheater. He seems to have composed no operas there. Around 1813 he was pensioned off because of his declining voice.

Schack composed almost all his operas for suburban theatres and travelling troupes. He was best known for the series of 'Anton' Singspiels that he composed with F. X. Gerl to librettos by Schikaneder. Anton, like the character Kasperl at the rival Theater in der Leopoldstadt, was a descendant of Hanswurst and Bernardon from Viennese comedies of the early and mid-18th century. In the 'Anton'

Singspiels and others like them – in contrast to the scenically and musically elaborate heroic-comic operas like *Die Zauberflöte* – the serious portions of the plot were played down, the central comic character became the focus of the story, and the music consisted most often of short numbers based on a popular folk style. Schack's *Der dumme Gärtner*, the first and most successful of the 'Anton' works, serves as a representative example. Several of the solos are strophic lieder with square-cut phrasing and simple melodies, while others depend on two- and three-part forms and a few have a two-tempo (slow-fast) format. The ensembles are the most extended numbers of the work; several changes of tempo, conversational interaction between characters and *buffo* -style patter set them apart from the solos and choruses. There is little or no use in the work of recitative, coloratura or complex orchestral writing.

Der dumme Gärtner, along with numerous other Viennese suburban Singspiels, found favour on stages throughout Germany. In some northern cities the texts of many of these works were revised while the music was retained. In the foreword to a revised libretto of *Der dumme Gärtner* (Leipzig, 1797) the editor explains that

The work's provincial veneer was always such an obstacle, that one could not perform it outside its fatherland; many connoisseurs and friends of comic opera often wished for an arrangement for other stages. Here is an attempt, in which the originality of this piece was retained as much as possible.

This type of treatment contrasted with the frequent practice in southern theatres (both national and suburban) of adopting librettos from the north but having them set to new music. Schack's regular collaboration with Gerl in composing operas was of a sort not unusual for the Theater auf der Wieden in the 1790s. Schikaneder regularly commissioned compositional 'teams' (another prominent duo was Ignaz von Seyfried and Matthäus Stegmayr) to set librettos written by himself or others: the most likely reason for this was the heavy production schedule, which demanded new Singspiels every month. Schack's recognition as an opera composer, resting mostly on the 'Anton' Singspiels and *Der Stein der Weisen*, declined rapidly after the 1790s, with the number of performances of his works steadily decreasing.

L.T.

Nancy Storace

Nancy [Ann Selina; Anna] Storace was born in London, on 27 October 1765; she died in Dulwich, on 24 August 1817. She was the daughter of Stefano Storace, an Italian double bass player, translator of Italian opera into English and adapter, and sister of Stephen Storace. A vocal prodigy, she appeared in Southampton in 1773 as 'a Child not eight Years old'; her first London concert was at the Haymarket Theatre in April the following year. On 29 February 1776 she appeared with the celebrated Caterina Gabrielli in the première of Venanzio Rauzzini's *Le ali d'amore*. Her teachers in London were Rauzzini and Sacchini. In 1778 she followed her brother to Italy where she began her career in *opera seria*, singing seconda donna roles, Phoebe and Ebe, in Bianchi's *Castore e Polluce* (1779, Florence); this was followed by appearances in revivals of comic opera (1780–81) in which she took both *prima seria* and *prima buffa* roles. In 1782 she sang in Milan, Turin, Parma, Rome and Venice. The first opera composed for her specifically was one of the most acclaimed of its time, Sarti's *Fra i due litiganti il terzo gode* (1782, Milan); Kelly, who sang with her in Venice at the Teatro San Samuele in 1783 recalled that she 'drew overflowing houses' and was 'quite the rage' and when 'she announced a benefit, the first ever given to any performer at Venice . . . the kind-hearted and liberal Venetians not only paid the usual entrance money, but left all kinds of trinkets, watch chains, rings, etc., to be given her'.

This celebrity caused the Viennese ambassador to Venice, Count Giacomo Durazzo, to engage her for the newly-organized Italian opera in Vienna the same year. For her début she sang the role created for her at the San Samuele, the Countess in Salieri's *La scuola dei gelosi*. During her first season at the Burgtheater, Storace sang in half of the 14 productions; her contract provided for a salary achieved by only the most sought-after singers of the day. In late 1783 she married the composer J.A. Fisher, but he apparently treated her cruelly and they soon parted; in 1786–7 she had a close relationship with Lord Barrard. Her years in Vienna (1783–7) are important for the roles that major composers (Paisiello, Martín y Soler, Mozart) created for her. Her early vocal training and her experience in serious opera in Italy had helped her acquire vocal and dramatic resources that she could integrate into her comic performances; composers responded with roles of stylistic richness and variety. Her vocal qualities can be inferred from her music in the greatest operas written for her, Mozart's *Le nozze di Figaro* and Martín y Soler's *Una cosa rara* (this latter the greatest popular triumph of Viennese music theatre). Both Susanna and Lilla exploit her formidable dramatic talents, her precise declamation and her preference for melodies within a limited vocal range and in *nota e parola* style. Mozart's sensitivity to Storace's low tessitura caused him to begin composing the role of Susanna below that of the Countess (subsequently reversed). Although Storace's music on occasion contained bravura elements, it is rarely ambitious in range or difficulty. Similar vocal writing is found in Mozart's other compositions for Storace, which include a single aria from the aborted *Lo sposo deluso* and the concert aria 'Chi'io mi scordi di te ... Non temer amato bene' (for her farewell concert in Vienna).

In February 1787 Storace, her mother, the composer Thomas Attwood and Michael Kelly left for London where on 24 April she appeared in Paisiello's *Gli schiavi per amore* at the King's Theatre, Haymarket, for which she was provided additional arias by her brother, Corri and Mazzinghi. Stephen wrote that his sister 'has had great opposition from the Italians – who consider it as an infringement on their rights – that any person should be able to sing that was not born in Italy'. In 1789 she moved to Drury Lane to join her brother for the 1789–90 season, and on 24 November 1789 she made her début as Adelia in her brother's *The Haunted Tower*, for which she received top billing (unusual for a woman on London playbills); its great success was in large measure due to its prima donna and her large-scale italianate piece, 'Be mine tender passion'. Other leading roles in operas by her brother included Margaretta in *No Song, no Supper*, Lilla in *The Siege of Belgrade* and Fabulina in *The Pirates*. There is reason to think she had a close relationship with the Prince of Wales in the early 1790s, when he, the Duke of Bedford and the Marquis of Salisbury attempted to hire her for their secret court theatre at the Pantheon concert hall in Oxford Street. She sang at the King's Theatre for a season in 1793. After her brother's death in 1796 she left Drury Lane and in 1797 she and her lover, the tenor John Braham, left for a tour of the Continent. Her farewell performance, and that of her friend Kelly, was at Drury Lane in *No Song, no Supper* in 1808.

After her death in 1817 Storace was underpraised by English writers. Burney called her 'a lively and intelligent actress' but said her voice had 'a certain crack and roughness' and 'a deficiency of natural sweetness'. Lord Mount Edgcumbe wrote that she was unfitted for serious opera and was undoubtedly most successful in comic parts: 'In her own particular line . . . she was unrivalled, being an excellent actress, as well as a masterly singer'. These evaluations suggest that it could not have been her virtuosity or purity of tone that made her voice so compelling to composers but rather that her intelligence, wit and charm inspired some of the most vocally and dramatically incisive music of its time.

P.L.G., B.M.

Therese Teyber

Theresa Teyber was born in Vienna, and baptized on 15 October 1760; she died in Vienna on 15 April 1830. She was the sister of Elisabeth Teyber, herself a soprano. A pupil of Bonno and Tesi, she made her début at the Vienna court theatre as Fiametta in Ulbrich's *Frühling und Liebe* (1778). Teyber was a popular portrayer of young lovers and artless girls and created the role of Blonde in *Die Entführung aus dem Serail* (1782); she also appeared with success in many other operas and Singspiels. The charm of her acting and singing was praised in contemporary reviews. She and her husband, the tenor Ferdinand Arnold, are reported to have performed together with much success at Hamburg, Berlin, Warsaw and Riga, though the chronology of these appearances is confused. Therese probably appeared as Zerlina in the later Viennese performances of *Don Giovanni* (1788) and is certainly the 'Mad:elle taäuber' ('Teyber') referred to in Mozart's letter of 29 March 1783.

P.B.

Louise Villeneuve

In 1787–8 the soprano Louise [Luisa, Luigia].Villeneuve sang in Venice in operas by Guglielmi and Martín y Soler; in Milan in 1788 her roles included Amore in Martín's *L'arbore di Diana*. She spent 1789–90 and 1790–91 in Vienna, making her début on 27 June 1789 as Amore, when she was admired for 'her charming appearance, her sensitive and expressive acting and her artful, beautiful singing' (*Wiener Zeitung*, lii (1789), 1673). Mozart supplied arias for her in Cimarosa's *I due baroni* (K 578) and Martín's *Il burbero di buon cuore* (K 582–3), and wrote for her Dorabella in *Così fan tutte* (26 January 1790), alluding in her Act 2 aria to her role as Amore. There is no evidence that, as is often stated, she was the sister of Adriana Ferrarese, who sang Fiordiligi. Zinzendorf noted in his diary (11 February 1791) that she caught the fancy of Leopold II. She appeared in Livorno in 1794.

D.L.

Dorothea Wendling

Born Dorothea Spurni in Stuttgart, on 21 March 1736; she died in Munich, on 20 August 1811. The daughter of a Stuttgart horn player, she was appointed a singer at the Mannheim court in 1752; on 9 January of that year she married the flautist Johann Baptist Wendling. Her first role was Hermione in Galuppi's *Antigona* (17 January 1753). In 1758 she sang the prima donna role in Holzbauer's *Nitteti* and for the next 20 years was the most celebrated soprano at Mannheim. Her salary, 1200 florins in 1759, increased to 1500 in 1778. She appeared in serious operas by Jommelli, Holzbauer, Piccinni and J.C. Bach, and took the title roles in Traetta's *Sofonisba* (1762) and Majo's *Ifigenia in Tauride* (1764). She also sang in the Italian comic operas performed at Mannheim in the 1770s, and appeared in more than 30 roles in 25 years. Mozart admired her voice and wrote the concert aria K486*a*/295*a* for her in 1778. Wieland, who heard her during rehearsals for Schweitzer's *Rosamunde*, wrote to Sophie La Roche: 'Her style of singing surpasses everything I have ever heard, even the famous Mara'. Heinse and Schubart praised her as one of the most expressive singers of the day, though the latter also mentioned an unfortunate 'warble'. She remained active after the court transferred to Munich in 1778, and created the title roles in Holzbauer's *La morte di Didone* (1779, Mannheim) and J.P. Verazi's *Laodamia* (1780, Oggersheim). She appeared as a guest in Munich, singing Calipso in Franz Paul Grua's *Telemaco* (1780) and Ilia in Mozart's *Idomeneo* (1781). After she left the stage, she continued to sing in concerts and taught singing in Mannheim and Munich. Her daughter, Elisabeth Augusta, also occasionally performed in comic operas at Mannheim and Schwetzingen.

P.C.

Elisabeth Wendling

Born Elisabeth Augusta Sarselli in Mannheim, on 20 February 1746, she died in Munich, on 10 January 1786. Her parents, the tenor Pietro Sarselli and his wife Carolina, were singers at Mannheim. She accompanied her future husband to Italy in 1760 and after her return to Mannheim in 1761 was appointed a court musician. She married Franz Wendling, the violinist and brother of Johann Baptist, on 1 December 1764. Beginning with the role of Cirene in Traetta's *Sofonisba* (1762), she was cast in the seconda donna roles at the Hoftheater, singing opposite her sister-in-law, Dorothea. She accompanied the court to Munich in 1778, and there created her most famous role, Electra in Mozart's *Idomeneo* (1781). She also sang the title role in Salieri's *Semiramide* (1782); her last role was Zelmira in Prati's *Armida abbandonata* (1785).

P.C.

Cities

Milan

The capital of Lombardy, Milan is the home of the most famous Italian opera house, the Teatro alla Scala, and has been a principal centre of Italian opera since the late 18th century, when it was the main city from which northern Italy was governed.

Religious processions with music and dialogue are known in Milan from the 14th century, and stage entertainments with music, song and dancing became popular at court during the 15th and 16th centuries. An important forerunner of opera was the eclogue *Arminia* by Giambattista Visconte and the *intermedi*, by Camillo Schiaffenati, were perhaps the first in Milan to include music in recitative style.

At the beginning of the 17th century Milan could offer few original theatrical productions, but it was ready to welcome those from other cities, in particular from Venice. Around the middle of the 17th century, however, the predominance of Venetian works in Milan gave way to operas by local composers, only for there to be a return to the Venetian repertory a few years later.

At the start of the 18th century, Austrian government replaced Spanish rule in Milan. This was the beginning of a new age of prosperity and peace which lasted until 1796 and saw a flowering of culture and the arts and an increasing addiction to spectacles and entertainments. Relations between Milan and Vienna were close and continuous, with exchanges of operas, musicians and singers.

On 26 December 1717 the new Regio Ducal theatre was inaugurated. For 59 years, until 25 February 1776 when it in turn burnt down, this was the centre of musical and social life in Milan. The city was still not a creative or dynamic force in opera, but rather an eclectic and receptive centre open to widely varying tendencies.

Comic opera was popular in Milan and from 1745 had its own spring season. Later the *opera buffa* season was fixed in the autumn and three different operas were produced, so that comic opera acquired the same importance as *opera seria*, two of which were performed between 26 December and the last day of the Ambrosian carnival, the Saturday after Ash Wednesday.

Maria Theresa, who acceded to the imperial throne in 1740, did not enjoy music or spectacular entertainment, but realized that the theatre was a social necessity in Italy and thought it wise to allow opera in Milan. The arrival of Francesco III d'Este, Duke of Modena, as governor of Milan in 1754, and even more the active presence of his minister plenipotentiary Count Firmian and the supreme chancellor Wenzel von Kaunitz, ensured a central role in city life for the Regio Ducal Teatro, which had been restored and improved at the expense of the Cavalieri Direttori in 1752.

In the second half of the 18th century Milan was one of the most enlightened of Italian cultural centres, with thinkers and men of letters such as the Verri, Cesare Beccaria and Giuseppe Parini; in instrumental music the innovations of Sammartini heralded Viennese Classicism. In opera, however, Milanese taste was still narrowly traditional, with little room for the innovatory ideas of Gluck and Calzabigi, whose *Orfeo* was received with admiration in Vienna in 1762. When the Cavalieri Direttori decided to produce *Alceste*, Gluck's music was rejected and a new score composed by P. A. Guglielmi. Parini had the task of revising Calzabigi's libretto, adding irrelevant arias to please the singers and trivializing the plot. Calzabigi was indignant, and Parini defended himself by saying that he had done the work 'to suit the unavoidable present circumstances of our theatre', which according to Calzabigi meant 'to draw out the performance to the ridiculous length of five hours and to be able to have supper during the performance'. Moreover, the insertion of ballets between acts of serious and even comic operas had become custom since about 1738. This then was the atmosphere in Milan when the young Mozart visited the city for the first time early in 1770.

At the palace of Count Firmian he met many musicians, including Sammartini, and was commissioned to write an opera for the Regio Ducal Teatro. He returned to Milan to conduct the opera, *Mitridate, re di Ponto*, on 26 December. There was an orchestra of 60, with Lampugnani at the harpsichord, and the singers included Antonia Bernasconi and Guglielmo Ettore. Mozart's next visit to Milan (21 August–5 December 1771) was in connection with the important commission he had received for a *festa teatrale*, *Ascanio in Alba*, to a text by Parini on the occasion of the marriage of Archduke Ferdinand of Austria and Maria Ricciarda Beatrice d'Este of Modena. The main work was *Il Ruggiero* by the 72-year-old Hasse to a libretto by the elderly Metastasio, performed in the Regio Ducal Teatro on 17 October 1771; *Ascanio in Alba* was given with greater success the following evening by Giovanni Manzuoli and Antonia Maria Girelli. Mozart was in Milan for the last time in 1772–3, when the third opera he wrote for the theatre, *Lucio Silla* to a libretto by De Gamerra (who had been appointed the theatre's poet in 1771), was performed on 26 December 1772, with Anna De Amicis and Venanzio Rauzzini.

At the turn of the 19th century Milan began to develop into a modern city based on the activity of a prosperous middle class, which eventually turned it into the most important industrial centre of Italy. Lombardy was returned to Austrian control in 1815; renewed Viennese connections resulted in a large patrician and upper class supporting cultural life.

A new era began with the success of Rossini (*La pietra del paragone*, 1812), who quickly came to dominate Italian opera along with Donizetti and Bellini; from then on, Milan's musical history became virtually identified with that of Italian opera, of which La Scala was perhaps the most notable centre (it was also at that time that cycles of Mozart operas began to be mounted there).

By the 1830s La Scala was one of the leading opera houses in Europe; 40 premières were given in that decade and in 1839 Verdi's first opera, *Oberto, conte di San Bonifacio*, was performed there. Ricordi bought the publishing rights, and the theatre's director, Bartolomeo Merelli, commissioned three more operas from the young composer. The first, *Un giorno di regno*, was a failure and was withdrawn after its first performance in 1840, but *Nabucco* (1842) and *I Lombardi alla prima crociata* (1843) were great successes; in fact, *I Lombardi* came to represent the drive towards unification, and the patriotic choruses often incited demonstrations in the theatre. Although Verdi is closely associated with La Scala, his career there was chequered, and his works until *Otello* in 1887 had their premières elsewhere (with the exception of revisions); there was hissing and chatter during the Milan performances of *La forza del destino*, *Un ballo in maschera* and *Aida*, and Milanese critics accused Verdi of not knowing how to write for singers and of imitating Wagner. The Requiem, written for Manzoni, was given at La Scala in 1874 only a few days after its first performance at S Marco, and Verdi did return to La Scala with the premières of his last two operas, *Otello* (1887) and *Falstaff* (1893). Many other Italian composers were presented at La Scala during the second half of the 19th century, including Petrella, Faccio, Marchetti, Boito, Ponchielli and Catalani. The works of foreign composers were also brought to the theatre and, after initial failure, Wagner's operas were enthusiastically received under Franco Faccio's direction.

Throughout the 19th century alterations and improvements were made to the theatre, the most important of which were the enlargement of the stage in 1807, the overall restoration in 1838, and the removal in 1857 of the tall houses that had made it impossible to have a perspective view of the façade. Gas lighting was installed in 1860 and electric lighting in 1883. There have traditionally been four annual seasons: Carnival to Lent (initially reserved for *opere serie*), and autumn, spring and summer, when *opere buffe* were mounted. The administration of La Scala had at first been supported by the proceeds of the dramatic company which used the theatre until 1803, but from 1806 to 1918 the theatre was supported, with varying success, by its joint owners: the state, then the city, box holders, impresarios and patrons. During the Austrian Restoration, the administration was in the hands of the government, but afterwards the theatre attracted such adventurous impresarios as Domenico Barbaia (1826–32) and Bartolomeo Merelli (1835–50 and 1861–3). In 1897 the city withdrew its subsidy and Duke Guido Visconti di Modrone formed a syndicate to take over the theatre's management, appointing Toscanini artistic director in 1898, with Giulio Gatti-Casazza as manager.

Milan continued to grow as a thriving industrial city supporting a wide range of musical activity. La Scala further expanded its prestige and, in addition to presenting the standard repertory and works by Puccini, Franchetti, Leoncavallo and Giordano, mounted the first Italian productions of many foreign works, including Tchaikovsky's

Yevgeny Onegin (1900), Strauss's *Salome* (1906), *Elektra* (1908) and *Rosenkavalier* (1911), Debussy's *Pelléas et Mélisande* (1908), Musorgsky's *Boris Godunov* (1909) and Falla's *La vida breve* (1934). After World War II several important works had their premières there, for instance J. J. Castro's *Proserpina e lo extranjero* (1952), Poulenc's *Dialogues des Carmélites* (1957), Pizzetti's *L'assassinio nella cattedrale* (1958) and *Il calzare d'argento* (1961), Stockhausen's *Donnerstag aus Licht* (1981), *Samstag aus Licht* (1984; see fig.7) and *Montag aus Licht* (1988), Berio's *La vera storia* (1982), Bernstein's *A Quiet Place* and *Trouble in Tahiti* (1984), Donatoni's *Atem* and Testi's *Riccardo III* (1987). Many other operas had their Italian premières in Milan, including Britten's *Peter Grimes* (1947), Prokofiev's *The Love for Three Oranges* (1947), Walton's *Troilus and Cressida* (1956) and Janáček's *The Cunning Little Vixen* (1958).

In 1920 the theatre had become a self-governing body, Ente Autonomo del Teatro alla Scala; Toscanini was reappointed artistic director and established a reputation for consistent excellence in performances during what was called 'the great Toscanini period'. He formed a new orchestra of 100 players and a chorus of 120; while the stage and auditorium were being reconstructed he took the company on a tour of Italy, the USA and Canada. His regime culminated in the company's visit to Vienna and Berlin in 1929.

After being seriously damaged by bombing in 1943, La Scala was one of the first buildings in Milan to be rebuilt after the war. It was reconstructed to the original designs (capacity now 3000) and was reopened on 11 May 1948 with a concert conducted by Toscanini including works by Rossini, Verdi, Boito and Puccini.

M.D.

Munich

In Munich, capital of Bavaria, opera as now understood began with courtly musical spectacles on mythological subjects and featuring allegorical characters, performed as acts of homage from about the mid 17th century. Until the later 18th century Italian court opera reigned supreme, but German Singspiel gained an increasingly firm foothold thereafter.

The origins of musical and theatrical life in Munich go back to the Middle Ages. From 1253 onwards it was the seat of the Wittelsbach dukes of Bavaria. Duke Albrecht III (1435–60), whose first wife, Agnes Bernauer, took an interest in music and literature, laid the foundations for theatrical development by encouraging the humanist *Schuldrama*. Munich reached a cultural peak on the occasion of the famous royal wedding of Duke Wilhelm to Renée of Lorraine in 1568. Contemporary accounts record that an Italian *commedia dell'arte* was presented for the first time with the cooperation of Orlando de Lassus, who also performed the musical interludes with instrumentalists and singers of the Hofkapelle. After a period of stagnation under Duke Wilhelm V 'the Pious' (1579–98), artistic pursuits at court began to revive; Bavaria was raised to the status of an electorate in 1623, and Ferdinand Maria (1651–79) and his highly gifted wife Adelaide of Savoy were responsible for the introduction of Italian opera.

Italian opera flourished during the first decade of rule by the artistically inclined Elector Maximilian II Emanuel (1679–1726). Even at this early date, German operas were occasionally performed, though German Singspiel could not have offered Italian opera any serious competition. The cultural life of Munich suffered a great blow when Maximilian Emanuel became governor of the Spanish Netherlands in 1691; the entire élite of the court, including the director of the Kammermusik Torri and the Konzertmeister E.F. Dall'Abaco, moved to Brussels with him. Only church and chamber music continued to be regularly performed at the ducal residence in Munich. The period between Maximilian Emanuel's return in 1715 and his death in 1726 restored the musical life of Munich to its former glory; despite French influences, however, Italian opera still predominated.

Although Elector Carl Albert (1726–45, Emperor Carl VII from 1742) also liked magnificence, unpropitious political developments (the reoccupation of Bavaria as a result of the War of the Austrian Succession) eventually made it impossible for him to maintain the high cultural standards previously established. Maximilian III Joseph (1745–77), however, raised a new monument to opera when he commissioned the Residenztheater, built by François Cuvilliés (hence, also known as the Cuvilliéstheater). It was ceremonially opened in 1753.

Count Joseph Anton von Seeau contributed to the development of musical drama in the city when he succeeded Count Joseph Ferdinand Maria von Salern in 1756 as Intendant of all the theatres (the Residenztheater, the Opernhaus am Salvatorplatz, the Redoutensaal, the Turnierhaus and the Färberbräu-Saal). While the Residenztheater was reserved for *opera seria* and ballet, middle-class audiences in particular were catered for in the old Opernhaus am Salvatorplatz. Mozart's *La finta giardiniera* had its première there in 1775, while *Idomeneo*, composed for Carnival 1781, was performed in the Residenztheater. Seeau's term of office saw a quantitative increase in productions. During Carnival, German Singspiels, usually translations of *opéra comique* and *opera buffa*, were performed on Sundays in the Salvatorplatz theatre, and court society then attended a ball in the Redoutensaal. Monday was set aside for *opera seria*, concluding with a ballet, Tuesday and Thursday for *opera buffa* (also with a concluding ballet), Wednesday and Friday for plays; only on Saturday was there no theatrical performance.

Now that *opera buffa* in German translation had become well established, from the 1770s onwards the German Singspiel finally made a breakthrough, after over a century of dominance by Italian opera. Theobald Hilarius Marchand introduced the *opéra comique* to Munich, and for the first time French influence really made itself felt, although it could not yet displace Italian opera. Not until the end of the 1780s can a decline in the popularity of *opera seria* be traced. The genre had one of its last successes with Vogler's carnival opera

Castore e Polluce (1787); in the same year Carl Theodor issued a decree prohibiting Italian opera. The Hof-National-Schaubühne, which opened that year with Anton Schweitzer's *Alceste*, set the tone. After 45 years in his post, Seeau left the Munich theatres in a state of remarkable mismanagement (the reasons are still obscure because the records have disappeared), and after his death in 1799 it was hard for much progress in theatrical affairs to be made under the direction of Josef Marius Babo. The ban on Italian opera was not lifted until 1805, a year before Bavaria became a kingdom.

The records indicate that Weber's Singspiel *Abu Hassan*, given its première in 1811 at the Residenztheater, met with a friendly reception. In the same year, however, King Max I laid the foundation stone of a new and larger Königliches Hof- und Nationaltheater; built in Max-Joseph-Platz to plans by the architect Carl von Fischer, it opened in 1818 but burnt down on 14 January 1823. Rebuilding began at once, with Leo von Klenze as architect. He made use of Fischer's plans and largely reconstructed the old façade, while adding new touches of his own.

In 1836 Franz Paul Lachner was appointed chief conductor and principal musical director; in practice, he was general musical director of Bavaria. Lachner, a close friend of Schubert, established Munich's reputation as an operatic centre. Initially he produced the works of Beethoven and Mozart, but soon concentrated on the work of such contemporaries as Spohr, Marschner, Lortzing and Flotow, and also extended the repertory to include French and Italian opera. With the first performance in Munich of *Ernani* in 1848 he began a series of productions of Verdi, who conducted several of the German premières of his own operas in Munich. Lachner had conducted the first Munich performances of *Tannhäuser* and *Lohengrin* in 1855 and 1858, but he retired when Wagner's connections with Munich became closer after 1864 through his friendship with King Ludwig II, and the city prepared to become a Wagnerian centre, as it were by royal decree.

In 1851 Franz von Dingelstedt became Intendant of the Nationaltheater, where plays had long been performed alongside opera. He paid special attention to spoken drama, and instigated the reopening of the Residenztheater to provide it with a stage of its own. When he left his post in 1858, the court musical director Karl von Perfall took over the direction of the court opera. He remained in the post until 1893, and his time in office thus covers the greater period of Wagnerian productions in Munich, coinciding with the reign of Ludwig II up to the time of the king's death in 1886. Hans von Bülow was Hofkapellmeister for part of that time, and he conducted the premières of *Tristan und Isolde* (1865) and *Die Meistersinger* (1868). In 1869 and 1870 Franz Wüllner, as principal musical director, gave the premières of *Das Rheingold* and *Die Walküre*. However, Munich could not continue to be so much of a Wagnerian centre, as relations between the composer and the king cooled and Wagner looked to Bayreuth. Perfall founded the Munich Opera Festival, whose origins and traditions constitute a chapter of great importance in operatic history up to the present day. The first summer festival was in 1875, with productions of operas by Mozart and Wagner. Two keystones of the continuing Munich operatic tradition were thus in place (another – Richard Strauss – was added later).

Perfall also tried to achieve continuity of conductors; he had appointed Hermann Levi from Karlsruhe in 1872, and Levi was to stay at Munich until his death in 1900. His influence on the musical life of the city cannot be valued too highly. He greatly increased the importance of the operatic festivals, purged the performance style of arbitrary additions or alterations perpetrated by contemporary taste, continued to promote the works of Mozart, Gluck, Weber and of course Wagner, and also encouraged young composers such as Peter Cornelius, Wilhelm Kienzl and Richard Strauss. While Ernst Possart was director of the Hoftheater (1893–1905) the Prinzregententheater was built, and a separate chapter in the history of opera in Munich began. Meanwhile Herman Zumpe and Felix Mottl had also occupied the post of principal conductor at the Hofoper. Both died in harness as conductors, Mottl in 1911 after his 100th performance of *Tristan*. With great personal commitment, Mottl had prepared the ground in Munich for Richard Strauss and his *Salome* and *Elektra*, thus completing the triumvirate of opera composers which forms the backbone of the Munich repertory, consolidated on 1 February 1911 when Mottl conducted the first performance in Munich of *Der Rosenkavalier*.

Bruno Walter was principal musical director from 1913 to 1922, followed by Hans Knappertsbusch in 1922 (the Hofoper was renamed the Bayerische Staatsoper in that year). Knappertsbusch and other conductors, either employed by Munich or performing as guest artists, brought renown to the Staatsoper, and extended the repertory at the Nationaltheater and the Prinzregententheater to include Strauss and Pfitzner.

Knappertsbusch resigned in 1935, and in 1937 Clemens Krauss became both opera director and general musical director. As musical interpreter, Krauss consolidated the house's connections with Mozart, Wagner and Strauss, but he also gave strong encouragement to Italian opera and became associated with Carl Orff and Werner Egk. The last notable events of this period to win fame internationally were the premières of Strauss's *Friedenstag* (1938) and *Capriccio* (1942), conducted by Krauss.

On the night of 3 October 1943 the Nationaltheater was destroyed during an air raid. Only the outer walls and the entrance façade remained. Operatic performances resumed after the end of World War II, in the renovated Prinzregententheater (seating 873). The Staatsoper began work again under its new director Georg Hartmann, from whom Rudolf Hartmann took over in 1952.

It was some time before the Nationaltheater was rebuilt. In the end it was possible to restore the 'famous and beloved house' (to use Rudolf Hartmann's description) only with considerable help from the citizens of Munich and the active participation of the city's artistic society. Deciding to rebuild and getting the reconstruction done took 18 years. The theatre (seating 2100) was reopened on 21 November 1963 with Rudolf Hartmann as Intendant and Joseph Keilberth as general musical director.

Since 1958 the company had also given regular performances in the new Residenztheater (seating 523), rebuilt – in the same style as the old theatre – on another site in the Munich Residenz after having been bombed in the war.

The repertory of the Staatsoper still rests on Mozart, Wagner and Strauss – during the 1980s complete cycles of Strauss and Wagner were performed – but operas from the Italian, Slavonic and Russian repertory are also given, as well as modern works. The season is from September to July, with the festival in July; the première of Penderecki's *Ubu Rex* was given at the 1991 festival.

J.L., K.J.S.

Prague

Prague, capital city of Czechoslovakia from 1918 and from 1992 of the Czech Republic, and formerly capital of Bohemia, has been an important operatic centre since the 18th century, first as an outpost of the Habsburg empire, and later as the focal point of Czech nationalism.

The first operatic performance in Prague took place on 27 November 1627 at the castle on the occasion of the coronation of Ferdinand III, when a company from Mantua presented 'eine schöne Pastoral-Comoedia', perhaps composed by G. B. Buonamente. This new art form was unconnected with any native tradition in Bohemia, but its history was naturally influenced by the political situation in the Czech lands in the 17th century. Following the resignation of Rudolf II in 1611 the imperial court had moved from Prague to Vienna; after defeat in the Battle of White Mountain (1620), the greater part of the non-Catholic nobility had to leave Bohemia. Courtly entertainment therefore found little room in Prague; the aristocratic culture that arrived from Vienna developed slowly, at the country seats of the nobility as much as in Prague itself. The imperial court was twice more situated in Prague during the 17th century, when operas were staged, among other works. Of great importance, over 40 years later, were the court festivities marking the coronation of Charles VI as Emperor of Bohemia (August 1723), which included the première of Fux's *Costanza e Fortezza*. The open-air stage was 63 metres in depth, and the sets and machines were designed by Giuseppe Galli-Bibiena.

The cultivation of Italian opera at the palaces of the aristocracy after 1650 is little documented, since nowhere was a long tradition established. There were theatres in the Eggenberg-Schwarzenberg palace at Hradèany (built in 1660), in the garden of Count Franz Anton Sporck's residence (built in 1701 and open to the public; until 1725 only spoken drama is documented), in the Clam-Gallas palace (after 1700), in the Kolovrat palace in the Old Town (1743), in the Wallenstein palace in the Little Quarter and (after 1770) in the Thun palace, also in the Little Quarter. It was to the Thun palace that the nobility invited the impresario Pasquale Bondini in 1781, and it was there that a castrato appeared for the last time in Prague.

The first opera impresario to work in Prague was apparently G. F. Sartorio, who was there between 1701 and 1705. He staged Italian operas to a paying audience at the Regnard house in the Little Quarter. In 1724 Count Sporck invited Antonio Denzio's Italian company to his summer palace at Kuks, and from 1725 to 1734 the same company also performed at his theatre in Prague. Denzio presented 57 operas by Vivaldi (several of them premières), Albinoni, Porta and others. During the period 1737–40 a company directed by the composer Santo Lapis performed in Prague, first at Count Sporck's theatre and later in the new theatre at Kotce known as the Comoedia-Haus or the Kotzen Opera (sometimes called simply the 'Nuovo Teatro'). This opened in 1738 or 1739 in a former commercial building; the stage measured 13 by 13 metres and the auditorium 46 by 13 metres. It was the main venue for performances (mostly of *opera buffa*) by Italian companies. The most important impresarios at Kotce were Angelo and Pietro Mingotti (1743–6), who put on operas by Pergolesi, Pinazzi, Galuppi, Vinci and Gluck; G. B. Locatelli (1748–57), who mounted the premières of Gluck's *Ezio* (1750) and *Issipile* (1752), as well as operas by Galuppi and others; J. F. von Kurz (1758–64) and his lessee Molinari, with operas by Galuppi, Auletta and Fischietti; and Giuseppe Bustelli (1764–81), who put on works by Galuppi, Piccinni, Guglielmi, Mysliveček and Kozeluch, while his lessees J.J. Brunian (1769–78) and Karl Wahr presented Singspiels, including *Die Entführung aus dem Serail* in 1782. The theatre at Kotce closed in 1783.

On 21 April 1783 the Nostitzsches Nationaltheater, built by Count F. A. Nostitz (1725–94) with a capacity of over 1000 and a stage measuring 18 by 16 metres, was opened; until 1862 it was Prague's main opera house. Among its early lessees were Bondini (1784–8) and Domenico Guardasoni (1788–1806). They both presented operas by Mozart: *Le nozze di Figaro* in 1786 and subsequent years, the premières of *Don Giovanni* (1787, commissioned by Bondini for royal wedding celebrations) and *La clemenza di Tito* (1791, commissioned by Guardasoni for the festivities surrounding the coronation of Leopold II), and a revival of *Die Zauberflöte* (1792). Guardasoni was the last impresario in Prague to maintain Italian as the language of performance. His productions included works by Cimarosa and Paisiello, as well as German Singspiels. In 1798 the theatre was purchased by the Bohemian Estates; as the Stavovské Divadlo or Ständetheater (Estates Theatre) it became a centre for German opera. C. M. von Weber worked there as conductor from 1813 to 1816, presenting, among other works, Beethoven's *Fidelio* (1814), the première of Spohr's *Faust* (1816) and a number of French operas. His *Der Freischütz* was performed in Prague 50 times between 1821 and 1823. From 1827 to 1857 the conductor was F. J. _kroup, who chose an exacting repertory: Meyerbeer (from 1835), Verdi (for the first time in 1849), *Tannhäuser* (1854), *Lohengrin* (1856) and *Der fliegende Holländer* (1856). Between 1850 and 1860 Meyerbeer, Donizetti, Flotow, Verdi, Mozart, Rossini and Wagner were the composers most frequently performed. Most of the aristocratic theatres had ceased to exist by 1800, but the nobility continued to support performances by the Prague Conservatory, which presented operas by Mozart between 1828 and 1831 at the theatre of Count Vrtba (*La clemenza di Tito*, 1828; *Die Entführung*, 1829) and later at the Dominican monastery (*Così fan tutte*, 1839) and at the Estates Theatre (*Don Giovanni*, 1842; *Figaro*, 1843).

The first serious attempts to stage opera in Czech occurred only in the late 18th century. Czech theatre had for a long time lacked the support of the nobility and the wealthy, and was starved of good professional forces. At Kotce Czech arrangements of Singspiels and, later, translations of Italian operas were presented, and after 1770 Bustelli and Wahr put on original operas in Czech. In 1786 Bondini's Vlastenské Divadlo (Patriotic Theatre) company began to perform in Czech and German at a new wooden theatre, and from 1789 to 1802 the same company presented about 50 works in Czech at the U Hybernů monastery, including Mozart's *Die Zauberflöte* in 1794 and operas by Süssmayr, Dittersdorf, Müller, Kauer and Tuèek.

For a time from 1862, opera in German was given only at the Estates Theatre, which had to cope with difficult operational problems. From 1885 to 1910 its director was Angelo Neumann, who substantially raised the standard, and in 1885–6 Mahler was conductor. Mozart operas continued to be performed here. But in 1888 the Deutscher Theaterverein opened the Neues Deutsches Theater as the chief German theatre in Prague. It was served by a series of outstanding conductors, including Otto Klemperer (1907–10), Alexander Zemlinsky (1911–27), Georg Szell (1929–37), and Karl Rankl (1937–8).

A speciality of the theatre were 'Maifestspiele' – opera cycles within which Italian seasons were also included during the periods 1899–1914 and 1927–35. The repertory was dominated by Wagner: 719 performances of operas by him were given during the years 1888–1918, as well as 337 of Verdi, 225 of Mozart, 154 of Meyerbeer and 108 of Bizet.

After 1945 the Estates Theatre became a second stage for the National Theatre under the name Tylovo Divadlo (Tyl Theatre; now the Estates Theatre) and continued to present only operas by Mozart and plays. In 1977–83 the National Theatre was reconstructed and the Nová Scéna (New Stage) built to present plays and, occasionally, chamber operas.

J.L.

Salzburg

From the 8th century until 1806 the Austrian city of Salzburg was the seat of a series of prince-archbishops, whose court became the centre of the city's musical life; it is specially noted in the 20th century for its festival.

The archbishop Marcus Sitticus von Hohenems, who reigned from 1612 to 1619, was half-Italian and cultivated economic and cultural links with Italy, especially with the court at Mantua. During his reign Salzburg enjoyed the first flowering of the Baroque: monody and opera were introduced, their earliest appearance north of the Alps, and in 1612 the famous exponent of the monodic style, Francesco Rasi, pupil of Giulio Caccini and a leading opera singer (he was probably Monteverdi's original Orpheus), visited Salzburg and dedicated a manuscript collection of monody to the archbishop. In 1614 a stage was erected in the archbishop's residence and inaugurated on 27 January with an Italian 'Hoftragicomedia', the first opera performance outside Italy. On 10 February the pastoral Orfeo was given, probably with music by Monteverdi.

The archbishop also created another remarkable setting for musical theatre, the Steintheater in the park at Hellbrunn (his summer residence outside Salzburg), the oldest surviving garden theatre in the German-speaking world. Guest performers from Italy probably joined local artists for Salzburg opera performances (the monodist Camillo Orlandi, for instance, was there in 1616). In 1617 the Benedictine Gymnasium was founded and with the university (1622) formed an important centre for drama and music. The Benedictine drama performed there developed during the 17th century and increasingly came to resemble opera.

Under succeeding prince-archbishops, music in Salzburg prospered; among composers active in the city were the Alsatian Georg Muffat (1678–90), the Bohemian H. I. F. von Biber (1670–1704) and the local composer Andreas Hofer (from 1653). All three composed dramatic music, which enjoyed new prominence, principally during the rule of Johann Ernst von Thun, for whose enthronement (1687) Muffat's opera *La fatale felicità di Plutone* was performed. Only the librettos of this and of Biber's *Alessandro in Pietra* (1689) have survived. The single surviving opera score from this period is that of Biber's *Chi la dura la vince*. Hofer, Muffat and particularly Biber also set to music a large number of Benedictine *Schuldramen*. At the beginning of the 18th century the most prolific composer of Benedictine drama was Matthias Sigismund Biechteler von Greiffenthal, in court service from 1688. Later, the Viennese deputy Hofkapellmeister Antonio Caldara came to Salzburg to compose operas and between 1716 and 1728 at least 16 of his operas and staged oratorios were performed there. His *dramma pastorale Dafne* probably opened the Heckentheater in the present Mirabellgarten in 1719.

The transition to the Rococo took place under J.E. Eberlin, who became court organist (1726) and Kapellmeister (1749); his compositions influenced a series of Salzburg court musicians, among them Leopold Mozart (court violinist from 1743 and deputy Hofkapellmeister from 1763), Michael Haydn (from 1763), A.C. Adlgasser (court organist from 1750) and Joseph Meissner (a court bass from 1747). W.A. Mozart was Konzertmeister (1769–77) and court organist (1779–81); his dramatic works given in Salzburg include the Latin intermezzo *Apollo et Hyacinthus* (1767, at the university), *La finta semplice* (1769), the serenata *Il sogno di Scipione* (written in 1771, probably performed on the inauguration of Archbishop Colloredo in 1772) and the *dramma per musica Il re pastore* (1775, these last three all at the archbishop's palace). In 1775, on the initiative of the archbishop but at the city's expense, the Ballhaus was converted into the prince-archbishops' Hoftheater, where for the most part travelling companies played, including those of Wahr, Schikaneder, Böhm and Weber. In 1803 the spiritual princedoms of Passau and Eichstädt had come under Salzburg's rule and their court musicians swelled the ranks of the musical establishment; the court was abolished in 1806.

In 1816 Salzburg changed from an episcopal seat to a provincial town, resulting in a stagnant cultural life. The former Hoftheater survived, as the Kaiserliche Königliche Nationaltheater, thanks to the public's love of the theatre. Singspiels by Weigl, Dittersdorf and

Wenzel Müller and operas by Rossini, Cherubini, Mozart and Weber (*Der Freischütz*, 1825) offered a varied musical fare, but with the departure from Salzburg of Michael Haydn's most gifted pupils – Weber, Neukomm and Wölfl – the city and its theatre lost an important source of musical impulse. Alois Taux's directorship (from 1839) coincided with the theatre's heyday. The Dommusikverein und Mozarteum was founded in 1841, for 'the promotion of all branches of music, but especially church music', and in 1870 the Internationale Mozart-Stiftung was established, with a broad programme for encouraging musical activity. The Nationaltheater was replaced in 1893 by the larger Stadttheater (inaugurated with Mozart's *La clemenza di Tito*), which after extensive exterior alterations was renamed the Landestheater in 1938; operas and operettas are given there during the winter months. A much-loved local institution is the Marionetten-Theater, founded in 1913, which with its accomplished performances (mainly of Mozart) to recordings has toured abroad many times.

In the 20th century, however, it is chiefly for the annual summer festival, held from the end of July to the end of August, that Salzburg is known. In 1967 Herbert von Karajan initiated an Easter Festival (Osterfestspiele), at which a new opera production is usually given; these have included the *Ring* (1967–70), *Fidelio* (1971), *Tristan und Isolde* (1972), *Die Meistersinger von Nürnberg* (1974), *La bohème* (1975, produced by Zeffirelli), *Lohengrin* (1976), *Il trovatore* (1977), *Don Carlos* (1979), *Parsifal* (1980), *Der fliegende Holländer* (1982), *Carmen* (1985), *Don Giovanni* (1987), *Tosca* (1988) and, after the death of Karajan, *Fidelio* (1990), directed by Peter Brenner and conducted by Kurt Masur. Georg Solti was appointed artistic director from 1992.

G.C.

Vienna

The capital of Austria, Vienna was formerly also the capital of the Austro-Hungarian monarchy and the Holy Roman Empire. It has been a great European centre of opera (Italian and French as well as German) since Cesti's *Il pomo d'oro* was given there in 1668, throughout the Viennese Classical period when most of Gluck's and Mozart's mature operas and Beethoven's *Fidelio* had their premières there, and throughout the 19th and early 20th centuries, though by that time less as a centre for new music (two Strauss operas apart) than as one where performances of high prestige were given. The Viennese court opera became in 1919 the Staatsoper, with its splendid house on the Ring built in 1869 and rebuilt in 1955; it is widely regarded as a centre of excellence, though its activities and its personalities have rarely been far from controversy. Vienna has also been a famous centre of more popular operatic entertainments, from the Singspiels of Mozart's contemporaries to the operettas of Johann Strauss and his followers.

For most of the first decade of her reign Maria Theresa (1740–92), Charles VI's daughter, was preoccupied with maintaining her throne in the face of invasion and consequently gave little attention to local spectacle. *Opera seria* productions at court became rare despite the presence of Metastasio, ceasing altogether after his and Hasse's *Ipermestra* of 1744. Italian opera continued in the Burgtheater in the Michaelerplatz (managed by impresarios; originally a tennis court, it was refurbished as a theatre in 1741). Works by court composers such as Bonno and Wagenseil alternated with pieces by foreign composers, notably Jommelli, Hasse and Galuppi. In 1747 the Galli-Bibiena opera house in the Hofburg was converted into two (still extant) Redoutensäle, for balls (the rooms were, however, occasionally used again for opera performances in the 19th century and the early 20th). The Burgtheater was renovated to designs by Nicolas Jadot, and reopened with Gluck's first work for Vienna, his *Semiramide riconosciuta* of 1748 (in whose title character the victorious empress could easily be recognized). Despite several remodellings, the

Burgtheater was to retain its small dimensions and intimate acoustics up to its demolition in 1888. The year 1747 saw the first performances in a new theatre in the Schönbrunn palace (the Schlosstheater), and in 1753 a small theatre was constructed in the garden of the Laxenburg palace to the south. In the Kärntnertortheater during this period a German-language troupe performed heroic-comic dramas and farces, often improvised and featuring local versions of *commedia dell'arte* characters. Some of these works included music (commissioned at a florin an aria) by the young Joseph Haydn. Viennese ballet during the 1740s and 50s was mainly in the hands of the choreographer Franz Hilverding, who, starting during the period of court mourning for Charles VI, undertook a reform of theatrical dance which soon had consequences for opera.

In 1752, prompted by the impresario Lo Presti's bankruptcy and the frequent indecencies in German comedies, the empress reconstituted the Viennese theatres under court control. She banned improvised pieces (only temporarily as it turned out) and, in a reflection of Austria's political rapprochement with France, substituted a company of French actors for the planned Italian opera company at the Burgtheater. This troupe's repertory soon came to include *opéras comiques* from Paris, arranged by Gluck. A resident of Vienna since 1750, he was made musical director of the Burgtheater in about 1754 by the theatre Intendant, Giacomo Durazzo. Gluck's own *opéras comiques*, as well as French imports (procured after 1759 through the playwright Favart), supplanted the expensive Italian opera during much of the Seven Years War. Several formal and stylistic features of this modest genre were of use to Gluck in composing his 'reform' works during the next decade.

Italian opera returned with the itinerant Mingotti troupe in 1759, but far more significant were the works celebrating the marriage in 1760 of Archduke Joseph to Isabella of Parma, in both Parma (an *opéra-ballet* by Traetta) and Vienna (operas by Hasse and Gluck). There was much interchange of personnel between the two courts' theatrical forces, both of which were headed by persons sympathetic to French spectacle. Isabella's birthday in 1761 was celebrated in Vienna with Traetta's *Armida*, based on Durazzo's prose adaptation of Quinault's libretto for Lully, and the next year the reform continued with Calzabigi and Gluck's *Orfeo ed Euridice*. Calzabigi was the focal point of the anti-Metastasian 'sect' described by Burney, which valued dramatic truth, theatrical illusion and continuity over poetic niceties and purely musical display. The abundant use of both chorus and ballet in *Orfeo*, unusual in *opera seria*, was a result of Durazzo's ability to combine at will the resources of the Burgtheater and the Kärntnertortheater (for which he was also responsible, both before the fire of 1761 and after the rebuilding in 1763). Metastasio's principal ally was Hasse, a special favourite of the empress, but there is also considerable evidence of support for Gluck from the imperial family. The German theatre, though benefiting from the example of the French actors, suffered financial neglect during this period. Musical plays were few, and translations of *opéras comiques* began only about 1764.

Durazzo was dismissed in 1764 during Archduke Joseph's coronation in Frankfurt as King of the Romans, and with Emperor Francis's death in 1765 the French troupe had to leave as well. (Subsequent French companies patronized by Chancellor Kaunitz and the high nobility, rarely performed *opéras comiques*.) The theatres were closed during the empress's protracted grief, and when they reopened it was again under a series of luckless impresarios. The bankruptcy of Giuseppe d'Afflisio in 1770 seriously affected the finances of Gluck, one of his associates. Opera reform continued with Calzabigi and Gluck's *Alceste* of 1767, which paid tribute to Maria Theresa as loving widow. But circumstances generally favoured neither *opera seria* nor experimentation. Musical theatre was now dominated by large-scale pantomime ballets, presented by Jean-Georges Noverre between 1767 and 1773, and by *opere buffe*, directed by Gluck's successor Florian Gassmann and after 1774 by Gassmann's pupil Antonio Salieri. Local librettists included both Calzabigi and his protégé Coltellini, but by 1773 Calzabigi had left Vienna in frustration and long-term subscribers such as Prince Khevenhüller were relinquishing their boxes on account of the shabbiness of theatrical offerings under the management of Count Koháry. Characteristically taking quick and drastic action, in 1776 Emperor

Joseph II suspended the agreement with the bankrupt Koháry's trustee, dismissed the Italian singers and their orchestra and installed the German actors in the Burgtheater, henceforth called a 'National-theater'. At the same time, he declared a 'Schauspielfreiheit' (an end to the court's monopoly on spectacles), allowing other companies or individuals to use the Kärntnertortheater – known as the Kaiserlich-königliches Hofoperntheater nächst dem Kärntnertor from 1776 – and (on free evenings) the Burgtheater, as well as other venues. Joseph and his new *Musikgraf*, Count Orsini-Rosenberg, managed the theatres directly, without an impresario.

At first Joseph's main concern was the spoken repertory; indeed, Lessing praised the lack of musical distractions at Vienna's National-theater. But audiences soon clamoured for opera, and Joseph accordingly sent his troupe's director, J.H.F. Müller, on a long recruiting trip for German singers capable of performing in *opéra comique* and *opera buffa*, not mere 'Liedsänger' as in much north German opera. The first Singspiel presented (in 1778) was *Die Bergknappen* by Ignaz Umlauf. Subsequent repertory consisted largely of translations from the French or Italian, but other local composers such as Franz Asplmayr and Salieri contributed as well. Dancers were lacking until a 1779 production of the pointedly chosen *Zémire et Azor* by Grétry showed the need for them. Also in 1779 the talented Gottlieb Stephanie ('the younger') replaced Müller as house poet and director of the Singspiel.

For the 1781–2 visit of the Russian Archduke Paul and his wife, the emperor and Chancellor Kaunitz decided on revivals of three major operas by Gluck as representing the best in Viennese musical theatre. Around the same time performances of a translation of Gluck's *opéra comique La rencontre imprévue* delayed and also influ-enced the closely related Singspiel *Die Entführung aus dem Serail* (1782) by Mozart, newly arrived in Vienna. Despite the phenomenal success of the latter work and nationalist sentiment against foreign spectacles, Joseph and the Viennese critics found that the National-theater offered too few Singspiels of too meagre a quality (musical and literary), especially when compared to French or Italian originals they remembered, and in 1783 Joseph ended the experiment and engaged an *opera buffa* company. The once-disgraced Count Durazzo, now imperial ambassador in Venice, was instrumental in recruiting these singers, who included the tenor Michael Kelly, *prima buffa* Nancy Storace and *primo buffo* Francesco Benucci, around whose comic talents the repertory was chosen or created. The singers quickly brought their acting into line with the recently raised standards of the German players, and were remembered by Caroline Pichler as the finest *buffo* company in Europe.

As his theatre poet Joseph engaged Lorenzo da Ponte, who at first collaborated with Salieri. The failure of their *Il ricco d'un giorno* and rivalry with Count Rosenberg's protégé Giambattista Casti led to a falling-out, and Da Ponte next worked with Vicente Martín y Soler, notably in *Una cosa rara* (1786), from which Mozart quoted in *Don Giovanni*. Casti collaborated with the visiting Paisiello in 1784 on *Il re Teodoro in Venezia*; influences from this work and the same composer's *Il barbiere di Siviglia* (performed 1783) are to be found in Mozart and Da Ponte's three operas. In his struggle to be heard in the Burgtheater Mozart suffered from cabals organized by Rosenberg's clique, notably in connection with *Le nozze di Figaro*. His three great comedies (including *Don Giovanni*, written for Prague) nevertheless won the approval of the Burgtheater Mozart suffered from cabals organized by Rosenberg's Viennese audiences, though performances of *Così fan tutte* (1790) were cut short by the emperor's death.

The *opera buffa* ensemble did not enjoy the undivided support of Viennese high society, or even of the emperor. In 1785 Joseph installed a 'Deutsche Opéra Comique' in the Kärntnertortheater as healthy competition for the Italians. Their performances quickly dwindled, ending in February 1788 with Mozart's *Entführung*, after which the theatre closed down. That same year, preoccupied by a Turkish war and irritated by singers' misbehaviour and greed, Joseph for a while contemplated dismissing the entire Italian company and making do with local talent. Advocates of German culture urged such an action, but were disappointed.

Joseph's successor, Leopold II, was initially aloof from theatrical affairs and concentrated on restoring order to his realms. But in 1791 he turned to opera in earnest, drawing on his experience as regent in Tuscany and in several ways returning to practices and genres of his mother Maria Theresa's reign. Leopold and his new *Musikgraf*, Johann Wenzel Ugarte, removed control of the theatres from the bureaucracy and made a fresh start on personnel, dismissing Da Ponte and his mistress, the soprano Adriana Ferrarese; Joseph Weigl replaced Salieri as director of the opera. Although plans to build a larger theatre were not realized, Leopold did reopen the Kärntnertortheater. He re-established both ballet and *opera seria* among the offerings, the latter in alternation with comic operas mostly less complex than those of Mozart and Da Ponte. Leopold first hired Caterino Mazzolà (adapter of Metastasio's *La clemenza di Tito* for Mozart) as theatre poet and then Giovanni Bertati, whose first libretto for Vienna was *Il matrimonio segreto* (set by Cimarosa, 1792).

Mozart, having received no preferment from the new emperor, in 1791 accepted an opera commission at his fellow freemason Emanuel Schikaneder's suburban Theater auf der Wieden (built 1787). *Die Zauberflöte* displays both masonic ideals and features typical of the popular musical and machine comedies dominating the fare at that theatre, which, like Karl Marinelli's Theater in der Leopoldstadt (founded 1781), owed its existence to Joseph's 'Schauspielfreiheit'.

Of the later 18th-century operas that have survived into the modern repertory, a disproportionate number were created in Vienna, despite widely varying tastes and forms of theatrical management. An explanation is suggested by Calzabigi, who in 1790 described the city's audiences as 'the distillation of all nations' and on the whole far more cultivated than their Italian counterparts. As the capital of a large and polyglot empire, Vienna was perhaps uniquely capable of producing such a golden age of opera.

Absent from the repertory after his death, except in Schikaneder's theatre, Mozart's operas began to reappear in the late 1790s. *Le nozze di Figaro* and *Don Giovanni* (as *Don Juan*) were given in 1798 (the former received four performances in Italian in 1807 and a few more in 1824–5, but German was the normal language for Mozart's Italian operas in Vienna in the 19th century, as it was for Gluck's works). *Die Entführung* was revived in 1801, and in the same year *Die*

Zauberflöte was staged at the court opera for the first time, in a production so inept that Schikaneder parodied its deficiencies in his own performances; with a new production in 1812 it became an established cornerstone of the repertory. *La clemenza di Tito* (as *Titus der Gütige*) and *Così fan tutte* (as *Mädchentreue*) shared about a hundred performances between 1804 and 1830, but *Idomeneo* (*Idomeneus, König von Creta*) disappeared after five performances in 1806 and was no more successful when put on again in 1819–20.

Between 1897 and 1907 Gustav Mahler held the directorship of the Hofoper. He was appointed over the head of Wilhelm Jahn (director from 1881 to 1897) by the *Obersthofmeister*, Count Liechtenstein. Mahler surpassed the achievements of his predecessor and made Vienna's opera the finest in Europe. In particular he conducted the five great Mozart operas in a stylistically more faithful manner, accompanying the recitatives on the piano and, later, the harpsichord.

In the period after World War II, the Viennese Mozart style became famous throughout the world, represented by the conductors Josef Krips and Karl Böhm, the director Oscar Fritz Schuh and singers such as Sena Jurinac, Hilde Konetzni, Wilma Lipp, Emmy Loose, Irmgard Seefried, Elisabeth Schwarzkopf, Ljuba Welitsch, Anton Dermota, Hans Hotter, Erich Kunz, Julius Patzak, Paul Schöffler and Ludwig Weber. Mozart's Italian operas, as well as most foreign works, were sung in German.

H.S., B.A.B, P.B., M.C., R.K, H.G.

Glossary,
Index of Role Names
and
Suggested Further
Reading

Glossary

Act One of the main divisions of an opera, usually completing a part of the action and often having a climax of its own. The classical five-act division was adopted in early operas and common in serious French opera of the 17th and 18th centuries, but in Italian opera a three-act scheme was soon standard, later modified to two in *opera buffa*. From the late 18th century, operas were written in anything from one act to five, with three the most common; Wagner's ideal music drama was to consist of three acts.

Air French or English term for 'song' or 'aria'. In French opera of the 17th and 18th centuries it was applied both to unpretentious, brief pieces and to serious, extended monologues, comparable to arias in Italian opera.

Alto *See* Castrato; and Contralto

Apoggiatura (It.) A 'leaning note', normally one step above the note it precedes. Apoggiatura were normally introduced by performers, in recitativevs and arias in 18th century opera, to make the musical line conform to the natural inflection of the words an (in arias) to increase the expressiveness.

Aria (It.) A closed, lyrical piece for solo voice, the standard vehicle for expression on the part of an operatic character. Arias appear in the earliest operas. By the early 18th century they usually follow a da capa pattern (*ABA*); by Mozart's time they took various forms, among them the slow-fast type, sometimes called rondò. this remained popular in Italian opera during most of the 19th century (the 'cantabile-cabaletta' type); even longer forms, sometimes in four sections with interruptions to reflect changes of mood, appear in the operas of Donizetti and Verdi. The aria as a detachable unit became less popular later in the century; Wagner wrote none in his mature operas, nor Verdi in *Otello* or *Falstaff* ; in Puccini, too, an aria is usually part of the dramatic texture and cannot readily be extracted. Some 20th-century composers (notably Stravinsky, in the neo-classical *Rake's Progress*) have revived the aria, but generally it has been favoured only where a formal or artificial element has been required.

Arioso (It.) 'Like an aria': a singing (as opposed to a declamatory) style of performance; a short passage in a regular tempo in the middle or at the end of a recitative; or a short aria

Azione teatrale (It.) A serenata-type genre of the late Baroque period, cultivated particularly at the Viennese court. Gluck's *Orfeo ed Euidice* was originally so described.

Baritone A male voice of moderately low pitch, normally in the range *A–f'*. The voice became important in opera in the late 18th century, particularly in Mozart's works, although the word 'baritone' was little used at this time ('bass' served for both types of low voice). Verdi used the baritone for a great variety of roles, including secondary heroic ones.

Bass The lowest male voice, normally in the range *F–e'*. The voice is used in operas of all periods, often for gods, figures of authority (a king, a priest, a father) and for villains and sinister characters. There are several subclasses of bass: the *basso buffo* (in Italian comic opera), the *basso cantante* or French *basse-chantante* (for a more lyrical role) and the *basso profundo* (a heavy, deep, voice).

Bass-baritone A male voice combining the compass and other attributes of the bass and the baritone. It is particularly associated with Wagner, especially the roles of Wotan (the *Ring*) and Sachs (*Die Meistersinger*).

Breeches part [trouser role] Term for a man or boy's part sung by a woman. The central examples are Cherubino in *Le nozze di Figaro* and Oktavian in *Der Rosenkavalier*, but there are many more, among them Verdi's Oscar (Edgar) in *Un ballo in maschera*, Fyodor in *Boris Godunov*, Hänsel, and the Composer in *Ariadne auf Naxos*. In Baroque opera numerous male parts were written for women but, with the issue confused by castrato singers, casting was less sexually specific.

Cadenza   A virtuoso passage inserted in an aria, usually near the end, either improvised by the singer or, as in Verdi's later operas, written out by the composer.

Canzone (It.)   Term used in opera for items presented as songs, sung outside the dramatic action, for example Cherubino's 'Voi che spaete' in *Le nozze di Figaro* (although Mozart called it simply 'Arietta'). Verdi used it several times, notably for Desdemona's Willow Song in *Otello*.

Canzonetta (It.)   A diminutive of Canzone, used in the same sense as that term; an example is Don Giovanni's serenade 'Deh viena all finestra'.

Castrato (It.)   A male singer, castrated before puberty to preserve the soprano or contralto range of his voice. The castrato figured in the history of opera from its beginnings: Monteverdi's *Orfeo* includes a eunuch in the cast. In the papal states, where women were banned on stage, castratos sang all female roles. They performed the heroic male roles which until the late 18th century were nearly always for high voices: Monteverdi's Nero, Cavalli's Pompey, Handel's Julius Caesar and Gluck's Orpheus were all sopranos or altos.

Castratos dominated the stage during the era of Metastasian *opera seria*. The singers were mostly Italian, but many achieved international reputations in England and the German-speaking lands. They often behaved with the capriciousness of prima donnas. Many, including most of those for whom Handel composed, were of contralto rather than soprano range. Mozart composed Idamantes (*Idomeneo*) and Sextus (*La clemenza di Tito*) for castratos. In the 19th century castrato roles appeared in a few operas by Rossini and Meyerbeer; thereafter the production of castratos came to be frowned upon. The last known was Alessandro Moreschi (1858–1922) who in 1902–3 made recordings in which the passionate yet curiously disembodied quality of his voice is apparent. The best castratos had high voices of great power, agility and penetration, and intense expressiveness; no one took exception to the use of castratos not only for heroic roles but also amorous ones.

Cavatina (It.)   In 18th-century opera a short aria, without da capo, often an entrance aria. Mozart used the term three times in *Le nozze di Figaro*. Later examples are Rosina's 'Una voce poco fà' in Rossini's *Il barbiere di Siviglia* and Lady Macbeth's 'Vieni t'affretta' in Verdi's *Macbeth*. Cavatinas often concluded with a Cabaletta.

Chaconne (Fr.)   A Baroque dance in triple metre and moderate tempo, often involving a ground bass, used in French opera, particularly as the final dance of a group (or of the entire work) in the late 17th century. Later examples appear in Gluck's *Orfeo ed Euridice* and Mozart's *Idomeneo*.

Coloratura   Florid figuration or ornamentation. The term is usually applied to high-pitched florid writing, exemplified by such roles as the Queen of the Night in Mozart's *Die Zauberflöte*, Violetta in Verdi's *La traviata* or Zerbinetta in Strauss's *Ariadne auf Naxos*, as well as many roles by Rossini and other early 19th-century Italian composers. The term 'coloratura soprano' signifies a singer of high pitch, lightness and agility, appropriate to such roles.

Comic opera   A musico-dramatic work of a light or amusing nature. The term may be applied equally to an Italian *opera buffa*, a French *opéra comique*, a German Singspiel, a Spanish zarzuela or an English opera of light character. It is also often applied to operetta or *opéra bouffe* and even musical comedy. Most non-Italian comic operas have spoken dialogue rather than continuous music.

Commedia dell'arte (It.) A comic stage presentation, developed in 16th-century Italy, characterised by the use of masks (or fixed parts), earthy buffoonery and improvisation. Its stock characters (Harlequin, Scaramouche etc.), or characters developed from them, have often been introduced into comic operas such as Pergolesi's *La serva padrona*, Mozart's *Le nozze di Figaro*, Busoni's *Arlecchino* and Strauss's *Ariadne auf Naxos*.

Continuo The continuous bass parts used in works of the baroque period and serving as a basis for the music, supporting the harmony. In opera, a continuo part will normally be played on a sustaining instrument (cello, double bass, viola da gamba, bassoon) and a harmonic instrument (harpsichord, archlute, theorbo, organ). Figures next to the notes indicated to the player what harmonies he should add. The use of continuo persisted in opera up to the end of the 18th century.

Contralto (It.) A voice normally written for the range *g"*. In modern English the term denotes the lowest female voice, but the term could also denote a male Falsetto singer or a Castrato.

In opera, true contrato (as distinct from mezzo-soprano) roles are exceptional. They occurred in the 17th century for old women, almost invariably comic, but in the 18th century composers came to appreciate the deep female voice for dramatic purposes. In Handel's operas several contralto roles stand in dramatic contrast to the prima donna, for example Cornelia in *Giulio Caesare*, a mature woman and a figure of tragic dignity. Rossini's important contralto (or mezzo) roles include Cinderella in *La Cenerentola*, Rosina in *Il barbiere di Siviglia* (original version), and the heroic part of Arsaces in *Semiramide*. In later opera, contraltos were repeatedly cast as a sorceress-like figure (Verdi's Azucena and Arvidson/Ulrica, Wagner's Ortrud) or an oracle (Wagner's Erda) and sometimes as an old women.

Da capo (It.) An instruction (usually abbreviated D.C.) to return to the head of a piece of music and repeat the first section. The 'da capo aria' was the standard aria form of the late Baroque and early Classical periods, especially in *opera seria*; it was generally understood that the repeated section would be ornamented. It was superseded by the 'dal segno' aria ('from the sign'). In which a sign part-way through the aria indicates the point at which the recapitulation should begin.

Dramma giocoso (It.) Term used in Italian librettos in the late 18th century for a comic opera, particularly for the type favoured by Carlo Goldoni and his followers in which character-types from the serious opera appeared alongside those traditional to comic opera. The *dramma giocoso* was not regarded as a distinct genre and the title was used interchangeably with others; Mozart's *Don Giovanni*, for example, is described on the libretto as a 'dramma giocoso' and on the scores an 'opera buffa'.

Dramma [drama] **per musica** [dramma musicale] (It.) 'Play for music': a phrase found on the title-page of many Italian librettos, referring to a text expressly written to be set by a composer.

Duet (It.) An ensemble for two singers. It was used in opera almost from the outset, often at the end of an act or when the principal lovers were united (or parted). Later the duet became merged in the general continuity of the music (Verdi, Puccini etc) or dissolved into a musical dialogue in which the voices no longer sang simultaneously (later Wagner, R. Strauss etc). The love duet had become characterized by singing in 3rds or 6ths, acquiring a mellifluous quality of sound appropriate to shared emotion. Often the voices are used singly at first and join together later, symbolizing the development described in the text.

Falsetto (It.) The treble range produced by most adult male singers through a slightly artificial technique whereby the vocal chords vibrate in a length shorter than usual. It is rarely used in opera.

Festa teatrale (It.) A serenata-type genre of the high baroque period, cultivated especially in Vienna; typically the subject matter was allegorical and the production part of a celebration of a court event.

Finale (It.) The concluding, continuously composed, section of an act of an opera. The ensemble finale developed, at the beginning of the second half of the 18th century, largely through the changes wrought in comic opera by Carlo Goldoni (1707–93), who in his librettos made act finales longer, bringing in more singers and increasing the density of the plot.

Intermezzo, intermezzi (It.) Comic interludes sung between the acts or scenes of an *opera seria* in the 18th century.

Key The quality of a musical passage or composition that causes it to be sensed as gravitating towards a particular note, called the keytone or the tonic.

Libretto (It.) 'Small book': a printed book containing the words of an opera; by extension, the text itself. In the 17th and 18th centuries, when opera houses were lit, librettos were often read during performances; when an opera was given in a language other than that of the audience, librettos were bilingual, with parallel texts on opposite pages.

Lieto fine (It.) 'Happy ending': term used for the normal, almost obligatory happy ending found in virtually all serious operas of the late Baroque and the Classical periods. Often it involved the appearance of a *deus ex machina* (the intervention of a benevolent deity) to resolve a dilemma happily.

Melisma A passage of florid writing in which several notes are sung in the same syllable.

Melodrama A kind of drama, or a technique used within a drama, in which the action is carried forward by the protagonist speaking in the pauses of, or during, orchestral passages, similar in style to those in operatic accompanied recitative. Its invention is usually dated to J.-J. Rousseau's *Pygmalion* (*c*1762). Georg Benda was its chief exponent in Germany; Mozart, influenced by him, wrote melodrama sections in his *Zaide*, Beethoven used melodrama sections in the dungeon scene of *Fidelio*; Weber used it, notably in *Der Freischütz*, Most 19th-century composers of opera have used it as a dramatic device, for example Verdi, for letter scenes in *Macbeth* and *La traviata*, and Smetana in *The Two Widows*. It has been much used by 20th-century composers, among them Puccini, Strauss, Berg, Britten and Henze.

Mezzo-soprano Term for a voice, usually female, normally written for within the range a–$f\sharp''$. The distinction between the florid soprano and the weightier mezzo-soprano became common only towards the mid-18th century. The castrato Senesino, for whom Handel composed was described as having a 'penetrating, clear, even, and pleasant deep soprano voice (mezzo soprano)'. The distinction was more keenly sensed in the 19th century, although the mezzo-soprano range was often extended as high as a $b\flat''$. Mezzo-sopranos with an extended upper range tackled the lower of two soprano roles in such operas as Bellini's *Norma* (Adagisa) and Donizetti's *Anna Bolena* (Jane Seymour). Both sopranos and mezzo-sopranos sing many of Wagner's roles.

The mezzo-soprano was often assigned a Breeches part in the era immediately after the demise of the Castrato, such as Arsace's in *Semiramide*; at all periods they have taken adolescent roles such as Cherubino (*Le nozze di Figaro*) or Oktavian (*Der Rosenkavalier*). The traditional casting however is as a nurse or confidante (e.g.

Brangäne in *tristan und Isolde*, Suzuki in *Madama Butterfly*) or as the mature married woman (e.g. Herodias in Strauss's *Salome*). Saint-Saëns's Delilah is an exception to the general rule that the principal female role (particularly the beautiful maiden) is a soprano.

Modulation The movement out of one key into another as a continuous musical process. It is particularly used in opera as a device to suggest a change of mood.

Motif A short musical idea, melodic, rhythmic, or harmonic (or any combination of those).

Musical comedy, Musical Term for the chief form of popular musical theatre in the English-speaking world. It developed from comic opera and burlesque in London in the late 19th century and reached its most durable form in the 1920s and 30s, particularly in th USA.

Music drama, Musical drama The term 'Musical drama' was used by Handel for *Hercules* (1745), to distinguish it from opera and Sacred Drama. In more recent usage, the meanings attached to 'music drama' derive from the ideas formulated in Wagner's *Oper und Drama*; it is applied to his operas and to others in which the musical, verbal and scenic elements cohere to serve one dramatic end. In 1869, Verdi distinguished between opera of the old sort and the *dramma musicale* that he believed his *La forza del destino* to be. Current theatrical practice tends to qualify this unity by performing music dramas with the original music and words but freshly invented scenic elements.

Number opera Term for an opera consisting of individual sections or 'number' which can be detached from the whole, as distinct from an opera consisting of continuous music. It applies to the various forms of 18th-century opera and to some 19th-century grand operas. Under Wagner's influence the number opera became unfash-ionable, and neither his operas nor those of late Verdi, Puccini and the *verismo* school can be so called. Some notable works can be considered number operas, such as Berg's *Wozzeck* and Stravinsky's deliberately archaic *The Rake's Progress*.

Opera buffa (It.) 'Comic opera': a term commonly used to signify Italian comic opera, principally of the 18th century, with recitative rather than spoken dialogue. Though now applied generically, it was one of the several such terms used in the 18th century.

Opera seria (It.) 'Serious opera': term applied to serious Italian operas, on a heroic or tragic subject, of the 18th century and the early 19th ('dramma per musica' is the more usual contemporary description'). Defined primarily by music historians out of sympathy with its musical and dramatic principals, 'opera seria' is often used in a derogatory sense. The classical *opera seria* is in three acts, has six or seven characters, consists primarily of arias in da capo (or shortened da capo) form in which characters express their emotional state, and recitatives, in which the action takes place, with occasional orchestral recitatives at dramatic highoipnts and sometimes duets; the topic traditionally involves a moral dilemma, typically a variant of 'love *versus* duty', and is resolved happily, with due reward for rectitude, loyalty, unselfishness etc. The most famous librettist was Pietro Metastasio, whose texts were set many times over.

Overture A piece of orchestral music designed to precede a dramatic work. By the mid-18th century the Italian type prevailed and the first movement had become longer and more elaborate; there was a tendency to drop the second and the third movements. In serious opera there was sometimes an effort to set the mood of the coming drama as in Gluck's *Alceste* and Mozart's *Idomeneo*; the famous preface to *Alceste* emphasizes the importance of this. In Mozart's *Don Giovanni*, *Così fan Tutte* and *Die Zauberflöte* the overture quotes musical ideas from the opera. Between 1790 and 1820, there was usually a slow introduction. The notion of tying the overture to the opera in mood and theme was developed in France and also appealed to the German Romantics. Beethoven made powerful use of dramatic motifs in his *Leonore* overtures while in Weber's *Der Freischütz* and *Euryanthe* overtures almost every theme reappears in the drama. Composers of French grand opera tended to expand the overture. For Bellini, Donizetti and Verdi the short prelude was an alternative, and it became normal in Italian opera after the mid-century. Wagner, in the *Ring*, preferred a 'prelude' fully integrated into the drama, as did Richard Strauss amd Puccini, whose prelude to *Tosca* consists simply of three chords (associated with a particular character). In comic operas and operettas the independent overtures lasted longer; the structure based on the themes from the drama became a medly of tunes. The 'medley' or 'potpourri' overture used by Auber, Gounod, Thomas, Offenbach and Sullivan can still be traced in musical-comedy overtures.

Pasticcio (It.)   Term for a work made up, at least in part, from existing works by a variety of composers; the practise, which began in the late 17th century and persisted for most of the 18th, arose from the need for commercial success, which was better assured if singers could be given their tried favoutites. A pasticcio was normally put together by a 'house' composer and librettist. Virtually all composers accepted the practice and partook of it, including Handel, Gluck, Haydn and Mozart.

Pastorale   A literary, dramatic or musical genre that depicts the characters and scenes of rural life or is expressive of its atmosphere. The pastoral tradition was important in early opera, such as Monteverdi's *Orfeo*, and Handel's *Acis and Galatea*; later it was parodied, as in Offenbach's *Orphée aux enfers* and Sullivan's *Iolanthe* (1882).

Prima donna (It.)   'First lady': the principal female singer in an opera or on the roster of an opera company, almost always a soprano. The expression came into use around the mid-17th century, with the opening of public opera houses in Venice, where the ability of a leading lady to attract audiences became important. Singers who became prima donnas insisted on keeping that title; when conflicts arose, manegerial ingenuity devised such expressions as 'altra prima donna', 'prima donna assoluta' and even 'prima donna assoluta e sola'.

Some prima donnas made it a point of their status to be difficult. Adelina Patti (1843–1919), at the height of her career, stipulated that her name appear on posters in letters at least one-third larger than those used for other singers' names and that she be excused from rehearsals. The need to meet a prima donna's demands shaped many librettos and scores, particularly because her status was reflected in the number and character of the arias allotted to her.

Primo uomo (It.)   'First man': the principal male singer in an opera or on the roster of an opera company. Just as a leading lady had been given the title 'prima donna', so a famous castrato would claim the title 'primo uomo'. His importance is evident in the roles he sang, which were generally on a par with those for the prima donna. In Handel's *Giulio Cesare* Cleopatra and Julius Caesar each have eight arias. At first 'primo uomo' referred to a castrato, but during the 18th century it came also to be applied to tenors.

Quartet   An ensemble for four singers. Quartets appear as early as the 17th century; Cavalli's *Calisto* ends with one and A. Scarlatti wrote several. There are quartets in Handel's *Radamisto* and *Partenope*. They appear in many *opéras comiques*. In *opera buffa* of the Classical era, when ensembles are sometimes used to further the dramatic action, quartets sometimes occupy that role: examples are the Act 2 finale of Mozart's *Die Entführung aus dem Serail*, where the sequence of sections shows the consolidation of the relationships between the two pairs of lovers, and in Act 1 of his *Don Giovanni*, where 'Non ti fidar' draws together the dramatic threads. The quartet in the last act of *Idomeneo* is however more a series of statements by the characters of their emotional positions, as is the quartet-for the 'wedding' toast in the finale of *Così fan tutte*. Another canonic quartet is 'Mir ist so wunderbar' from Beethoven's *Fidelio*. Verdi wrote a quartet in *Otello*, but his best-known example is the one from *Rigoletto*, an inspired piece of simultaneous portrayal of feeling.

Quintet An ensemble for five singers. Quintets, except within ensemble finales, are rare in the operatic repertory. Notable exceptions are the two in Mozart's *Così fan tutte*. The only substantial ensemble in the sense of a number where the characters sing simultaneously in Wagner's late operas is the famous quintet in *Die Meistersinger von Nürnberg*, a rare moment in his operas where the dramatic action is suspended an the characters take emotional stock.

Recitative A type of vocal writing which follows closely the natural rhythm and accentuation of speech, not necessarily governed by a regular tempo or organized in a specific form. It derived from the development in the late 16th century of a declamatory narrative style with harmonic support, a wide melodic range and emotionally charged treatment of words. During the 17th century, recitative came to be the vehicle for dialogue, providing a connecting link between arias; the trailing off before the cadence (representing the singers being overcome with emotion), leaving the accompaniment to provide the closure, became a convention, as did the addition of an apoggiatura at any cadence point to follow the natural inflection of Italian words.

By the late 17th century a more rapid, even delivery had developed, a trend carried further in *opera buffa* of the 18th century. Recitative was sung in a free, conversational manner. Plain or simple recitative, accompanied only by Continuo, is known as *recitativo semplice* or *recitativo secco* (or

simply *secco*), to distinguish it from accompanied or orchestral recitative (*recitativo accompagnato*, *stromentato* or *obbligato*), which in the 18th century grew increasingly important for dramatic junctures. In France, the language demanded a different style, slower-moving, more lyrical and more flexible.

Recitative with keyboard accompaniment fell out of use early in the 19th century. Recitative-like declamation, however, remained an essential means of expression. Even late in the 19th century, when written operas with spoken dialogue were given in large houses where speech was not acceptable (like the Paris Opéra), recitatives were supplied by house composers or hacks (or the composer himself, for example Gounod with *Faust*) to replace dialogue: the most famous example is Guiraud's long-used set of recitatives for Bizet's *Carmen*. With the more continuous textures favoured in the 20th century, the concept of recitative disappeared (as it did in Wagner's mature works), to be replaced by other kinds of representation of speech. *Sprechgesang* may be seen as an Expressionist equivalent of recitative.

Rescue opera Term used for a type of opera, popular in France after the 1789 Revolution, in which the hero or heroine is delivered at the last moment either from the cruelty of a tyrant or from some natural catastrophe, not by a *deus ex machina* but by heroic human endeavour. It reflected the secular idealism of the age and often carried a social message. Some rescue operas were based on contemporary real-life incidents, among them Gaveaux's *Léonore, ou l'amour conjugal* (1798) and Cherubini's *Les deux journées* (1800), both to librettos by J. N. Bouilly. The former was the source of Beethoven's *Fidelio*.

Ritornello (It.) A short recurring instrumental passage, particularly the tutti section of a Baroque aria.

Romance Term used in 18th- and 19th-century opera for a ballad-like type of strophic song. It suited the sentimentalism of *opéra comique*, and in Germany was used in Singspiel, notably by Mozart (Pedrillo's 'Im Mohrenland' in *Die Entführung aus dem Serail*) and later Weber ('Nero, dem Kettenbund' in *Der Freischütz*); Italian examples include several by Verdi, notably Manrico's 'Deserto sulla terra' (*Il trovatore*) and Radamès's 'Celeste Aida' (*Aida*).

Scena (It.), **Scène** (Fr.) Term used to mean (1) the stage (e.g. 'sulla scena', on the stage; 'derrière la scène', behind the stage), (2) the scene represented on the stage, (3) a division of an act (*see* Scene). In Italian opera it also means an episode with no formal construction but made up of diverse elements. The 'Scena e duetto' is a typical unit in opera of the Rossinian period. A *scena* of a particularly dramatic character, often (though not invariably) for a single character, may be described as a 'gran scena', e.g. 'Gran scena del sonnambulismo' in Verdi's *Macbeth*.

Scene (1) The location of an opera, or an act or part of an act of an opera; by extension, any part of an opera in one location. (2) In earlier usage, a scene was a section of an act culminating in an aria (or occasionally an ensemble); any substantial (in some operas, any at all) change in the characters on the stage was reckoned a change of scene, and the scenes were numbered accordingly.

Serenata (It.) A dramatic cantata, akin to a short opera, usually on a pastoral, allegorical or mythological topic and given in honour of a person or an occasion. From *sereno* (It.), 'a clear night sky', referring to the usual performance circumstances, the term was used in the 17th and 18th centuries for works performed in courtly or aristocratic surroundings, lavishly set and in a quasi-dramatic manner. The serenata was popular in Venice and Rome, and outside Italy in Vienna.

Set piece An aria or other numbers clearly demarcated from its context.

Sextet An ensemble for six singers. Sextets are rare in the operatic repertory, except within act finales, but there are two notable Mozart examples: the recognition scene in Act 3 of *Le nozze di Figaro* and the central scene of Act 2 of *Don Giovanni*. The most celebrated operatic sextet is that at the climax of Donizetti's *Lucia di Lammermoor*.

Singspiel (Ger.) Literally, a play with songs; the term was used in 18th-century Germany for almost any kind of dramatic entertainment with music. In operatic usage, Singspiel means a German comic opera of the 18th or early 19th centuries, with spoken dialogue. The genre was particularly popular during the late 18th century in Vienna and Northern Germany (especially Leipzig). In its early days it was influenced by the English ballad opera. The most significant examples are Mozart's *Die Entführung aus dem Serail* and *Die Zauberflöte*.

Soprano (It.) The highest female voice, normally written for within the range $c'-a''$; the word is also applied to a boy's treble voice and in the 17th and 18th centuries to a castrato of high range. The soprano voice was used for expressive roles in the earliest operas. During the Baroque period it was found to be suited to brilliant vocal display, and when a singer achieved fame it was usually because of an ability to perform elaborate music with precision as well as beauty. The heroine's role was sung by the most skilful soprano, the prima donna; to her were assigned the greatest number of arias and the most difficult and expressively wide-ranging music. The highest note usually required was *a* and little merit was placed on the capacity to sing higher.

The development of the different categories of the soprano voice belongs to the 19th century, strongly foreshadowed in the variety of roles and styles found in Mozart's operas (although type-casting was not at all rigid: the singer of Susanna in 1789 created Fiordiligi the next year). It was a consequence of the divergence of national operatic traditions and the rise of a consolidated repertory. Italian sopranos of the age of

Rossini and Bellini developed a coloratura style and the ability to sustain a long lyrical line (the coloratura soprano and the lyric soprano); later, in Verdi's time, with larger opera houses and orchestras, the more dramatic *spinto* and *lirico spirito* appeared. In Germany the dramatic or heroic soprano was already foreshadowed in Beethoven's Leonore and Weber's Agathe; Wagner's Brünnhilde, demanding great power and brilliance, was the climax of this development. French *grand opéra* developed its own style of lyric-dramatic soprano. The operetta too produced a light, agile voice of its own.

Soubrette (Fr.) 'Servant girl': a stock character of 18th-century French opera and by extension the kind of voice appropriate to a shrewd and spirited young woman. Examples include Serpina in Pergolesi's *La serva padrona*, Susanna in *Le nozze di Figaro*, Despina in *Così fan tutte* and Adele in *Die Fledermaus*. The type of voice called for is light and sharp in focus, with clear diction.

Stretta, Stretto (It.) Term used to indicate a faster tempo at the climactic concluding section of a piece. It is common in Italian opera: examples include the end of the Act 2 finale of Mozart's *Le nozze di Figaro* and Violetta's aria at the end of Act 1 of Verdi's *La traviata*.

Strophic Term for a song or an aria in which all stanzas of the text are set to the same music. The term 'strophic variations' is used of songs where the melody is varied from verse to verse while the bass remains unchanged or virtually so. The form was popular in early 17th-century Italy; 'Possente spirito', sung by Monteverdi's Orpheus, is an example, and Cavalli occasionally used the form.

Tenor The highest natural male voice, normally written for within the range *c–a"*. Although the tenor voice was valued in early opera – a tenor, Francesco Rasi (1574–after 1620), sang Monteverdi's Orpheus

(1607) – heroic roles in middle and late Baroque opera were assigned to the castrato. Tenors took minor roles, such as the old man (sometimes with comic overtones), the lighthearted confidant, the mischievous schemer or the messenger, or even a travesty role of the old nurse. By the 1720s, important roles were occasionally given to tenors, and by the Classical era the voice was more regularly used in central roles. Such roles as Mozart's Bassilio, Ottavio, Ferrando and Titus – comic, docile lover, more virile lover, benevolent monarch – define the scope of the voice at this period.

A creation of the early 19th century was the *tenore di grazia*, a light, high voice moving smoothly into falsetto up to *d"*, called for by many Rossini roles. With the increasing size of opera houses, and the changes in musical style, the *tenore di forza* was called for. The tendency continued as, with Verdi's operas, the *tenore robusto* developed. For the German heroic tenor roles of the 19th century, especially Wagner's, a more weighty, durable type was needed, the Heldentenor. The lighter tenor continued to be cultivated for the more lyrical French roles. Many of the great tenors of the 20th century have been Italians, and made their names in Italian music, from Enrico Caruso (1873–1921) to Luciano Pavarotti to these the Spaniard Plácido Domingo should be added.

Terzet, Trio An ensemble for three singers. Terzets or trios have been used throughout the history of opera. there is an example in Monteverdi's *L'incoronazione di Poppea*; Handel used the form several times, notably in *Tamerlano, Orlando*, and *Alcina*, and Gluck wrote examples in the closing scenes of his Italian reform operas. Mozart's include three (one in *Don Giovanni*, two in *La clemenza di Tito*) which are akin to arias with comments from two subsidiary characters. There are two in Weber's *Der Freischütz* and several for very high tenors in Rossini's serious operas. The form was much used by the Romantics, among them Verdi, who wrote three examples in *Un ballo in maschera*.

231

Tessitura (It.) 'Texture': the part of a vocal compass in which a piece of music lies – whether high or low, etc; it is not measured by the extremes of range but by which part of the range is most used.

Tonal Term used for music in a particular key, or a pitch centre to which the music naturally gravitates. The use of tonalities, or the interplay of keys, can be an important dramatic weapon in the opera composer's armoury.

Trio *see* Terzet

Vaudeville (Fr.) A French poem or song of satirical or epigrammatic character common in the 17th and 18th centuries; vaudevilles made up much of the repertory at the annual Paris fairs of St Germain and St Laurent. As the *opéra comique* developed from these ventures, more original music was added. The French *comédie en vaudeville* had an international influence.

Vaudeville final (Fr.) Placed at the end of an act or play, the *vaudeville final* reassembled on stage all the important characters and required each to sing one or more verses of a vaudeville, usually with a choral refrain. This style was common in French opera and *opéra comique*. The influence of the *vaudeville final* may be seen in other genres, and continued into later periods, as in Gluck's *Orfeo*, Mozart's *Die Entführung aus dem Serail*, Rossini's *Il barbiere di Siviglia*, Verdi's *Falstaff*, Ravel's *L'heure espagnole* and Stravinsky's *The Rake's Progress*.

Index of role names

Aceste (tenor)	*Ascanio in Alba*
Agenor/Agenore (tenor)	*Il re pastore*
Alexander (the Great)/Alessandro (Magno) (tenor)	*Il re pastore*
Alfonso, Don (bass)	*Così fan tutte*
Allazim (bass)	*Zaide*
Almaviva/Almaviva, Count (baritone)	*Le nozze di Figaro*
Almaviva, Countess (soprano)	*Le nozze di Figaro*
Amyntas/Aminta (soprano)	*Il re pastore*
Anna, Donna (soprano)	*Don Giovanni*
Annius/Annio (soprano)	*La clemenza di Tito*
Antonio (bass)	*Le nozze di Figaro*
Apollo/Apollon (treble)	*Apollo et Hyacinthus*
Arbaces/Arbace (tenor)	*Idomeneo*
Arbates/Arbate (soprano)	*Mitridate*
Arminda (soprano)	*La finta giardiniera*
Ascanio (soprano)	*Ascanio in Alba*
Asdrubale, Don (tenor)	*Lo sposo deluso*
Aspasia (soprano)	*Mitridate*
Aufidius/Aufidio (tenor)	*Lucio Silla*
Aurelia (soprano)	*L'oca del Cairo*
Barbarina (soprano)	*Le nozze di Figaro*
Bartolo/Bartolo, Dr (bass)	*Le nozze di Figaro*
Basilio, Don (tenor)	*Le nozze di Figaro*
Bastien (tenor)	*Bastien und Bastienne*
Bastienne (soprano)	*Bastien und Bastienne*
Belfiore, Count (tenor)	*La finta giardiniera*
Belmonte (tenor)	*Die Entführung aus dem Serail*
Bettina (soprano)	*Lo sposo deluso*
Biondello (tenor)	*L'oca del Cairo*
Blonde (soprano)	*Die Entführung aus dem Serail*
Bocconio (bass)	*Lo sposo deluso*
Calandrino (tenor)	*L'oca del Cairo*
Cassandro (bass)	*La finta semplice*
Cecilius/Cecilio (soprano)	*Lucio Silla*
Celia (soprano)	*Lucio Silla*
Celidora (soprano)	*L'oca del Cairo*
Cherubino (mezzo-soprano)	*Le nozze di Figaro*
Chichibeo (bass)	*L'oca del Cairo*
Cinna (soprano)	*Lucio Silla*
Colas (bass)	*Bastien und Bastienne*

Suggested further reading

The New Grove Dictionary of Opera, edited by Stanley Sadie (London and New York, 1992)

*

CATALOGUES, BIBLIOGRAPHIES, LETTERS, DOCUMENTS, ICONOGRAPHY

E. Anderson, ed.: *The Letters of Mozart and his Family* (London, 1938, 1985)

O.E. Deutsch: *Mozart: die Dokumente seines Lebens, gesammelt und erläutert* (Kassel, 1961; English translation, 1965, 1966; supplement 1978)

O.E. Deutsch: *Mozart und seine Welt in zeitgenössischen Bildern* (Kassel, 1961) [in German and English])

W.A. Bauer, O.E. Deutsch and J.H. Eibl, eds.: *Mozart: Briefe und Aufzeichnungen* (Kassel, 1962–75)

H.C.R. Landon, ed.: *The Mozart Compendium* (London, 1990)

BIOGRAPHIES, STUDIES OF LIFE AND WORKS

A. Einstein: *Mozart: his Character, his Work* (English translation, New York, 1945: German original, 1947, 1960)

W. Hildesheimer: *Mozart* (Frankfurt, 1977; English translation, 1982)

S. Sadie: *The New Grove Mozart* (London, 1982)

C. Peter: *Mozart and his Circle: a Biographical Dictionary* (London, 1993)

S. Maynard: *Mozart, a Life* (London, 1995)

J. Rosselli: *The Life of Mozart* (Cambridge, 1998)

LIFE AND WORKS, PARTICULAR PERIODS AND ASPECTS

C. Rosen: *The Classical Style: Haydn, Mozart, Beethoven* (London, 1971, 1973), 183–325

A. Tyson: *Mozart: Studies of the Autograph Scores* (Cambridge, MA, 1987)

H.C.R. Landon: *1791: Mozart's Last Year* (London, 1988)

H.C.R. Landon: *Mozart: the Golden Years, 1781–1791* (London, 1989)

OPERAS

E.J. Dent: *Mozart's Operas: a Critical Study* (London, 1913, 1947, rev. 1991)

B. Brophy: *Mozart the Dramatist: a New View of Mozart, his Operas and his Age* (London, 1964, 1988)

C. Gianturco: *Le opere del giovane Mozart* (Pisa, 1976, enlarged 1978, English translation, enlarged, as *Mozart's Early Operas*, 1981)

W. Mann: *The Operas of Mozart* (London, 1977)

F. Noske: *The Signifier and the Signified: Studies in the Operas of Mozart and Verdi* (The Hague, 1977)

C. Osborne: *The Complete Operas of Mozart* (London, 1978)

S. Kunze: *Mozarts Opern* (Stuttgart, 1984)

R. Angermüller: *Mozart: die Opern von der Uraufführung bis heute* (Fribourg, 1988; English translation, 1988, as *Mozart's Operas*)

D. Heartz: *Mozart's Operas* (Berkeley, 1990) [with T. Bauman]

N. Till: *Mozart and the Enlightenment: Truth, Virtue and Beauty in Mozart's Operas* (London, 1992)

M. Hunter and J. Webster, eds: *Opera buffa in Mozart's Vienna* (Cambridge, 1997)

Individual operas

J. Rushton: *W.A. Mozart: Idomeneo* (Cambridge, 1993)

T. Bauman: *W.A. Mozart: Die Entführung aus dem Serail* (Cambridge, 1987)

W.J. Allanbrook: *Rhythmic Gesture in Mozart: Le nozze di Figaro and Don Giovanni* (Chicago, 1983)

A. Steptoe: *The Mozart-Da Ponte Operas: the Cultural and Musical Background to 'Le nozze di Figaro', 'Don Giovanni' and 'Così fan tutte'* (Oxford, 1988)

N. John, ed.: *The Marriage of Figaro* (London, 1983) [ENO opera guide]

T. Carter: *W.A. Mozart: Le nozze di Figaro* (Cambridge, 1987)

J. Rushton: *W.A. Mozart: Don Giovanni* (Cambridge, 1981)

N. John, ed.: *Don Giovanni* (London, 1983) [ENO opera guide]

N. John, ed.: *Così fan tutte* (London, 1983) [ENO opera guide]

B.A. Brown: *W.A. Mozart: 'Così fan tutte'* (Cambridge, 1995)

J. Chailley: *'La flûte enchantée', opéra maçonnique: essai d'explication du livret et de la musique* (Paris, 1968; English translation, 1972)

N. John, ed.: *The Magic Flute* (London, 1980) [ENO opera guide]

P. Branscombe: *W.A. Mozart: 'Die Zauberflöte'* (Cambridge, 1991)

J. Rice: *W.A. Mozart: 'L clemenza di Tito'* (Cambridge, 1991)